INDUSTRY
CLOTHING
CONSTRUCTION
METHODS

INDUSTRY CLOTHING CONSTRUCTION METHODS

Mary Ruth Shields
Lincoln College of New England

Fairchild Books
An imprint of Bloomsbury Publishing Inc

BLOOMSBURY
NEW YORK · LONDON · OXFORD · NEW DELHI · SYDNEY

Vice President and General Manager, Fairchild Education & Conferences Division: Elizabeth Tighe Executive

Editor: Olga T. Kontzias

Associate Acquisitions Editor: Amanda Breccia

Editorial Development Director: Jennifer Crane

Senior Development Editor: Joseph Miranda

Creative Director: Carolyn Eckert

Production Director: Ginger Hillman

Senior Production Editor: Elizabeth Marotta

Editorial Services: Progressive Publishing Alternatives

Editorial Management: Marsha Hall

Ancillaries Editor: Noah Schwartzberg

Copyeditor: Progressive Publishing Alternatives

Cover Design: Carolyn Eckert

Cover Art: Jacket photograph by Stephen Mark Sullivan; other photographs by Carolyn Eckert Illustrators: Susan

Brereton, Ron Carboni, and Progressive Publishing Alternatives

Text Design: Renato Stanisic

Director, Sales and Marketing: Brian Normoyle

Fairchild Books

An imprint of Bloomsbury Publishing Inc

1385 Broadway	50 Bedford Square
New York	London
NY 10018	WC1B 3DP
USA	UK

www.bloomsbury.com

FAIRCHILD BOOKS, BLOOMSBURY and the Diana logo are trademarks of Bloomsbury Publishing Plc

First published 2010

Reprinted 2015

Copyright © 2011 Fairchild Books

Library of Congress Cataloging-in-Publication Data

2009926331

ISBN: 978-1-56367-726-7

GST R 133004424

CH13, TP09

Table of Contents

Extended Table of Contents

Preface

A fter having been asked countless times by students which stitch or seam to use for a particular garment, I have written *Industry Clothing Construction Methods* to help you solve those dilemmas quickly and with confidence.

Successful, independent designers possess a level of mastery with machines, tools, and construction techniques that allows them to move beyond concerns or thoughts about those tools and techniques to expressing their fashion voice. Successful merchandisers in large companies must use their knowledge of fashion construction to ensure that the apparel manufactured represents the company's brand image and budget while still meeting the desires of their customers. Buyers need to choose apparel that will meet the retailer's construction requirements for durability and design. Confidence in your own skills will allow you as a fashion industry leader to go beyond those skills and rise to the tasks at hand. Modern designers, buyers, planners, and merchandisers must be agile, aggressive, and results-oriented.

The structure, format, and styling of this book make it an essential tool for achieving those goals. *Industry Clothing Construction Methods* is a tool for success, so it is built like a tool that you always reach for because it is dependable, functional, and makes creating easier. As a tool, it has two basic functions: to assist you in managing information, time, processes, people, materials, and money in an apparel industry setting and to allow you to progress through your decisions and tasks more quickly, with less confusion. The material in this book is a hybrid between the industrial methods used in a large factory with highly specialized machinery and a small workroom with access to a lock stitch machine, 2 or 3 thread overlock, 4 thread mock safety stitch overlock and/or a 5 thread safety stitch, a blind hemmer, and gravity feed iron with board plus basic garment construction tools. The content of the book has been written with the assumption that these tools and machines are available. Garment engineering concepts are present throughout the book to ensure that your apparel is constructed in the correct, most cost effective order without specialized machinery such as welt pocket makers and sleeve setting machines.

Once you have practiced the samples and absorbed the written information, you will be ready to move on to the challenges of employing the construction techniques and machinery that are continuously being developed in the apparel manufacturing industry. New trends in technology and manufacturing methods will be easier to learn with a solid foundation in the construction techniques and concepts in this book. New ideas in garment design—shapes, silhouettes, details, hemming styles, and finishes—and ways to reuse old ideas are forever evolving. Being confident in your apparel construction skills will allow you to take advantage of these trends with confidence. You will be able to make the correct choices about construction quality level when you are planning lines, designing garments, or purchasing them. You will have a construction method vocabulary to draw upon when you are trying to meet the desires of your customer, no matter what their level of investment in apparel, no matter what your manufacturing budget is, and no matter what style you are called upon to do. I have created *Industry Clothing Construction Methods* to help you discover and apply the clothing construction methods required to achieve the right quality level for the apparel you are designing or buying. The concept of quality in the apparel industry is a very complex one. In order to make the right choices about apparel construction, you'll need to understand the effects issues such as consumer preferences, brand image, manufacturing costs, and timing will have on your quality decisions. Therefore, we will discuss these issues and more.

The introduction and Chapters 1 and 2 will provide you with the essential information you will use, together with your knowledge of garment construction, to make educated decisions. You will learn what foundation materials, threads, and tools to employ in your garments and how proper construction techniques can enhance their combination with fashion fabrics. We will discuss the concepts of batch and lean manufacturing, how to avoid the seven types of waste, and how workers fit into the manufacturing equation. This knowledge will support the design, quality, and, therefore, the brand image of the apparel you will create or buy, allowing you to excel as a fashion professional. Chapter 3 covers the stitches and seams used in this book which have been selected for their versatility and to give you alternatives for a variety of price points. The construction Chapters 4–11 are arranged by garment instead of by technique so that you will understand the basic garment sewing order for each item. For cross reference purposes, all of the techniques from these chapters are listed in alphabetical order in the Appendix, with their page numbers, so that you may access them quickly. Boldfaced terms from the chapters are also arranged alphabetically with their definitions for you in the Appendix for easy access. The Appendix also includes a chart about interlining categories, listings of machine needle information, a chart featuring information about dealing with difficult fabrics, plus a very useful chart detailing important information about the stitches used in this book.

In addition to the information in the Introduction and in each chapter there are pull outs to stress important concepts and tip boxes for added techniques and concepts. Two industry profiles, one from a unique, private designer who creates small exclusive lines, and one from a large manufacturer which employs the latest in industry technology, have been included to show how the methods and concepts in this text are applied in the fashion industry. The flow charts which are located at the beginning of Chapters 4–11 are an important tool for you to access when you need to know the sewing order of a garment quickly. Industrial notations for each stitch and seam are included in Chapters 3–11 so that you will become familiar with them. These notations are also gathered together in a chart in the Appendix. Resources for equipment, tools, notions, and soft goods are listed there as well. Look for further reading on material covered in this text in the bibliography.

AN ADDITIONAL WORD TO TEACHERS

Industry Garment Construction Methods is intended for the student who is at an introductory level in their professional fashion education. I have designed the book to work in a variety of curriculum models including design studio, line planning, merchandising, and buying. The content included in the book gives a general overview of the fashion industry and includes construction techniques with a focus on the issues mentioned above. This content will enable the student to connect the nuts and bolts of garment construction methods with the theory behind garment engineering, quality control, eliminating waste in the production process, and brand image. Students in all curriculums will have the foundation to make the correct decisions on which techniques to use for construction and the garment industry factors which influence these decisions. Each of these concepts is discussed in the introduction and related to the materials in Chapters 1 and 2 plus the construction methods in Chapters 4 through 11. While the garment construction text is comprehensive, it includes general methods that are applicable to an infinite variety of industry applications at price points from budget to designer signature. Because of the constantly advancing nature of the fashion industry, there is no way that any one text could possibly cover all the permutations of construction choices, machines, materials, and tools that are and will become available. I have endeavored instead to provide a firm foundation of concepts and methods that the student will use to move their career forward with your able assistance. I have not included information about pattern drafting; the book already assumes that design students have either learned to do that or been provided with patterns, that merchandisers will delegate this task, and that buyers are not usually concerned with this step.

Because I am and have been a teacher of garment construction, apparel line planning, brand image, and quality concepts for over 20 years, I know what it's like to attempt to teach from a text that is indecipherable, causing you to waste time interpreting what the author was trying to relay instead of enjoying the process of learning with your students. I have written *Industry Garment Construction Methods* with the intention of supporting you in your journey with them. I encourage you to give me feedback on the structure and content of the book so that the next edition will be an even better resource for you.

The content is organized according to garment order with the addition of a flow chart in the beginning of Chapters 4 through 11 to affirm correct sewing order. Pull outs in the Introduction are there to aid in highlighting essential concepts. Additional ideas are arranged for easy access in tip boxes throughout the book including specific techniques and extra concepts. These are included in the listing of techniques in the Appendix so that you may direct the students to look there for what they need. ASTM information is supplied to the student in Chapters 3–11 and is directly related to the instances when each stitch and seam is employed to facilitate the use of the book as a resource.

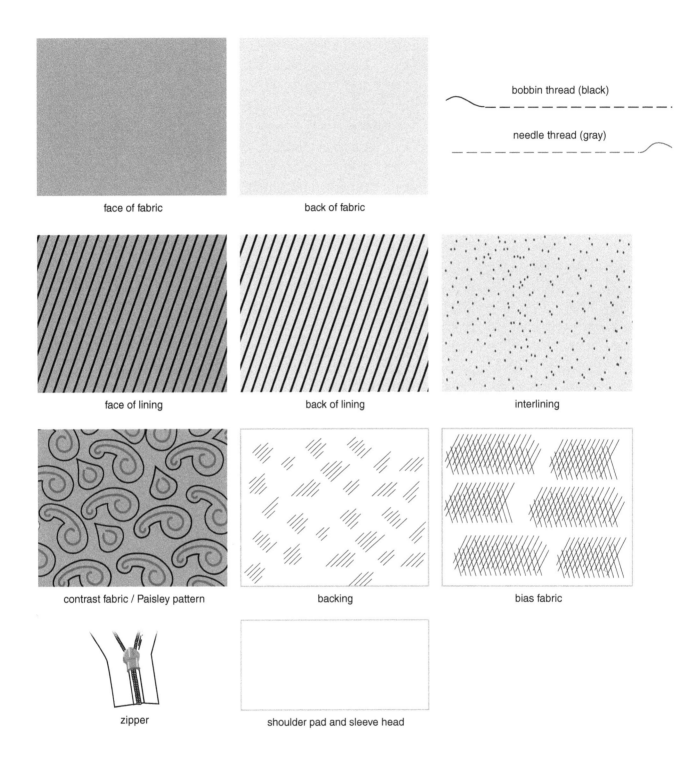

face of fabric

back of fabric

bobbin thread (black)

needle thread (gray)

face of lining

back of lining

interlining

contrast fabric / Paisley pattern

backing

bias fabric

zipper

shoulder pad and sleeve head

Acknowledgments

It is very important for me to recognize the people whose names are not on the cover of this book. Without their knowledge and support, I would not have been able to get the ideas and words that I am so passionate about into book form for students and professors to access.

First, I would like to thank the staff at Fairchild, including Olga Kontzias for her gracious introduction to the world of publishing and Jennifer Crane for sticking with the project to the finish line. Thanks also to the most patient and cheerful Joe Miranda, always ready with the right answer, and to Progressive Publishing Alternatives for their tireless attention to detail. I am grateful also to Elizabeth Marotta and Carolyn Eckert for picking up the artwork pieces, reassuring a worried author, and creating a beautiful, accessible setting for the words and concepts in this book.

To all my fashion colleagues including Nancy, Jennifer, and Tina, thanks for your input and encouragement. To Jack, Ron, and Roula, thanks so much for the technical, emotional, and scholarly support. And thanks especially to Susan, the originator of the illustrations in this book: you will never be far from my heart. To my "comrades" Linka, Jennifer, Tammy, and Lisa—turns out that writing a book is a creative practice after all. Who knew? Thanks for being the amazing women you are and sharing yourselves with me. I am especially grateful to Michelle for treating a worn-out writer with joyous love and hugs. And most important of all, eternal thanks to Dad and Alice for bringing me up right.

This book is dedicated to my most
awesome sons

for sharing their mom with "the book."

Thanks for sticking with me,

cheering me on,

and sharing my love of fashion.

Yes, it's really done now.

Introduction

B efore you begin using this book, let's discuss some fashion industry terms so that we can communicate more easily. These terms are fully defined for easy reference in the Appendix.

INDUSTRY OVERVIEW

Fashion Terminology

A designer transforms the basic shape of a style into a unique expression of fashion, frequently referred to as a design. In the retail sector, groups of designs that fit under a certain style, such as dressy trousers, are given a particular style number that may be used to track them through the process of design, manufacturing, and sale to the retail consumer.

Designers design and buyers choose apparel that has been constructed of fabric. Fabrics, also known as textiles, are predominantly created from yarns or fibers and may be knitted, woven, or combined in some other manner, such as fusing. In *Industry Clothing Construction Methods*, we discuss construction techniques that are best suited for woven fabrics. Construction in the apparel industry usually means joining fabrics and notions, such as zippers or snaps, together to create a wearable shape. Often, trims—including laces, braids, piping, appliqués, and so on—are also added. Construction is accomplished by sewing on a variety of sewing machines and other machinery designed to perform specialized functions, such as attaching a pocket or a button.

The basic style choices available to the designer have not changed for centuries. The age-old trouser, skirt, jacket, blouse, vest, dress, and other forms for women still exist in modern Western societies, but the look of those garment forms, as interpreted by designers, changes with prevailing cultural whims. What is "in fashion" today may or may not have been acceptable in the past and may or may not be acceptable in the future. The majority of people in a society (such as the United States) or groups within that society (such as Orthodox Jewish women in the United States) decide what is "in fashion."

Divisions of Apparel Manufacturing

Almost everything that is available in a department store, designer boutique, or independent retailer today is ready-to-wear. Ready-to-wear is available in many price ranges and is always ready to be purchased and worn off the rack. Minor alterations may be needed, but the garment is created in a specific design and size before the customer enters the retail store. Custom apparel may or may not be designed ahead of time. It is sized and sewn especially for the individual who is purchasing the item, using mostly machine-sewn construction techniques. Couture fashion is the highest quality apparel available to the fashion consumer today. It is created and constructed by a small number of fashion houses and is available only to the lucky few fashion aficionados who can afford this level of quality. The exclusive fabrics, trims, and findings; the construction and finishing techniques executed almost entirely by hand; and the one-of-a-kind designs reflecting the creative voice of the designer blend to create truly unique pieces of art.

Benefits and Features in Apparel

Prior to the early 1970s, designers and department stores determined what was in fashion for ready-to-wear and therefore what would be available for the consumer to buy. After the cultural movements of the 1970s and 1980s (detailed in the "Quality" section) in Europe and the United States, the consumer became the major controlling force in ready-to-wear fashion. This shift in the direction and functions of the fashion industry from designer-initiated fashion to consumer-initiated fashion did not happen overnight. It did not completely transform every aspect of every designer's offerings each fashion season, but it did fundamentally alter the behavior of many designers, merchandisers, and buyers, who began to listen to the customer's needs and wants rather than dictating fashion directions.

Designers heard the consumer say that apparel should offer benefits. Consumers believe that apparel benefits should help them achieve their goals as individuals, such as feeling more self-confident, gaining respect, saving time and money, attaining comfort during leisure time, attracting a lover, fitting into a social group, or expressing themselves. The task for a fashion professional, then, became determining what features should be included in the garments to achieve those apparel benefits. The core of the designer's, merchandiser's, or buyer's craft in the ready-to-wear industry is to find the right combination of features—silhouette, fit, shape, color, line, fabric, texture, price, and so on—that entice customers to look, try on, and feel satisfied with their apparel purchase.

The expression of an original design concept using those features created by the designer or chosen by the merchandiser or buyer is the foundation of that craft and is what keeps fashion new, moving forward, and forever relevant. The actual features of a garment may also be described as intrinsic attributes. These may include the color or texture of the fabric, the width of a hem or a sleeve, the design interest created by the placement of seams, and the style and fit. Other intrinsic attributes might be the method of care used to clean the garment, the fact that the pant comes with a coordinating belt, or the way the fabric keeps you cool when you are exercising. The benefits of some intrinsic attributes are best appreciated after the customer has purchased the garment. The industry professional must carefully evaluate the intrinsic attributes of a garment, because these features will influence the type and quality of fabrics, trims, and notions used; the construction techniques chosen; and how and in what order they are applied.

Just as intrinsic attributes offer benefits to the customer, so do **extrinsic characteristics**. An extrinsic characteristic is one that is not an actual part of the garment but is definitely part of the customer's thoughts about the item. Extrinsic characteristics often have more to do with the customer's initial decision to purchase the garment than the actual features do. They might include how a woman feels a seam detail accentuates her figure, the positive image in a college graduate's mind of interviewing for a job in that new suit, or the feeling of belonging a teen has when wearing a shirt displaying a fashionable brand logo.

Merchandisers

Merchandisers are also aware of benefits and features. In large manufacturing firms that produce wholesale apparel, merchandisers create a **merchandising calendar,** which they and other members of the company, such as designers and **specification writers** (also known as *spec writers*), use to manage the hundreds of tasks necessary to complete a fashion **line** and to set deadlines for those tasks to be completed. Merchandisers use the calendar to direct the functions of creating, producing, and delivering the apparel to ensure that all members of the company perform their duties in a timely manner so that apparel in the line is produced efficiently and arrives in the retail store on time. In smaller companies, merchandisers themselves may perform many of the duties needed to ensure the successful completion of the line. Such duties might include researching current fashion trends, consulting previous seasons'

Consumers believe that apparel benefits should help them achieve their goals as individuals.

sales figures from their retail stores, the **sourcing** of fabric and labor for production, or reviewing garment **prototypes** for approval. In small, private boutiques, the designer may also perform these tasks.

Brand Image

Many of the tasks that merchandisers complete are related to **brand image**. Merchandisers and designers are conscious of how their construction choices reflect and affect the brand image of the apparel and the company producing or selling the apparel. As consumers, when we think of the idea of a brand, we consider many aspects of that brand in just a few short minutes. We may have a picture of a symbol (the Nike Swoosh), of the product itself, or of a garment style such as jeans. Almost simultaneously, we may also think of a commercial we saw on television or an ad in our favorite fashion magazine featuring a spokesmodel in a pair of designer jeans. Or perhaps we heard about the jeans from a friend who had an opinion about their fit, or we remember seeing the same jeans in the store. We may have formed an opinion of them based on what our experience was with the atmosphere and sales associates in the store. All of these aspects of a brand lead to the formation of expectations related to the apparel brand. When these expectations are met by successful decision making, the customer will purchase more products and remain loyal to the brand.

Quality Concepts

When we think of a brand, one of the aspects of the apparel that we consider is quality. **Quality** may be evaluated by the consumer as how well the garment fits, how durable the garment is, and how well it performs the function for which it was purchased. The benefits and features that we understand as being part of the brand—the brand's intrinsic attributes and extrinsic characteristics—are all perceived as part of the brand quality and are experienced directly through the intrinsic attributes of the apparel.

Designers and merchandisers can directly affect the brand image you experience by the decisions they make about construction issues in each product, such as the type of construction method, the time it takes to complete the construction technique, the cost of that technique in time and materials, and the accuracy with which the techniques are performed. The seams or seam finishes that are chosen, the stitch length used in the seams, the type of thread chosen to sew the seams, the hem width on the garment, and more must be decided before the garment goes into production; this ensures that the garment offers the benefits that the customer desires.

Merchandisers must also decide how much production time each construction choice will take. More complicated construction methods may take more production time, which should be calculated into the merchandising calendar if this extra time is acceptable to the company and will not reflect badly on the company's image. However, if the extra time means a delay in the production of the apparel, a construction technique that takes less time to complete may be substituted to enable the garment to be delivered on time. This less-expensive choice must still comply with the consumer's desire for garment durability.

Fashion professionals try to predict how much an item will cost to produce before it goes into production. If this precosting is done effectively, the added costs of more materials or more expensive

> *Quality may be evaluated by the consumer as how well the garment fits, how durable the garment is, and how well it performs the function for which it was purchased.*

construction methods can be budgeted for or removed from the project to contain the cost of the garment. Merchandisers must also ensure that the level of accuracy in the chosen construction methods meets the needs of the consumer. Some consumers see hanging threads and unequal seam widths as a symbol of low quality, while others may not notice them at all. All of the construction issues mentioned and more determine the quality of the garment. A garment that is produced at the right level of quality at the right wholesale price and that arrives in the store on time will stand a much better chance of pleasing the customer so much that he or she will leave the store without it.

Buyers

Buyers are also concerned with the quality of the apparel they are purchasing for retail sale. They may purchase finished garments from wholesale manufacturers, or they may collaborate with the merchandisers in a garment company to design apparel that meets their needs specifically. Either way, buyers will consider how construction techniques affect the retailer's brand image because of their relation to garment appearance, durability, performance, costs, and, ultimately, the preferences of their customer.

Stages in the Fashion Manufacturing Process

The fashion industry is made up of many businesses that work together to produce the apparel we wear. The production of apparel in the 21st century is a global effort. Designers, merchandisers, and buyers have the capability to source the materials and labor for their products to whoever can provide what they need. The company they choose to get their materials from or to do their construction must suit their budget, produce the amount they believe they can sell, and deliver it on time and at the quality level their customer demands.

Electronic Data Interchange allows companies to communicate instantaneously with their partners at any level of the apparel process, from the manufacturer or farmer producing the fibers to the retail customer as the end user, making sure that customers have endless variety in the latest fabrics and styles at their favorite fashion retailer. Many of the companies in the manufacturing process specialize in one area of production, such as spinning yarn or dyeing fabric. Increasingly, larger companies are emerging that are vertically integrated. These companies will perform more than one part of the process, such as creating the chemical mixture for a manufactured yarn, spinning and dyeing the yarn to their customer's specifications, and then knitting that yarn into fabric for the customer's knit dresses.

Fibers

Fibers are the most basic building material of fabrics. When manufacturing apparel, selecting the fiber is the first chance you will have to ensure that the garment you make will have the benefits that your customers desire, both when they are purchasing the apparel

and later, when they are using it at home or work. The fiber choices you will make as a fashion professional directly affect the quality and performance of the garment being manufactured. All fibers have certain advantages and disadvantages that make them ideal for some apparel but unsuitable for others.

Natural fibers are farmed all over the world and are either protein based, like sheep's wool or silk (Figure I.1), or cellulosic based, like cotton or linen (Figure I.2).

Natural fibers are distinguishable from manufactured fibers, because the basic structure of the fiber is not changed with heat or chemicals, nor are the fibers formed mechanically. Their original form may be treated to clean it or make it easier to work with, but they are then spun into yarn in their original structure.

Man-made fibers may be created from many different chemical combinations such as nylon and acrylic or from natural materials such as wood and bamboo that are chemically altered and are then mechanically formed into fibers or a continuous filament, which is then spun into yarn (Figure I.3).

Occasionally, fibers that are natural or man-made may also be fused or felted together to create a nonwoven fabric.

Yarn

Yarn is a linear formation of filaments or fibers that is used to knit or weave a fabric. The choice of which yarns to use in your apparel also gives you a chance to positively affect the quality of the finished product. There are many different yarn structures, from a single smooth strand to multiple strands, in many unique formations that create textural effects in fabric (Figure I.4).

These textural effects can improve the hand, or feel, of the fabric for the customer. Is it rough, soft and flowing, limp and clingy, softly textured, or stiff and crunchy? The feel of the fabric in customers' hands when they are evaluating a garment on the rack and then when they are trying on the garment strongly influences their purchasing decision. Yarns also affect the durability of the fabric and therefore the satisfaction of customers as they use the garment. The structure of some yarns—diameter,

slipperiness, looseness of spin, and so on—also affect the construction techniques used to sew fabrics together.

Fabric

Knitted and woven fabrics are created from yarns. The way the yarns are arranged in the knit or weave depends on the style of garment being made, the use of the garment (once a week or once in a lifetime), what the customer's expectations are for the garment's performance (does it need to impress by being silky and shiny, or does it need to wick moisture from the skin during exercise?), the fit of the garment (close and slinky or structured and tailored), and the care

FIGURE I.4 An assortment of yarn types.

and durability of the garment over time (Figure I.5).

Some woven structures are soft and supple, and some are full and stiff. Some knits are smooth and thin, and others are thick and textured. You will choose many fabrics to work with over your fashion industry career. *Industry Clothing Construction Methods* contains the information you need to be successful in your work. Learning and mastering the apparel construction methods in this book will enable and encourage you to create beautiful apparel in any fabric. You will find tables in the Appendix that will help you cope with several aspects of using a variety of fabrics in apparel. Chapter 9 includes information on sewing with leather.

Dyeing and Printing

Dyed yarns can make up fabrics, but some fabrics are dyed and/or printed after being woven or knitted. Dyeing a yarn or fabric means that the color will penetrate into the depths of the yarn, which usually ensures that the color will not wear off (but may fade). Printing may also penetrate into the yarns but is primarily a surface treatment and may wear off in poorer-quality apparel. The order in which these steps are executed depends on the quality level chosen for the textile, the finished garment, and the types of dyeing or printing methods used. More information about these processes is available in the texts listed in the bibliography.

FIGURE I.5 An assortment of fabrics showing different drapes and textures.

Yarn, Fabric, and Garment Finishing

Yarns, fabrics, and garments may then be finished with a variety of methods, both mechanical and chemical, to further ensure their capacity to satisfy the retail customer. A mechanical finish might enhance a fabric's fluffy softness; a chemical finish might allow it to be flame retardant. Mechanical and chemical finishes may also be done after the fabric is sewn into apparel and may also be executed by hand, as in the case of distressing jeans.

Construction

Once the knit or woven fabric is prepared to be sewn, apparel construction begins. Many factors influence the chosen methods of construction, how the interior of the garment is finished, and any decorative construction details. Most important among these factors are the opinions and attitudes of the customer. These factors also include the amount of money necessary to pay for the materials used to accomplish those methods, finishes, and details; how long it will take to complete them; what machinery is available to make them; and if the machine operators have been or can be trained to complete them efficiently. Designers, merchandisers, and buyers who are trained in all the possible methods, finishes, and details available to them can confidently choose what satisfies the customer and their own goals. All of the preceding concepts will be more thoroughly discussed in the "Quality" section.

Price Categories in Fashion Apparel

Positioning

At times, it's convenient to categorize apparel in terms of how much it sells for at retail. For example, discussing apparel in terms of "price points" can help a fashion professional decide on the positioning of a new design against the competition, especially with regard to construction quality. When successful manufacturing decisions are made, the costs of manufacturing the garment are kept within a budget that allows the wholesaler and the retailer of the garment to make a profit high enough to keep their businesses moving forward day to day. This profit comes from making the garment cheaply enough so that it can be sold at a price that satisfies both the customer and the retailer. You can look at it this way: The manufacturer works backward from the selling price to determine how much to spend on making the garment.

How does a fashion professional determine this selling price? They look at the positioning of the garment in the store and the geographical market where it is being sold. This does not mean how it is hung on the hanger or on what shelf it sits, waiting for the customer to buy it. *Positioning* means how the garment relates to others like it in style, complexity of design, fabric, quality, and price. Fashion professionals must price their garments with their customer and these other products in mind. Will their customers be looking only in one store for a low price and reasonably good quality because they are on a strict budget? Or do the customers care more about brand, no matter where they find it, and are willing to pay whatever it takes to get brand recognition from their friends? Or are they somewhere in between, shopping around among many choices of the same style to find the right level of price and quality that will cause them to pull their credit card from their wallet?

Competition in the fashion industry is fierce. As mentioned before, shoppers have many options when they are out shopping. When considering the positioning of their styles, fashion professionals are confronted with the huge range of prices at which one style may sell. Jeans, for instance, may be purchased at prices ranging from $20 to $250 or more. Prices and the accompanying attributes of the product, such as quality of fabric; complexity of embellishment; the care taken when designing for a particular figure type; and designer, garment, or store brand image will place a style in a certain price category. The retail selling price, along with the brand image of the product, can be a quick, commonly used way for the consumer to decide on the quality of the apparel. Although consumers often use price to determine quality, doing this is often not reliable and can be risky.

This superficial relationship between price and quality is also not a dependable measure for the fashion professional of consumer willingness to buy. Consumers all have opinions about what value means to them—that is, the relationship between quality and price. Determining the fine points of your customers' feelings about this relationship is, at best, an educated guess. The price categories are as follows, from most to least expensive: couture, designer signature, bridge, better, moderate, budget, and category killer. We give examples of labels at each price point; however, the examples are by no means the only ones in each category, nor do they only sell apparel in the category in which they are listed.

Couture

Currently, only a few design houses practice the beautiful arts of couture fashion, as defined in the "Fashion Terminology" section. They include such labels as Ralph Rucci, Christian Dior by John Galliano, Chanel by Karl Lagerfeld, and Christian Lacroix.

Designer Signature

New designer signature labels, on the other hand, seem to be appearing with every new fashion season. Designers at this ready-to-wear price point are free to express their own statement, influenced perhaps by trends identified by outside sources and by what they have sold successfully in the past, but more so by their own unique inspirations and expression. Their loyal clients follow them because the designer often caters to their brand expectations. If the designer does go off in an unexpected direction, their clients know that they will still be able to exercise their own fashion sense to pick and choose which of the designer's styles suit their own lifestyle and wardrobe. Many of the most recognizable fashion labels reside at this price point, such as Donna Karan, Stella McCartney, and Diane von Furstenberg, but there are many lesser-known labels of equal if not better quality in workmanship and design, such as Tom and Linda Platt.

Bridge

In the 1950s, it occurred to many designers that they could make additional money by cashing in on the influence of their own names at a lower price point than their signature labels. Thus, apparel licensing was born. These bridge lines, like all other licensed lines, allow a whole new target market of consumers to take part in a fashion dream that they could not otherwise afford. Licensing is a cooperative venture between a designer with name recognition and a manufacturer whose name is not well known to consumers. The manufacturer supplies the consumer with a lower-priced line of apparel that shares a similar design appeal and name with the designer's signature line but is often made with simpler designs, lower-quality fabrics, and faster construction techniques. Lower costs to the licensed manufacturer means they can keep the price low for the consumer. Their sales are increased by the power of the designer name. The designer benefits by being paid a licensing fee and perhaps a portion of the profit without having to struggle with the planning that goes into creating a lower-priced line that involves an entirely different set of concerns. One of the most well known of these lines is DKNY, modeled after the designer signature line of Donna Karan. There are other companies that manufacture their own apparel sold at this price point without licensing. They include the independent designers Eileen Fisher and Elie Tahari, plus chain companies such as Talbots and Ann Taylor.

Better

Bridge is so named because it "bridges" the price levels between designer signature and better, formerly the next lowest price level before bridge came into being. Better is sold mostly at department and independently owned specialty stores and is considered to be a perfect price point for the solidly upper-middle to middle-class consumer, especially those who depend on brand names for quality. Many of the labels at this price point feature designs, fabrics, colors, and prints that do not require as large a leap of imagination by the average consumer. Customers can easily see how the pieces will fit on them and into the wardrobe they already own. The fabrics and construction are dependable and usually long-lasting. Labels at this price point include Jones New York, plus chain retailers like bebe and Banana Republic.

Moderate

Apparel at a moderate price point can be found at chain department stores and chain specialty stores. Fashion professionals design or buy items by relying on their knowledge of what their customer expects from their brand according to quality and styling; what has sold best in the past; and what the forecasts in fabrics, styling, and colors are for upcoming seasons. Needless to say, the apparel styles may be dependably predictable. Customers frequent these stores because they can rely on finding the expected every time they enter, and they know the apparel is constructed to last. New lines are frequently introduced, often once every month, to keep up with consumers' demand for new styles to excite them. Labels at this price point include Ann Taylor LOFT, J. G. Hook, "Vera" by Vera Wang, and J. Jill.

Budget

Examples of budget apparel include Mossimo at Target, Arizona at JCPenney, Covington at Sears, or Apt. 9 at Kohl's; examples can also be found at stores such as H&M, Zara, or Uniqlo. This price point is a reliable buy for middle- to lower-middle-class consumers, featuring designs and fabrics that range from the tried-and-true to right-on-trend and fashion forward. But they also tend to attract the consumer who usually can be found at high-end department stores purchasing ready-to-wear from labels like Armani and Calvin Klein. In the last several decades, a certain attraction has emerged to purchasing trendy, low-priced garments to mix with designer labels. Garments may feature interesting prints and sewn details, but the construction is occasionally poor. Most of the garments are wash-and-wear.

Category Killer

At an even lower level than budget, the consumer finds a price point labeled by some as category killers, because these items are priced at the lowest level possible in their style category to kill the competition. The most well-known seller of these products is Walmart, although Kmart and Forever 21 also compete in this category. The goal for these retailers is to offer every conceivable style that the customer could know about, and to have as many as possible on the selling floor at a time, for the cheapest price that can be found. For these consumers, quality of construction comes after price in their decision-making process, if it is considered at all. Some of the labels may be national, such as Wrangler, but many are manufactured to be sold under the store's label or may be labels that are unfamiliar to the consumer. In some stores, national brands may sell under their own name but may manufacture apparel at a lower quality level that costs them significantly less to make so they can sell the garments at a much lower price point.

Brand Image and Pricing

Brand image can be seen as confusing the entire quality-of-construction-compared-to-cost-of-construction subject, because many designer brands are much more expensive than the level of construction quality would seem to suggest. This is a matter of positioning. Many designers feel that in order to be taken seriously, they need to price their apparel within range of their competition and for the environment in which it is being sold to "position" it. They do not want their apparel to be seen as too "mass market" or as not exclusive enough compared with the other designer goods being sold at the same department store or boutique.

Retail price is not always an indicator of construction quality, although this used to be the case. As Karl Lagerfeld says, "We live in a time when expensive and inexpensive—not cheap, I hate that word—can live very well together. It's the first time in fashion this has happened."[1] The goal for many fashion consumers is getting that designer look or making their own fashion statement for the best possible price. Instead of being proud of exclusivity, they are proud of the designer "deal." The goal still remains, though, that you will need to buy or create fashion that speaks to the consumer's needs and wants with regard to design, construction quality, and price, and you will need to present your fashions to them when they are ready to buy.

The Value Equation

When considering the concept of quality in apparel, it is important to also have an understanding of the idea of value as you and your customer will understand it. This word is tossed around constantly in the fashion industry by both fashion professionals and consumers. But what does *value* really mean in the apparel industry? What does value have to do with quality?

Value Equation for the Consumer

We can go a long way toward explaining the customer's and the apparel maker's ideas of value by using a simple equation. As customers, our equation would be the following: value = intrinsic attributes + extrinsic characteristics + investment. That is to say, when the actual, physical properties of the garment, added to the extrinsic benefits (such as the consumer's personal image) of the garment, plus the investment in time, effort, and money it takes to

Retail price is not always an indicator of construction quality, although this used to be the case. As Karl Lagerfeld says, "We live in a time when expensive and inexpensive—not cheap, I hate that word—can live very well together. It's the first time in fashion this has happened."[2]

acquire the garment are equal to what the consumer feels is a "good" value or a "fair" price, then they will be satisfied and purchase the garment. Consumers' perception of the garment as a "good" value will change to a "not good" value if the physical properties of the garment are considered inadequate; if the benefits do not fit their needs; or if they have to invest too much time, money, or energy into getting the garment. If they are dissatisfied in some way, they will not purchase.

Keep in mind, though, that different customers will have different ideas of what a "good" value is and what level of construction quality makes a "good" value. Your job as a designer, buyer, or merchandiser is to know what your customer considers to be a good or fair value for their investment so that you can create fashions for them; or if you already have your product, you will know enough about them to find them and market to them. Customers view quality as being an element of value. They see the quality of a product on a continuum between terrible (very bad value) and exceptional (very good value). The quality of a garment will not be judged alone but as one of many pieces that the customer will consider consciously or unconsciously when deciding to make a purchase.

A customer's idea of quality can also be understood from the standpoint of **risk**. The value equation represents a customer's level of risk tolerance. As mentioned before, customers invest time, money, and effort into getting the garments they want. They also invest in their self-image when wearing the apparel. Customers choose how much money, time, and effort they want to risk when purchasing a garment. If the risk is too great—that is, the garment costs "too much"—they will not purchase. If they feel the garment will positively affect their image in the eye of their peers, purchasing the garment is seen as being less of a risk.

Value Equation for the Fashion Professional

The value equation for the professional maker or buyer of the apparel is significantly different. For the maker, the equation is as follows: value = objective adherence to quality standards + cost of production. For the buyer, the equation is as follows: value = objective adherence to quality standards + cost of apparel at retail. Fashion professionals are in the business of satisfying the customer or finding the customer who will be satisfied by what they are creating or buying. As the end user of the garment, the customer's needs and wants are the ultimate determiner of the standards that the maker uses and that the buyer adheres to. These standards include fabric, finishing, and construction choices. As you will see in the "Product" section below, the quality level of these standards is measurable and will be objectively evaluated for success.

The second half of this equation is cost, which is incurred by the maker to produce or the buyer to purchase the garment. Although the maker and buyer are

---

VALUE EQUATION FOR THE CONSUMER

We can go a long way toward explaining the customer's ideas of value by using a simple equation format. The equation would be the following: value = intrinsic attributes + extrinsic characteristics + investment. That is to say, when the actual, physical properties of the garment, added to the extrinsic benefits (such as their personal image) of the garment, plus the investment in time, effort, and money it takes to acquire the garment are equal to what the consumer feels is a "good" value or a "fair" price, then they will be satisfied and purchase the garment.

---

concerned with the desires of the end user, their ultimate concern is how to satisfy those desires while maintaining their brand image plus turning as much of a profit as possible. If they cannot cover the cost of making or buying the garment and generate a profit, they will not be able to pay their bills or grow their business.

◇◇◇◇◇◇◇◇◇◇◇◇◇◇◇◇◇◇◇◇◇◇◇◇◇◇◇◇◇◇◇

QUALITY

The importance of choosing construction methods at the correct level of quality for your apparel cannot be underestimated. The impact of your choices will affect every aspect of your product, whether you designed it or bought it. These customers' choices and their reasoning behind them represent a core dilemma for designers, merchandisers, and buyers in today's fashion industry: What level of construction quality should I choose for the apparel I am creating or buying? Let's consider this statement: "The most significant intrinsic cues for fashion goods may be styling and color. Manufacturers, retailers, and consumers that favor styling . . . may overlook other intrinsic factors such as quality of materials and construction. The wearable life of a fashion garment may be only a few weeks; therefore, intrinsic characteristics that affect durability are less critical."[3] If construction quality isn't as important as the design or color of the style, then why should you care about the quality of construction you use? For that matter, why *don't* customers care about the quality of the construction? Shouldn't they? Today's consumer is likely to purchase fashions in any retail location at any price point that

offers them what they are looking for in fit, style, silhouette, print pattern, color, fabric, or any other intrinsic attribute that is seen or felt during initial contact with the garment. Extrinsic characteristics such as brand will also influence a purchasing decision, although they seemingly have nothing to do with construction. What customers think is acceptable or "good" quality construction changes with their demographic facts and psychographic choices as well as their motivations for purchasing the apparel and in what situations they intend to wear it. Seems very confusing, doesn't it? We will discuss these concepts more thoroughly later in this introduction. In this section, we will take an in-depth look at quality from three perspectives: the product, the customer, and the maker.

The Product
Intrinsic Attributes
As we have discussed before, apparel has intrinsic attributes that are physical parts of it. These attributes can be measured objectively according to how well they fulfill the quality goals required for that product. The intrinsic attributes are part of the experience the customers have when they investigate the garment using their senses. They also are part of that customer's perception of the product's brand image, and they affect the level of risk the customer sees in purchasing that garment: Does the garment appear to be fashionable and well made? When they try it on, do they notice missing buttons or loose threads and unfinished seams, or is the garment lined and well fitting? Will purchasing it be money well spent? The retailer must be sure to inform consumers about the intrinsic attributes of the product to increase its salability and to lower the consumer's perception of risk. Catalogs,

---

Structure is a combination of silhouette, the shapes that make up the silhouette, fit, and construction techniques.

print ads, and knowledgeable salespeople are great tools to achieve this goal.

The structure of the garment makes a significant first impression on the customer. Structure is a combination of silhouette, the shapes that make up the silhouette, fit, and construction techniques. Customers must see it as being functional according to the need or want they are fulfilling. Good-quality, successful structure results in a satisfied customer. Poor-quality structure will lead to customer disappointment and your garment staying on the rack.

Durability, or the expected lifetime of the garment or its construction, is another intrinsic attribute that consumers use to evaluate apparel. The level of quality that you require for your garment must match the expected lifetime of that garment. As we will discover in the section on the Consumer, a poorly made but very trendy, inexpensive skirt is still considered to be a good buy if the customer expects to use it only once for a few hours. On the other end of the quality spectrum, an expensive garment that is easily identified as being a designer item and is well made is expected to be more durable. If the durability of the garment does not meet the customer's expectations for the designer's label, then purchasing it might be considered a bad investment and a repeat purchase might be less likely. The customer recognizes that the features that make a garment durable, such as quality-construction decisions (linings or enclosed seam finishes, evenly stitched buttonholes that are not fraying, and topstitching that is not coming undone, etc.), will add to its wearability and will justify the investment.

Closely related to durability is the attribute of reliability. For the consumer, reliability also relates to the physical characteristics of the garment but, more specifically, to the likelihood of the sewn

Durability, or the expected lifetime of the garment or its construction, is another intrinsic attribute that consumers use to evaluate apparel.

elements failing in the garment. Consumers may expect the crotch seam on a pair of dress pants to last until they no longer want to wear them. If the seam bursts when they first put them on, then the brand image of the company that sold them the pants will be damaged in the eyes of consumers. They may give the company another try, or they may regard the purchase of garments from that company as being too risky. Repeat purchases of your apparel depend on the proper balance between the level of sewn quality you choose and the expectations of your customer.

Customers who have experience with the level of quality that your brand represents will also be expecting conformance to that level of quality. They will be unaware that you have set quality standards for durability in the fabric and construction methods you employ, but they will be aware of the benefits those standards offer them. If consumers' first priority is finding the lowest price around and quality of construction is a distant second (if they consider it at all), the construction choices you have made will keep that price low and will allow you to deliver the fashions they crave more quickly. If price is not a concern and beautiful fabrics and unique design are what your customer demands, then the construction methods you choose will allow you to flawlessly execute that unique design in that specialty fabric.

For the consumer, reliability also relates to the physical characteristics of the garment but, more specifically, to the likelihood of the sewn elements failing in the garment.

Customers who have experience with the level of quality that your brand represents will also be expecting conformance to that level of quality.

The **performance** of the garment construction works in tandem with the fabric and fabric finishes that you choose. Every garment is expected to meet the needs of customers and help them attain the goal for which they purchased it. Construction may have to be extremely durable, as in the case of active wear for sports enthusiasts. Or the performance may need to be a stylishly slimming seam with an added decorative topstitching on a business pantsuit for an upscale gallery owner who is meeting a new client. Either way, the ability of the garment to satisfy customers' needs is an aspect that they will discover after they have taken the garment home and used it. That's when they will judge the performance of your construction choices.

After they have used the garment, customers will also judge its **serviceability**. *Serviceability* refers to the refurbishing of the garment, or the method that should be used to clean it. The fabric and fabric finishes you have chosen for your garment are the chief aspects that will determine this, but construction choices also have an impact. The ability of your seam finishes, pocket and zipper applications, hems, button sewing, and so on, to be able to withstand machine washing, if that is the method of care for the garment, may be a make-or-break benefit for your customer. The thread you use should

The performance of the garment construction works in tandem with the fabric and fabric finishes that you choose. Every garment is expected to meet the needs of customers and help them attain the goal for which they purchased it.

not shrink when washed or discolor when dry-cleaned.

Extrinsic Characteristics

As we discussed before, every garment has extrinsic characteristics that are not actually a physical part of the garment. However, they are just as important—and at times even more important—to customers, and therefore to you, as the intrinsic attributes, especially at the moment of their decision to purchase. Extrinsic characteristics are very subjective and are almost impossible to accurately measure. They exist because of the benefits the customer perceives the apparel to have. Purchasing apparel is often a very emotional transaction; therefore, extrinsic characteristics are frequently a more powerful factor in determining whether the customer will purchase your garment. They influence customers' experience with the garment and their perception of the risk they will take when purchasing and wearing it. The more satisfactory extrinsic characteristics the garment has, the more appealing it is and the more likely it is to be purchased. The factor of risk will be lower from the consumer's point of view.

Extrinsic characteristics are formed by the intrinsic attributes of the product. Your design of the style, its silhouette and lines of seaming; the fabric, its texture, color, or print motif; and the construction as seen in the seam finishes, topstitching, or embellishment all contribute to the customer's aesthetic impression. Just as with intrinsic attributes, you must inform the customer about the extrinsic characteristics. This is often done with a suggestive ad campaign or in-store visual display.

The aesthetic appearance of your garment must be pleasing to your customer. They will be using it in a tangible way to express their self-image to others and to reassure themselves about their appearance. They may be using the garment's extrinsic characteristics with the hope of creating a symbolic representation of who they want to be. They could be using the garment to help them feel confident that they are appropriately dressed for a certain occasion or that they belong to a chosen group.

The Customer

You and every other professional involved in the design or purchasing of garments for retail sale inhabit a unique spot in the fashion industry. You are both a consumer and a seller of apparel. Your experience at the receiving end of the apparel industry gives you a unique perspective into the dialogue that occurs between that industry and the customers who support it. This dialogue is both a conversation and an intriguing guessing game between you—the fashion industry professional—and your customers. As a designer, buyer, or merchandiser, you are making a particular statement about what you think your chosen customer should be wearing at a particular time of a particular year in a particular environment. Your statement may be very unique, unlike anyone else's, or it may look very similar to other garments. You may leave the customer guessing as to what it is you are saying, or you may know what the customer wants to hear from you and try to say something he or she will easily understand.

Whatever your statement is, to achieve a degree of success, you will need to define who you are talking to. You will want to know information about your customer. Someone knew about you, didn't they? Chances are very good that the fashions you purchased were designed with you in mind and put into the store where you love to shop at just the right time, in just the right quantities, and at just the right

After they have taken the garment home and used it, customers will also make a judgment on the serviceability of it. Serviceability *refers to the refurbishing of the garment, or the method that should be used to clean it.*

price to entice you to purchase them. As a fashion industry professional, you will be well served if you remember the person at the other end of your conversation! In this section, we will discuss what you need to know about your customer—their perceptions, attitudes, and assessment of your product; why it is important to know about their needs and wants and what they invest when they purchase your product; and how these affect their decisions about quality.

Customer Information

The information we want to know falls into three categories: demographics, psychographics, and psychological motivations. Information from these categories will give us insight into how customer preferences affect construction quality. There are many excellent books that go into great depth on these topics. Several are listed in the Appendices. Our discussion will center on basic, introductory concepts and how they will influence the construction choices you will be making.

Customers have many reasons for choosing apparel. We want to know information about consumers and their reasoning to help us learn how to influence their apparel-buying habits. Obviously, we want them to buy *our* apparel. But not everyone in our society is going to want to purchase our designs. We want to talk to, design, and buy only for people who will. We can use the information we gather to help us find those people and influence them by selling compelling designs. We want to understand their preferences in apparel and what aspect(s) of the apparel is the most important to them. Will it be the cost or the brand name, the comfort or the embellishment, the durability or the silhouette? "Products are developed and marketed to suit groups of target customers in terms of styling, fit, fashion, quality, and value."[4]

Demographics. **Demographic** facts include such information as age, ethnicity, gender, religious practice, place of residence, level of education, income level, marital status, and size of family. This information can be used to separate or "segment" people into groups that would be more likely to purchase what we are selling based on what styles we sell, what our designs look like, or how much they retail for. But how can these facts influence which construction methods we choose for our apparel? Let's look at two examples.

A 40-year-old single mother of four school-aged children lives in an urban area and works as a maid in a high-rise hotel. She is currently taking college Internet classes to become a paralegal. We can assume that she has a limited income based on where she works and because she is going to school and taking care of four children. Her apparel-purchasing choices may be almost unlimited, because she lives in an urban setting. To help her maintain her budget, she most likely would decide between two options: She may purchase the cheapest garments she can find no matter what the brand name or construction techniques used to make them; she will just replace them with another inexpensive garment if the seams come undone. Or she may spend more money on apparel that has

Demographic facts include such information as age, ethnicity, gender, religious practice, place of residence, level of education, income level, marital status, and size of family.

a brand name she has experience with. She knows these items may cost more, but in the past, the construction of the garments has held up well enough to be passed down from one child to the next, thereby saving money in the long run. How could your choice of construction methods influence her purchasing decisions?

Sales also depend on customers at the opposite end of the price-point scale with a different demographic profile. Take, for example, a single woman, aged 25, who is out of college and working as a graphic designer at a large marketing firm. She has no children and a sizeable income, which she need spend only on herself. She lives in the same urban area as the woman in our previous example and therefore has many options when it comes to apparel shopping. She purchases a trendy budget garment to wear to a party, because it has to last only one night. So what if the hem comes out on the skirt? She was planning to throw it out after the party anyway. On the other hand, she might also shop for an elegant winter coat to wear to work. Because this is a sizeable investment that she intends to wear for several seasons, she will choose one from a well-known designer brand her friends have raved about. She knows it will be carefully made, fully lined, and have high-end details. How will this customer be influenced by your garment construction decisions?

In both consumer examples, the difference between a "throwaway" garment verses an investment piece relies heavily on the quality of the construction. The fast-paced, profit-oriented industry you are entering no longer thinks of quality as "the preserve of high fashion or expensive clothing, but . . . a feature of all market segments, and that the level of quality in all apparel should meet the specific requirements and tastes of all types of customers."[5]

Psychographics. The **psychographic** choices that consumers make can also be studied to attempt to predict their apparel-purchasing decisions. These attitude, interest, and opinion choices include what activities they do in their leisure time, what media they read, what stores they frequent, what their opinions are about society, what music they listen to, and what their attitudes are about the environment. As we have discussed before, consumers have needs and wants that they often look to apparel to fulfill. Consumers may be segmented according to psychographic choices into groups that prefer a particular level of quality or even a particular type of seam or seam finish in the apparel they purchase. Take, for example, consumers who participate in rigorous physical pastimes such as mountain biking, running, or downhill skiing. Each of these groups has specific requirements for the garments they wear during those activities. This type of high-tech apparel often requires special seaming techniques to contribute to the performance and comfort of the garment. Customers usually purchase these garments based on how well they perform and how long they last, not on how much the garment costs.

Consumers also have opinions and attitudes about the apparel that we are making. Of course, consumers have opinions and attitudes about many things, some of which affect the type of fashions they will buy, but we are going to concentrate on how they relate to our apparel and its construction specifically. A consumer's attitudes and opinions about the category of products we sell and the individual fashions in that category will initially be formed by their demographic background, such as their ethnicity, their childhood and family life, their religious practice,

and their level of education. Those attitudes will then be modified by their feelings and concerns and by the society they live in, including current demographic facts like where they live, their marital status, and family size. Their opinions can also be changed by the marketing efforts of fashion professionals that they are exposed to. For example, a young woman's opinions and attitudes about the revealing fashions worn to nightclubs might be negative if her conservative, religious family lived in a rural town in the Midwest. But if she then attends college in a large city such as Boston, she may be exposed to different attitudes about the category of club wear through new friends, magazines, and newspaper ads. It is important for her to have positive feelings about the fashions she is purchasing. She may adopt a more relaxed opinion about this apparel and may end up accepting this category of apparel enough to try wearing it herself. If her family was of modest means, she may have grown up making her own apparel or wearing hand-me-downs from other family members. In that case, she would have an opinion about how a garment at a certain price point should be constructed. She may have been unaware of how expensive designer goods can be and so opt for low-priced garments that are constructed well. In this example, we can also see that her social class and culture have influenced her purchasing decisions. Her new attitudes may be influenced through marketing by brands that she is unfamiliar with but also by her past experiences of shopping environments and the performance of fashions she has already purchased.

Psychological aspects. The psychological motivations that influence apparel-purchasing decisions are just as important, and possibly even more so, as demographic facts or psychographic choices. An apparel professional should carefully consider what motivates the customers who make up their targeted market. The psychological motivation we are most concerned with is the customer's reason for purchasing apparel in general or buying a particular garment. In many cultures, the most basic motivation might be to avoid being nude in public or to protect oneself from the weather. But beyond that need, there are obviously more needs and wants that influence apparel purchases.

Achieving a goal is another very strong motivator. An apparel choice may be made to realize the goal of getting a better job or a promotion, to garner respect from associates at work, or to attract a long-term partner. Another extremely important goal is to fit in with one's family or one's peers at work or in a social or religious group. This goal is very compelling to consumers, because they are dealing with their self-image.

Consumer Self-Image

All people have images of who they think they are that include many aspects of their being. This self-image "picture" is influenced by environment, the people around them, their own personality, and their wants and needs. When they are ready to make a decision on a fashion purchase, their self-image exerts a strong influ-

The psychographic choices that consumers make can also be studied to attempt to predict their apparel-purchasing decisions. These attitude, interest, and opinion choices include what activities they do in their leisure time, what media they read, what stores they frequent, what their opinions are about society, what music they listen to, and what their attitudes are about the environment.

ence on that decision. After all, they risk damaging their self-image if they make an inappropriate choice. Everyone wants to have a positive self-image and to be satisfied with the picture in their heads. Your job as a fashion professional is to offer garments that customers feel will enhance their self-image, thereby causing them to purchase. Seams that are poorly constructed with loose stitching, puckering, and hanging threads will not enhance anyone's self-image. Seams and seam finishes that are well placed and neatly sewn, with the possible addition of a design detail in seam construction or a higher level of quality, will result in more sales to customers who feel the garment represents them well and will be an asset to their image.

Designers, merchandisers, and buyers should also be aware of the transformative ability of fashion. The designs you choose to sell will often be selected because customers see these fashions as having the ability to transform them into someone they are not or someone they wish to become. As Dana Thomas states, "brands (are) now in the business of selling dreams."[6] Customers may want to see themselves as a successful executive, their favorite sexy movie star, or more physically fit. The construction methods you choose to build and shape your garments will create and enhance their transformative qualities. Will that zipper application look more biker chick or more pop starlet? Will that pocket application fit more with a streamlined exercise suit or a tailored business suit? How will you seam that sheer chiffon so that it enhances the customer's vision of herself as a sultry movie star of the 1940s?

Fashion is many different things to many people. Not only must fashion satisfy the needs and wants of today's consumer, but also it must appear in the store faster and at a very competitive price. Remember, the value equation for the customer only works if they feel that they have made a fair investment of time, money, and energy to get the product. In addition, they are investing their self-image into the purchase of the garment. They must be able to see themselves as expressing their own fashion voice while at the same time fitting in with their social, family, or work groups.

Because of the revolutionary activities of such fashion luminaries as Yves St. Laurent, Liz Claiborne, and Donna Karan, women now feel that they can create their own style and be their own "designer" to invent a look that will uniquely enhance their self-image. Because of this new attitude, and the related decline of couture, women can also combine fashions from the best designers seen in the best department stores at designer signature prices with fashions from Target, Zara, and H&M at budget price points. "The emergence of luxury designer fast fashion has finished off whatever division was left between high-end and low-end fashion. These days, the rich buy Isaac Mizrahi designs at Target while the middle market shops at Gucci."[7]

The impact this has had on the construction of fashion in the 20th and 21st centuries is both profound and permanent. Although there is still an exclusive market for designer ready-to-wear, which has been constructed without regard for the cost or amount of time taken to complete the work (Ralph Rucci's Chado line is the perfect example), most fashion ready-to-wear—from designer labels to budget—works with a more profit-centric view of quality; that is, the construction quality that best represents the brand and does not compromise its image must be balanced with the cost of producing that level of quality. Also, the speed with which the apparel gets to market is

The psychological motivations that influence apparel-purchasing decisions are just as important and possibly even more so than demographic facts or psychographic choices.

considered. Shortening the time between when the garment is designed and when it lands on the retail rack is essential to maximizing profits. Has construction quality suffered in the fast-paced, trend-pumped, profit-centered fashion industry of today? It has changed, yes, but your view on whether it has suffered depends on your perspective, how long you've been in the industry, what company you work for, and what the needs of your customers are.

Consumer Perception

Fashion professionals must also take the perceptions of their customer into account when deciding on apparel quality. As a designer, merchandiser, or buyer, you can minimize the level of risk the customer associates with purchasing your apparel by using the aesthetics of your garment to appeal to their physical and mental perceptions. Your garment must arouse the senses of the customer. How will you enhance your garment in the eyes of the consumer by your choices of silhouette, colors, hand, textures, lines, and shapes? What construction techniques will impact their emotional response and promote their self-image—feminine princess seams, ruffles, and pleats, or tailored collars and welt pockets with flaps? What benefits will the fit and construction have for them?

Along with their sensory and emotional perceptions of your garment, your consumer will also experience them in a cognitive way. They will acquire knowledge about your product from people they know who have tried it and from advertisements, salespeople, the store displays, and the product itself. They will read the tags on it, which might tell the customer about the garment's construction. They may flip up the hem on a skirt to see if it is lined or not. When they try it on, they will evaluate the fit and the comfort. Their cognitive evaluation may also have a symbolic element, which we discussed before. They will then use this knowledge together with their sensory experience and their emotional response to how they look in it to decide whether to buy the garment.

Outcomes of Consumer Purchasing Decisions

There may be several outcomes once consumers are done with their evaluation. They may be satisfied, in which case they will purchase the garment. If their experience with the garment meets their standards of quality after using it, such as the seams, hems, and trims staying sewn, then you will have established a good relationship with them. If they are dissatisfied with the garment, then they will not purchase it or will purchase and then return it with a complaint. During the use period of this process, the construction methods you chose will really have a chance to impress your customer. They will be judging the quality of your garment, and therefore your brand, according to the durability, reliability, performance, and conformance standards that you have set, the standards that you determined would please your customer. At the end of the purchase and use cycle, the customer will discard the garment in some way. If you have maintained your level of quality, then they will become a loyal customer and purchase repeatedly.

The Maker

As a maker of apparel, you will need to arm yourself with knowledge of many issues related to the manufacturing process to ensure your success. These issues include what strategies are available to you for controlling the manufacturing process; what factors impact your customer, brand image, and positioning; what materials, skills, knowledge, energy, and tools will be used in the manufacturing process; what the benefits of creating the apparel will be for you; and what costs you will incur and how you will control them. Obviously, we understand that designers and merchandisers are engaged in making decisions about the quality of the garment's construction from the start. For the purposes of this book, if you are a buyer, we will assume that you are purchasing apparel that has specifically been created for you, that you have had a hand in designing or redesigning the garments, or that you are making the decisions about what apparel to accept for sale at retail. We will also assume that you, as a fashion professional, are making a quantity of apparel in a workroom or factory.

Strategies

As an apparel maker, your products will arrive at the store more quickly and at the quality level you have chosen if you adopt a strategy for its manufacturing. Two strategies you might choose include process focused and product focused.[8]

Process focused. In a process-focused format, the maker concentrates on ensuring that the garments are being manufactured using construction methods that meet the level of quality the customer requires. The successful selling of the garment is ensured by choosing the most advantageous processes with which to manufacture it. The fashion professional must also keep waste to a minimum in the manufacturing process. For example, employing untrained workers who are prone to making mistakes in construction or using a low-quality thread that is prone to breakage will cause both time and money for wages to be wasted during the manufacturing process. The only way to correct such a circumstance is to redo the garments, which wastes time, money, and materials. If the garment's poor quality is left uncorrected, the customer may perceive the lack of quality, if not at the point of purchase, then during the usage stage. This damages the brand image and negatively affects the positioning of the apparel. The fashion professional will be keeping track of what processes are being used; how they are being performed; and when improvements are called for, whether they are made rapidly and consistently. It is especially important that costs are being controlled during the process to ensure that the apparel generates a profit for the company and is sold at the retail price that is most competitive. Controlling costs also contributes to successful positioning against competing garments and to a positive, reliable brand image.

Product focused. The product-focused strategy centers on intrinsic traits of the garment to ensure success rather than on the process used to manufacture it. As discussed before, these traits are physical, such as construction, fit, comfort, color, and texture, and are performance related, such as durability, reliability, performance, and conformance to standards. Consistency is a major factor in determining quality and value. "Manufacturers establish quality standards that result in garments of a particular quality level. . . . Not all garments must be the highest quality, but garments should be of the highest quality for which the customer is willing to pay."[9]

Benefits to the Maker of Manufacturing Apparel

Whatever the strategy, fashion professionals will consider what benefits manufacturing the apparel will have for their business and for the consumer. Producing garments with a quality of construction that will both generate profit for the maker and satisfy the customer will preserve the company's brand image and market reputation. Choosing the right quality of construction will also ensure that the customer feels a lower level of risk associated with buying the garment, which results in customer goodwill and repeat sales.

Makers must also consider the positioning of the garment against the competition in their marketplace, as discussed earlier. Correct positioning will prevent the customer from wanting to substitute other garments for theirs. It will also insulate their garments from the competition represented by current rivals and any new entrants into the market in their product category.

Considerations

Remember, the fashion professional will find that fulfilling consumers' preferences will sell more apparel. Does this mean you should design only what the customer wants without regard for your own fashion voice? Not necessarily. But incorporating your chosen consumer's implied or explicit preferences into your fashions or making sure that you have thoroughly explored the marketplace and clearly defined the customer who will see your fashions as essential to his or her wardrobe will only lead to more sales without compromising your design ideas. Whichever way you approach the fashion marketplace, remember that features are the name of the game in fashion. Those features must have benefits that are relevant to the customer's needs and wants. You must objectively measure the level at which you have fulfilled those needs and wants with each style you produce with the customer's viewpoint foremost in your mind. Fashion professionals should inform the customer about

Tom and Linda Platt are the epitome of successful independent designers. Their refined ready-to-wear collections are carried at major department stores such as Lord & Taylor and are featured in their own exclusive showroom in Manhattan. Tom and Linda have built a visionary outlook on fashion that their clients adore for its fresh, humorous twists on the everyday.

Tom and Linda met while students at Pratt Institute, and both graduated from Syracuse University. The Platts began their industry education as assistant designers learning workroom techniques and garment engineering, practicing what they learned by creating fashion miniatures in period costume for the extravagant Christmas windows at Lord & Taylor in New York. When the time came to begin their own line in 1982, they dedicated their efforts to studying and defining "what made clothes modern." The Platts came to the conclusion that dresses were the "simplest, most practical, [yet] most modern garment in the world." They realized that in this, the "sewing machine era," women wanted pure fashions with a "dress-making approach" that uses fabric to caress the body. Tom and Linda developed seven styles that they actually sewed themselves, 16 dresses a day. Now the Platts "buy fabrics that we love and use them as simply as we can." At the time of this interview, the Platts were on their 76th collection, producing 50 to 70 pieces in a line, including day dresses, separates, coats, and cocktail dresses. In their studio in midtown, the Platts work out the designs themselves, create the patterns and marker on a computer, and complete the cutting by hand, keeping a careful eye out for fabric defects. Two gifted sample makers who have been in their employ for over 15 years help with feedback and input on construction and sewing order issues for especially intricate pieces, such as their signature "chicken wing" sleeve. "When we go to production we need to say, 'can this be made, is this practical, how can I stream line this . . . where can we take a step out?'" The pieces are then taken to a factory down the street to be constructed into small garment runs. After completion through pressing, the garments come back to the design room for inspection. "Every square inch of every garment" is inspected individually to ensure the high level of quality that the label is known for. Does he think quality is still important to the fashion industry? "Absolutely! I think people are maniacal about quality."

Tom Platt relates that their fashion house doesn't worry about quality control, because it's "second nature" to them; they "are a product-oriented company; we are all about the product; it's part of our hearts here." In their design house, Platt relates, "we have a much higher price point. We cannot mechanize (the garment-making process) because every time we go about making a garment, we're going to do it a little differently. . . . Our basic social need in the world is to communicate." Through fashion, Tom Platt believes he can "communicate with my customers by making clothes for them that perhaps change their perception of themselves and make them feel a certain way or look a certain way. They get positive feedback from their friends and relatives and even if I've never spoken to them, I've had a very intense and intimate communication with them."

the features and benefits of the fashions they are promoting, especially the quality of construction. Linking the quality of construction to the price of the garment helps lower the consumer's perception of risk in purchasing your apparel.

Contributions

Many physical and conceptual components go into the manufacturing of apparel. Before the actual manufacturing process begins, buyers, merchandisers, and independent designers will analyze past sales figures for the previous season's fashion lines to determine what sold, how well it sold, and when it sold. They must answer quality- and construction-related questions, such as what the cost was of producing this specific garment and how much income a style represented for the company. Did the construction of the garment hold up well according to the customer's usage patterns, or were there returns due to construction faults? What about this design's construction appealed to the customer the most? Did the factory where the garment was produced have difficulties with the manufacturing process, and if so, is there a factory that could do a better job at a better price? How has the market for the garment changed? Are there any new entrants to the market with higher construction quality, and if so, how are the garments from that company priced? Do the customers require new benefits from the garment, and if so, what are they, and how will the manufacturing process be changed to meet those new customer requirements?

Also, fashion professionals will most likely seek information on the upcoming trends in fashion that impact construction, including silhouettes, shapes, details, and fabrics. If your customers are aware of what is coming up in fashion and expects your brand to offer them apparel choices that include those trends, then incorporating them in your styles may sell more garments. Being able to work with a variety of fabric weights and garment detailing may mean purchasing different sewing equipment or tools, training workers to perform different tasks, and having different materials on hand. The impact of these changes may be felt both in the costs of producing those new shapes or details and in the time needed to complete them. Fashion professionals must be aware of those effects and plan for them accordingly.

In addition to the decisions mentioned above, merchandisers, independent designers, and buyers must also use their fashion construction knowledge and skills to identify what apparel will satisfy the needs and wants of their customer. To successfully manufacture those designs, they must decide what techniques should be used to construct them at the level of quality that suits their brand image, that will keep costs down, and that will get the fashions to the store at the right time. Many buyers, designers, and merchandisers use the services of a product engineer to help them define the most timely, cost-efficient construction methods to use and the order in which those processes should be completed. For the buyer, and in some situations the designer and merchandiser, the product engineer may already be an employee of the factory where the apparel is being manufactured. Depending on the size of the factory, workroom, or design studio, the merchandiser or designer may perform the duties of product engineer, often with the help of an experienced sample sewer.

Product Engineering

The process of product engineering begins with the preferences of the retail consumer. Based on consumer preferences, fashion professionals determine the features of the garment that affect construction, including the pieces used to make the shapes and silhouette of the garment; the fabric; and the types of stitches, seams, and seam finishes to be used.

Garment pieces are the smallest part used in construction, such as a fly facing for the front of a pair of jeans, the strip of fabric used to construct a sleeve placket, or the pocket flap on a jacket. "Pieces make components which are the basic sections of garments, including top fronts, top backs, . . . sleeves, collars."[10] Each component is studied to determine the number of pieces needed to construct it and what materials will be needed to complete it.

Determining the "operation breakdown" is the next stage in analyzing components.[11] An operational breakdown determines the sequence of assembly, resulting in a list of steps for the production process of that component. It is essential to quality and timeliness of construction that the process begin with the smallest pieces, which are joined to create ever-larger components that are joined to each other when the process cannot proceed any further without doing that. For example, the sequence of assembly for a blouse sleeve might be to pleat the bottom of the sleeve, complete the placket, sew the underarm seam, attach the

previously completed cuff, and then execute the buttonholes and apply the buttons. One of the most strategic concepts during this analysis step is to keep flat the component or garment being sewn during as many steps as possible. It is much easier to work with a small, flat item than with a large, bulky item that is in a circle; that is, it will be much easier to sew a complex welt pocket to a jacket front alone without the front being sewn to the jacket back at the side seams and shoulders. Another way to express this concept of operational breakdown is "pieces + pieces = components, components + components = garments."[12] (In this text, there are flow charts at the beginning of each chapter that give you a basic sewing order for the garments featured in the chapter.)

Once the methods of construction are determined, they are analyzed according to how many steps are needed to complete them, what additional materials may be needed besides thread, what handling and pressing steps are required for that construction method, and what additional training, tools, or machinery are necessary. These factors are carefully considered to determine the cost of making the garment. If necessary, they will be changed or deleted from the process to keep the garment within budget.

The level of quality, as guided by consumer preferences, will also be a factor in product-engineering decisions. As we have already seen, consumer preferences in quality and retail price will affect the types of seams and seam finishes that are used. These choices, in turn, affect the sewing steps to be executed, the order in which these steps are done, and the level of accuracy demanded of the workers. "The specific construction sequence for assembling a particular apparel product varies depending on the product and the manufacturer making it."[13]

After this planning period, which also includes pattern making, marker making, choosing fabrics, and foundation materials, the fabrics, linings, interlinings, and interfacings are cut as needed. For certain styles, foundation materials are attached by sewing or fusing to their respective pieces. Trims may then be applied at this point or later when certain components are finished. "Components are usually assembled simultaneously by different sewing machine operators."[14] After the components have been joined to complete the garment, final finishing steps may be done to complement the look or performance of the garment. These finishing steps fall loosely into two groups: chemical and physical. Chemical finishes for completed garments may include dyeing or sizing or adding an antiwrinkle treatment. Physical finishes might include distressing either by tumbling with pumice or hand distressing with sandpaper or might include applying heat transfers. When finishes are completed, the garment may go directly for a final pressing plus trimming, which includes snipping of thread ends, tagging, and packaging.

Batch Manufacturing

The fashion industry has undergone radical changes during the last 40 years or so in the United States and abroad. In this introduction, we have discussed the idea of fashion having changed from a designer-centered industry to a customer-centered industry. One of the most significant changes has been the increasing speed of the fashion manufacturing process. Instead of seeing collections in stores only four times a year, consumers can now choose from a collection every month at certain price points from some retailers and designers. Many consumers expect this now and may not visit retailers who do not turn over fashions quickly enough to keep them entertained. Not only that, but fashion professionals must also maintain the same level of quality and quantity each time customers shop. These current influences have encouraged manufacturers to adopt methods of manufacturing that originated in other industries and that have also faced time and quality constraints. One of the most important of these methods is known as "lean" manufacturing.

Since fashion manufacturing began during the Industrial Revolution, the batch method has prevailed as the most frequently employed technique to produce apparel. Batch manufacturing is characterized by the way the garment pieces flow through the process and how the production floor is arranged (Figure I.6).

Basically, in the batch methods, workers are assigned a particular part of the process to complete. They work on "batches" of pieces instead of one piece of the garment at a time to complete their part of the process. In order to keep track of the batch (usually by means of a computerized, bar code-based system), the batch being worked on does not leave a worker until all the identical pieces from that batch are completed. Workers are paid by the number of pieces they complete each day.

FIGURE I.6 Batch manufacturing process.

Another way to express this concept of operational breakdown is "pieces + pieces = components, components + components = garments."[15]

If one worker is faster than another, then they will complete their batches faster and get paid more. Small pieces are prepared and sewn together before being attached to larger components of the garment. Workers and their equipment, such as fusing machines, sewing machines, and rivet setters, are positioned on the floor, usually in a line, so that the batches travel over the shortest space possible from one worker to the next. All of the necessary pieces for finishing a component should arrive simultaneously at the operator completing that component.

The problem with the batch system is that sometimes that does not happen. If two people working on a piece for the same component do not finish at the same time, those two batches of pieces will not arrive at the component sewer at the same time. *All* of the pieces in the batch need to be completed before the batch can move on to the next worker. Therefore, the completion of the component is delayed, which subsequently delays the work of each person, piece, and component down the line. Additionally, simply having

to transport the batches via human or automated transportation from one worker to the next adds time. In manufacturing, especially in the highly competitive apparel market, wasted time is wasted money. "Minutes of make," the amount of time it takes to complete a job on the line, is calculated down to the 1/1,000th of a minute. Although minutes of make vary with the level of construction quality specified for the garment, higher quality means a longer time to make. Time is still equated with profitability.

Lean Manufacturing

Lean manufacturing allows the manufacturer to make the same amount of money in less time because production is faster (Figure I.7). The thought processes of management and workers, the placement of equipment, and the order of production are all fundamentally different.

In lean manufacturing, the focus is on the elimination of waste during and after the production process. Waste for apparel manufacturers means money out of their pockets. Reducing or eliminating waste is accomplished by a remarkable rethinking of the core concepts of apparel manufacturing. In general lean-manufacturing concepts, the forms of waste are labeled as

* overproduction,
* waiting,
* transporting,
* inappropriate processing,
* unnecessary inventory,
* unnecessary and/or excess motions, and product defects.

A lean manufacturing "cell" or "pod" in an apparel factory has all the machines needed to complete one component or garment arranged together in a circle or block format. Each worker is trained in

FIGURE I.7 Lean manufacturing process.

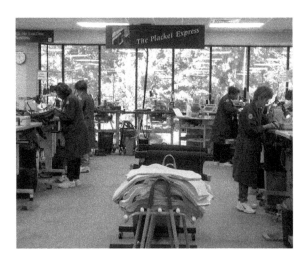

all of the processes, on all of the machines in the pod. The pieces are handed off one at a time to the next member of the pod, so there is a never-ending flow of pieces or components. If there is a delay in the flow, then the cross-trained workers can move to another machine to correct the delay. Since all of the workers are invested in completing the whole component or garment, they are all concerned with the same goal of turning out quality work in the shortest time possible and are more likely to see errors so they spend less time redoing work. The workers in cells are paid a salary with bonuses when production exceeds targeted goals.

Lean manufacturing can cut **throughput** time quite drastically, often cutting months down to a few weeks; this means less time between the placement of an order and its completion. Therefore, there can be a reduction of garments in inventory, which means a lower cost for storing and transporting them. The pods can go on to manufacture another order more quickly, so **replenishment** is faster for retailers. They will be able to sell more garments in season when the trend is hot and the consumer's need is at its peak.

Waste in Apparel Manufacturing

As mentioned in the preceding section, lean manufacturing developed around the idea of reducing waste in manufacturing. The problem of waste in apparel manufacturing is not limited only to time spent waiting for garment parts to arrive. Obviously, materials such as fabric, thread, and foundations, as well as time, are wasted when a construction step needs to be redone due to defects by workers. The possibility of defects means that the garments being made need to be inspected, which involves time and motion.

Waste can also occur if the fabric is not cut efficiently. Markers are made to best use the fashion and foundation fabrics. Motions made by workers can be wasted while completing a construction step or moving a piece or component to another spot on the production floor. Inventory of materials are being wasted if they are not used right away. Your buttons may have been paid for already, but if you are not using them immediately, you are wasting money and space for storing them. Finished garments will not make you money sitting in your warehouse waiting for someone to buy them. The key is to make them right before they are needed to avoid the waste of overproduction.

Overprocessing is an area of waste that can be avoided by employing a product engineer to streamline the manufacturing process and by having the correct tools to quicken the process without compromising quality. For example, adding a bias binder attachment to a lockstitch machine will save hundreds of hours in production time and will enhance quality over trying to apply bias binding to a Hong Kong seam by hand. The guiding concept to keep in mind about lean manufacturing is that your customer probably will not care what you had to go through to make the apparel they are purchasing. The majority of them will want to have the best quality for what they feel is the most reasonable price no matter what the process was that got the apparel to their favorite store. Anything that you as a manufacturer can do to deliver that will ensure your success.

Sourcing

Fashion professionals must also take part in many activities to ensure that their apparel is manufactured to the quality standards that their customer requires.

One of the most essential activities is sourcing. Buyers take part in sourcing activities when they are looking for apparel to buy. Designers, depending on the size of the company they work for, may look for fabrics, trims, and notions to make their designs become real. Materials need to meet the quality levels, aesthetic needs, and brand image of the manufacturer while being able to be delivered on time at the right wholesale price. Merchandisers may look for manufacturers to make the apparel created by their com-pany. The Appendix lists many great texts that go into depth on this topic. We will focus on the sourcing of labor and the questions that a fashion professional will need to answer about construction.

As mentioned before, apparel companies need to have their garments made with a particular level of quality, at a particular cost to them, within a particular time frame to allow on-time delivery for sale to the retail consumer. Fashion professionals who are employed by a garment-manufacturing factory may have

INDUSTRY PROFILE: HOW JOSEPH ABBOUD, AN AMERICAN APPAREL COMPANY, WRITES ITS OWN SUCCESS STORY

Is apparel manufacturing in America still on the decline? Not according to Joseph Abboud, which recently began exporting its high-quality men's suits and furnishings to its first retail shops in China. "We've all heard about how apparel manufacturing is one of so many industries to move in recent years from the U.S. to China. We're pleased to be moving in an exciting new direction by bringing the fine craftsmanship of a Joseph Abboud suit 'Made in America' to Chinese customers."[16]

How does an American institution turn around a failing New England mill, add employees when everyone else is cutting jobs, and break into the fickle but immense apparel market in a country hungry for all things upscale and American? By maintaining quality and taking the customers' wishes to heart and then combining them with modern thinking aided by cutting-edge manufacturing technology.

Joseph Abboud Manufacturing Corporation, under the watchful eyes of Anthony R. Sapienza, president and chief operating officer, and Rick Motta, VP of operations, has embraced lean-manufacturing methods and computerized machinery to optimize their time and the skills of their unionized workforce.

The process of suit manufacturing starts 2 years ahead with choosing the finest wools, cashmeres, silks, and blends for the selected styles. The designer works with the highly skilled tailor at the mill to fit jackets to the customer size demographic. The tailor makes samples and prototypes at the mill, and spec sheets are drawn up at the mill in consultation with the designers from the corporate headquarters in New York City. Then the pedal hits the metal with the use of the Gerber Accumodel digitized grading system, which fits the jackets to the target customer—aged 35 to 55—and the Gerber Silhouette system linked to the Marker system, which creates the layout of the pattern pieces to maximize use of the costly fabrics. Computerized spreading machines spread the materials; 30 pairs of fabric layers, 120 linings, or 50 fusible interlinings are then simultaneously cut by the Gerber system. Most of the construction machines used in the mill also have computerized components that control the stitch functions, adding to the workers' productivity.

Brand image, quality, and time are the guiding mantras of the Joseph Abboud mill. This results in a "commitment to distinctive quality and the sophisticated styling that is the hallmark of the Joseph Abboud label. . . . Our goal has always been to consistently design and manufacture the finest menswear in the marketplace."[17] To reach that goal here in the United States, Joseph Abboud has chosen to apply lean-manufacturing methods along with computerization to minimize waste.

Time does make a difference in profitability, especially when you are measuring it down to .001 of a minute! Time, or "minutes of make," helps determine the quality level of the product. "Quality tailoring methods make the suit," in this case.[18]

Lean manufacturing techniques and an investment in an Eton Unit Production System[19] have shaved the time needed to manufacture an exceptional suit from 6 weeks to one! Relocating their shipping facility from New Jersey to the mill in New Bedford has reduced transportation time for retailer order fulfillment as well. Many operators are cross trained on multiple machines and operations so that they may move to a process that is stalled or backed up to prevent delays. As with many garments, quickly manufacturing a suit lowers the carrying costs, results in faster replenishment and reduces lead time. The closer a suit is manufactured to the time it sells, the more accurate the decision of how many suits need to be made. They also realized that outsourcing production, the favored strategy of many retailers, carried with it hidden costs. Chief among them: The company would lose control over the shipping time and would probably be forced to make more merchandise than needed because of production minimums mandated at many overseas factories.[20]

In addition to their ready-to-wear line, demicouture suits are made using the Joseph Abboud Personal Style System, which is a perfect fit with the lean-manufacturing philosophy. In this system, the customer visits a retailer such as Nordstrom, picks a suit model, and is professionally measured for limited alterations; then their information is sent directly to the mill in New Bedford. Their "demicouture" suit is completed by the lean-manufacturing cell and shipped to the retailer for pickup in less than 2 weeks.

In the lean-manufacturing pods, quality is also better, as mistakes are caught sooner and are then redone, repaired, or recut. Pod members are responsible for their own quality control, which contributes to a sense of ownership in the process.

As Mr. Marty, staff president and CEO of Joseph Abboud, has said, "The consumer rules. He wants what he wants when he wants it, and he wants it gift-wrapped with a smile. We have to be responsive to today's market."[20]

all the labor they need in house, or they may choose to look elsewhere for certain parts of the construction process or to have a lower-priced companion garment made to supplement their regular line. They will consider the costs of what needs to be done and will consider if they can spare the time it would take for their own workers and machines to do the work, if they have the machines and trained employees to do the tasks, and if it would make better sense financially to have an outside vendor do the work. If they have all the garments made in their own factory, they will know the skills of the workers and the machines, tools, and other equipment available to them. If they choose to have apparel made elsewhere, they will have to explore the capabilities of each labor vendor they consider to make sure that the vendor can do the work while meeting deadlines and quality specifications.

Machines and Tools

As discussed before, the apparel industry has become increasingly competitive. In order to speed up production and reduce waste in the form of defects, manufacturers have employed very specified machines to complete garment-construction tasks. These machines range from versatile lockstitch machines, which can complete many tasks, to highly specialized machines that may only sew on a belt loop with a bar tack. The manufacturers who choose these specialized machines invest in them because they produce only one item, such as jeans.

Some tools are found in any workroom or manufacturing floor, such as thread nippers, but there also may be specialized forms for pressing garment parts that are shaped specifically for a certain style of suit jacket. The tools and machines employed

in garment construction are more fully explored in Chapter 2.

Costs

Before any fashion is manufactured, it undergoes the process of costing. Regardless of whether you are an independent designer for your own boutique or a merchandiser for a major private label, you must consider the impact of your construction decisions on the cost of making the garment. Analysis conducted to cost a garment requires an in-depth understanding of apparel materials and production. The apparel professional is challenged to choose the best alternatives among many options.[29] Buyers also consider how much they will pay for the apparel that the wholesaler is offering them. Even if they are not directly participating in construction decisions, the buyer's cost of goods is directly related to how much it cost the manufacturer to make the style being considered.

We have previously discussed the costs of manufacturing apparel—specifically, how those costs influence the retail price of the garment and its value in the eyes of the consumer. Let's take a minute to discuss some of the decisions involving construction that a fashion professional will make that impact costs.

The raw materials you choose for the garment needs to be handled and constructed using certain techniques to achieve the appropriate quality effect. For example, fine, translucent chiffon with a soft hand is more difficult to handle than cotton broadcloth and requires finishing techniques that could range from simple four- or five-thread overlocking at a low quality level to French seaming at a higher, more costly quality level. Working with stripes, plaids, and border prints also requires more handling and presents less room for error.

THE SEVEN MANUFACTURING WASTES

Waste elimination is one of the most effective ways to increase the profitability of any business. Processes either add value or waste to the production of a good or service. To eliminate waste, it is important to understand exactly what waste is and where it exists. While products significantly differ between factories, the typical wastes found in manufacturing environments are quite similar. For each waste, there is a strategy to reduce or eliminate its effect on a company, thereby improving overall performance and quality.[21]

The seven wastes are:

1. Overproduction. Manufacturing product just before it is needed reduces the waste of "overproduction." JIT (just in time) manufacturing also reduces the material expenses related to producing a product that will not be immediately paid for by customers. The factory should "produce only what can be immediately sold/shipped."[22] JIT production also cuts down on the storage costs represented by excess inventory.

2. Waiting. Arranging the manufacturing floor for the quickest flow between processes reduces the waste of "waiting." The traditional arrangement of a garment factory includes batches moving from one operator to the next. Using the concepts of lean manufacturing to improve factors such as material flow, length of production run, and the distance between workers reduces waiting time.[23]

3. Transporting. Reducing the time, energy, and cost needed to move pieces from one operator to the next cuts down on the waste of "transporting." Not only can excess moving of materials waste time and energy, but also it adds no value to the product and can sometimes cause pieces of the product to become damaged or lost.[24] Situating the correct operators next to each other greatly eases the costs of transporting.

4. Inappropriate processing. Identifying and investing in the machinery and tools required to complete the needed operations reduces the costs of "inappropriate processing." Often, a simpler, less expensive machine is more versatile than a high-priced piece of technically advanced equipment that only completes one operation. Also, good garment engineering can identify steps that can be combined or eliminated, which cuts back on inappropriate processing.[25]

5. Unnecessary inventory. Having the right amount of material on the manufacturing floor for your production needs creates less "unnecessary inventory." Too much inventory on the floor takes up space that could be used for production and gums up the speed of the process. Optimizing the flow from the materials such as cut fabric, shoulder pads, thread, etc., to the operator and the flow from one operator to the next reduces unnecessary inventory.[26] So does making sure that manufacturing materials arrive right before they are needed from outside suppliers.

6. Unnecessary/excess motion. Workers who move less and whose movements are more comfortable can work longer and are more effective. "Unnecessary/excess motion" should be eliminated by conferring with operators and management to optimize productivity.[27]

THE SEVEN MANUFACTURING WASTES (continued)

7. Defects. Materials such as fabric, thread, and foundations, plus time, are wasted when a construction step needs to be redone due to defects by workers. The possibility of defects means that the garments being made need to be inspected, which involves time and motion. A commitment to quality-control methods practiced throughout the organization are essential to cutting back on defects. "As world-class organizations have come to realize, customers will pay for value added work, but never for waste."[28]

If the apparel is being manufactured for a consumer at a certain quality level at a particular price point, that consumer will expect patterns to be matched. This activity results in higher production costs due to the extra time and handling.

The complexity of the construction process directly impacts the expense of producing the garment. The number of pieces and components needed for the garment and the overall number and types of seams add time, materials, and handling costs. Adding trims may require additional training for workers, added time to apply them, and materials. More sophisticated equipment may be needed for applying trims; for other complex construction activities, such as applying bias binding to seam edges; or for speeding processes that are essential to construction, such as button sewing. Apparel professionals are constantly faced with pressure to control costs of labor, materials, and overhead to maintain profitability.[30]

Trained workers must be able to work at a profitable speed while maintaining the quality level that is expected. Training or retraining workers also requires an initial investment in time, especially when you are cross-training on several pieces of equipment for lean manufacturing. Construction quality-control activities are the responsibility of the machine operators, managers, or quality-inspection workers. Consistency is a major factor in determining quality and value. "Manufacturers establish quality standards that result in garments of a particular quality level."[31] Everyone engaged in constructing the garment has an investment in ensuring that the quality level expected, determined with the retail customer's wishes in mind, is fulfilled. However, the cost of maintaining the set level of quality must be balanced with the expense of producing that level of quality. In search of higher profits in a highly competitive market, fashion professionals are increasingly choosing construction methods that will improve the profitability of each design, usually with the added benefit of getting the product to the customer faster. The hope is that the changes made will not be noticed by the customer, or if they are noticed, will still be tolerated and not result in lost sales at the point of purchase or after the garment has been worn. This quote from Dana Thomas in *Deluxe: How Luxury Lost Its Luster* sums up the situation for many of today's brands: "Lowering costs was a more delicate problem. How could luxury brands slash the production cost of their goods and maintain the same high level of quality? In fact, they couldn't. There had to be concessions. Some cut corners in ready-to-wear. . . . Soon that became the industry standard."[32] The decisions made by the professionals working for these labels reflect the constant demand for apparel that represents the company's brand image and generates a profit while satisfying the customer's fashion needs.

~~~~~~

CONCLUSION

Ultimately, what does *quality* mean for ready-to-wear fashion professionals and their customers? Is it trendy, cheaply constructed designs that satisfy the consumer's immediate urge to have something new to wear to a party this evening? Or is quality a fulfillment of the customer's ultimate dream of owning a piece of timeless designer apparel featuring hand-sewn embellishments? As you have learned from reading this introduction, quality is both. In this new fashion era, every consumer is creating his or her own "look," his or her own fascinating mixture of new and old, inexpensive and costly, inexpensively made and luxurious. Well-designed fashion of dependable quality at affordable prices, offered on an ever-changing retail sales floor, has become accessible to all. "In the end, good fashion isn't about price," Karl Lagerfeld said. "It's about taste."[33]

Where quality is concerned, for both the maker and the customer, the impact of the construction techniques chosen on the garment retail price is just as important as the look of the construction. To many customers, the retail price is even more important than the way the construction looks. Retail customers strive to create a signature look that represents their own fashion statement. They now judge themselves by the label inside the garment and how successful they are at representing their inner selves and aspirations more than how much something cost them. In retail ready-to-wear, price is no longer the guarantee of quality construction that it used to be, and customers realize this.

You will decide what is necessary to meet the needs of your customer and your need to create that special garment. In the end, the quality level of construction you choose will become an integral part of your fashion statement.

~~~~~~

KEY INDUSTRY TERMS TO KNOW

Back tacking: Stitching backwards a few stitches at the beginning and/or end of a line of stitching to prevent it from unraveling.

Basting: A line of temporary stitching used to hold garment parts together before being sewn permanently.

Batch: A group of apparel parts, usually more than 10 at a time, passed from one operator who has completed their task to the next operator on a garment assembly floor. Also refers to the method of garment manufacturing that uses these "batches" of pieces.

Benefits: What goal the apparel satisfies *for* the customer such as keeping them within their budget, preserving their image at work, or making them comfortable while lounging at home.

Better: An apparel price point just below designer and above bridge.

Binding folder: A sewing machine attachment which transforms strips of bias cut fabric into a double folded binding to finish the raw edge of a fabric.

Bobbin: A spool like device for neatly holding a quantity of the lower thread on a sewing machine.

Brand: A conglomeration of all of the images and experiences that a customer has had with a business entity or a product.

Bridge: An apparel price point just below better and above moderate.

Budget: An apparel price point just below moderate and above category killer.

Buyers: Individuals in the apparel industry whose job it is to select merchandise for a retail store within a predetermined budget while keeping the current trends, retailer brand image, and customer preferences in mind.

Category killer: The lowest apparel price point just below budget.

Conformance: Adherence to a standard of quality in materials, processes, and workmanship during manufacturing.

Construction: The joining of fabric, trims, and notions in the apparel industry to form wearable shapes by sewing, using metal parts such as rivets, or gluing.

Costing: The process of estimating how much of a monetary investment will be necessary to make a particular garment. This estimate may be done before and/or after a sample garment is made and before production begins.

Custom: A garment that is made for a specific individual using their measurements and often their choice of materials.

Defects: A flaw in a manufactured item such as a fabric, notion, or the finished garment which prevents it from being of the best quality.

Demographics: Data collected about customers used to help define their preferences in relation to products and consuming behavior.

Design: The process of a product produced by an artist working in the realm of apparel production. A design is the individual's interpretation of a style. Designs may also be produced by a group of individuals in a large corporation.

Designer: An industry professional who interprets a style to create their own vision of fashion. Designers may take their own artistic ideas, inspirations from the world around them, the customer's preferences, available materials, and current trends into consideration when creating their designs.

Designer signature: The highest price point available for sale in mass quantities at retail apparel stores just below couture.

Durability: The stability of a product such as a notion, fabric, or a garment represented by how long it lasts without sustaining damage or looking worn.

Easing: A small amount of fullness, less than gathering, added to a seam. The fabric fullness should only be visible in the seam allowance of the garment.

Electronic Data Interchange: The process of transferring data from the manufacturer to the retailer to speed the production and sale of apparel. EDI shrinks the amount of time between when the garment starts as a concept to when it is taken home by the customer, thereby helping to make the garment more saleable.

End user: Another name for the retail apparel customer who is assumed to be the last person to purchase and use the garment.

Extrinsic: A characteristic of a garment that is not an actual part of the garment but is part of the customer's thoughts and beliefs about the garment. An example of an extrinsic characteristic of a garment would be that it is trendy, or is accepted by a certain peer group.

Fabrics: A predominantly flat, sheet-like formation of fibers and/or yarn that is woven, knitted, or nonwoven, and is used in the production of apparel.

Fashion: As a noun, this word is used as a synonym for the words "apparel" and "garment," but can also be used to mean the type of apparel that is worn by the majority of a certain group of individuals in a particular society, meaning that the prevailing fashion for women to wear to night clubs in America will not be the fashion for women to wear in the jungles of the Amazon.

Features: Actual physical qualities of the garment such as fabric type, construction, and fabric finish.

Feed teeth: Part of a machine used in garment construction which moves the fabric through the machine in the manner necessary to assist in stitch formation.

Fibers: An extremely slender, natural or man-made material measuring from less than an inch to several inches in length, which is spun into yarn and then knitted or woven together to create fabric. Fibers may also be meshed together by mechanical means without spinning to form fabric.

Finish: A mechanical or chemical process used on fabric after dyeing or printing, or on a finished garment to add qualities which make it more saleable and appropriate for customer use, such as wrinkle resistance or brushing.

Foundation materials: Materials such as buckram, flannel, and batting which change the hand of the finished garment usually for the purposes of making the fabric stiffer, hiding inner construction, or reinforcing areas that will receive stress while the garment is worn.

Grade: To alter a pattern up or down in size from the original pattern.

Hand: The qualities of a fabric that contribute to how it feels such as fiber, yarn, weave, drape, or fabric finish.

Haute couture: A title applied to fashions created almost completely by hand with the highest attention to detail, often for a single individual. The title may only be used by designers who have been given permission by the Fédération française de la couture, du prêt-à-porter des couturiers et des créateurs de mode (*French Federation of Fashion and of Ready-to-Wear of Couturiers and Fashion Designers*) to use the title.

Inappropriate processing: One of the seven forms of waste characterized by the use of over-designed, too-expensive equipment and/or too many or too complicated steps to complete a product. Inappropriate processing is usually avoided by utilizing the simplest, least expensive machines which may be able to perform a variety of tasks and reduce the number of steps in making the product.

Interfacings: The home sewing term for the garment industry's products called interlinings.

Interlinings: Materials attached by sewing or fusing with heat and moisture to the inside of a fashion fabric to add body or stiffness to a garment area for styling purposes and to increase durability.

Intrinsic: An actual part of a garment or the actual attributes of that part such as the fabric or the texture, hand, or color of the fabric.

Lean: A theory of manufacturing which focuses on the elimination of waste in the production process. Waste can be classified as anything during the process that doesn't directly add value to the product in the customer's eyes. The elimination of waste simultaneously lowers the price and production time of the product while raising the level of quality and, hence, the level of value. Lean manufacturing routinely employs manufacturing units or "cells" instead of the batch assembly line.

Licensing: A cooperative venture between a designer with name recognition and a manufacturer whose name is not well known to consumers. The manufacturer supplies the consumer with a lower priced line of apparel that shares a similar design appeal and name with the designer's signature line but is often made with simpler designs, lower quality fabrics, and faster construction techniques. This allows sales at a lower price point called "bridge" which encourages another segment of fashion consumers to purchase products.

Line: A group of garments which usually share a common inspiration plus various characteristics such as fabrics, colors, shapes, and use.

Linings: Fabrics that are attached inside a garment such as a jacket or skirt to make the garment easier to slip on, and to preserve its shape, construction, and outer fabric.

Lock stitch: A stitch formed in a straight line by a needle and a bobbin thread.

Make: The quality level of the garment as evidenced by the styling, fabric, and stitching used.

Manmade fibers: Materials not produced in nature which are used in the spinning of yarn or the making of fabric. Examples include polyester, rayon, and nylon. (see **Fiber**)

Marker making: The arrangement of pattern pieces on a given fabric width prior to cutting. Considerations are made for the most cost effective use of the fabric while maintaining quality.

Merchandisers: Individuals in the garment manufacturing process who engage in a variety of jobs while planning, coordinating, and producing lines of apparel or coordinating other individuals who are performing those tasks. Visual merchandisers function in the retail fashion realm where they are responsible for creating displays designed to make fashion products more appealing to the customer while at the same time representing the retailer's brand image.

Merchandising calendar: A calendar used by a garment manufacturing firm to keep the processes and personnel employed in the production of apparel on track so that the apparel is delivered on time.

Moderate: An apparel price point just below bridge and above budget.

Natural fibers: Materials used for the production of yarn and fabric that are either cellulosic or protein-based and are grown from a natural source. Examples include wool, silk, and flax. (see **Fiber**)

Needle: A very slender, round bar of metal that has been formed into a shape with a point at the lower end and an eye above it ending in a thicker diameter at the top called a shank. Needles will have a variety of point, eye, and shank configurations to suit

the fabric and thread being used,
the type of machine, and
the process being performed.
The purpose of the needle is to bring
the thread through the fabric during
stitch formation.

Notions: Materials used in the
production of apparel excluding fabric
and trims. Notions include metal
hardware such as snaps or hooks and
eyes; plastics, wood, or shell such as
buttons; or combinations of those with
fabric such as zippers.

Over lock: A type of sewing machine
which employs one or more needles
and one or more loopers to sew a seam,
finish the edge with over casting, and
cut off the raw edge of the fabric
simultaneously. Overlocks may also
be called "sergers," and may be used
to only finish the edge of a fabric, as a
merrow machine.

Overproduction: One of the seven forms
of waste which is seen in the production of too much merchandise to be
sold in a given amount of time. Also
known as "excess inventory," overproduction may be solved by understanding customer needs in a timely manner
so that only the amount to be shipped
is produced.

Pattern making: The creation of paper
or computer-generated patterns which
are the shape of garment pieces.
The pattern pieces are used to cut the
garment fabric to the correct shape and
size required for garment construction.

Performance: The way in which a
garment fulfills the needs of the customer. This term is most often used
to describe garments with special
properties such as the ability to wick
sweat away from the body, keep the
wearer warm, or reduce wrinkles. But
it can also be used to refer to other

characteristics such as fit for a
specific figure type or styling such as
in a swimsuit or wedding gown.

Piping: A tubular trim consisting of a
cord covered with bias fabric which is
sewn into a garment seam.

Positioning: How a product compares
to others like it in the marketplace
according to price, styling, and quality.

Process focused: A manufacturing
strategy in which the maker concentrates on the methods used to ensure
that the garments are being manufactured at the level of quality the customer requires by choosing the most
advantageous processes with which to
manufacture it.

Product engineer: A professional in
the manufacturing field who studies
the parts of a product, the machines
used to manufacture it, and the order
in which the processes are completed
to make sure that the product is being
made in the most cost-effective way
possible at the appropriate quality level.

Product focused: A manufacturing
strategy in which the maker concentrates on making sure that the
garment has the intrinsic traits the
customer prefers to ensure success
rather than on the process used to
manufacture it.

Prototype: A sample garment made
to test design decisions such as fabric,
construction methods, and fit.

Psychographics: Information
about the attitudes, interests, and
opinions of customers used to
understand their product and
consuming preferences.

Quality: A judgment of suitability to
purpose by a manufacturer or customer. Individuals and manufacturers
have standards which they expect the
attributes of an object to adhere to.

If an object is seen as meeting those standards, it is judged as being of "good quality."

Ready to wear: Apparel that is available to the end user to wear immediately, off the rack, with a minimum of changes to the garment structure, such as hemming.

Reliability: The dependability of an object; whether or not the object consistently meets the user's expectations.

Replenishment: The activities associated with ensuring that more of a previously sold product is available for the customer to purchase.

Retail: The final level of sales to the product's end user.

Risk: The likelihood that an object will not meet expectations. Customers may spend money, time, and effort on acquiring a piece of apparel. They expect that piece of apparel to live up to their expectations.

Stay stitching: A line of lock stitching done inside the seam allowance to prevent a curved or bias edge from stretching.

Sample sewer: A fashion industry professional practiced in the art of garment construction who produces a first version of a garment to check it for product engineering concerns, fit, and costing before production begins.

Seam allowance: The distance between the cut edge of the fabric and the innermost line of stitching, usually ½" to 1/4".

Serviceability: How a garment is refurbished; the method that should be used to clean it.

Seven areas of waste: Areas of manufacturing, as identified by the theories of lean manufacturing, which can be examined to ensure that the product is made in the most cost effective, quickest way possible without sacrificing quality.

Sizing: Adding a chemical finish to a fabric or to finished apparel to stiffen the product to make it easier to handle or have more appeal on a hanger.

Source: Businesses which provide materials or workmanship to the apparel industry.

Sourcing: The process of finding the appropriate companies in apparel manufacturing that can deliver the correct level of quality at the best price in a timely manner.

Specification writers: Fashion industry professionals who are responsible for compiling numerical data about a garment to aid in its production. Data may include lengths of seams, neck hole sizes, cuff widths, distances between belt loops, etc.

Stitches: Connections between threads created by the motions of machines usually completed in a linear direction for the purpose of attaching two pieces of fabric together but can also be done for decorative purposes.

Stitch length: The number of times the needle penetrates the fabric to form a stitch in a given distance. Stitch length is controlled by adjusting the setting of the feed teeth on the machine.

Stitch width: The distance between two sides of a single stitch or group of stitches.

Structure: The form a garment takes which is a combination of the silhouette, the shapes that make up the silhouette, fit, fabric, foundation fabrics, and construction techniques.

Style: A basic garment shape which is interpreted by a designer to become a fashion. For example, the basic button-down dress shirt can be redesigned to have french cuffs, decorative tucks, or princess seams to make the shirt more fitted. The word *style* can also be used to refer to an individual's combination of apparel, which reflects their personal attitudes about fashion.

Textile: A synonym for "fabric."

Thread tension: The degree of pressure put on a thread in a machine. Thread tension controls the quantity of thread given to the stitch-forming mechanism.

Throughput: The process of moving materials through the manufacturing processes.

Transporting: The movement of materials within the manufacturing process, i.e. from one machine operator to another, or to the movement of finished apparel from manufacturing to the retail sales floor. It can be one of the seven areas of waste if not managed properly to reduce the time taken to transport materials or goods.

Trims: A material which may be woven, knitted, crocheted, beaded, braided, etc. and that is made predominantly of yarn or fabric. Trims include ribbons, fabric ruffles, piping, and various kinds of cording, braids, tape, bias strips, laces, and appliqués.

Unnecessary/excess motion: One of the seven forms of waste which occurs when operators or other personnel on the factory floor are engaged in movements that do not add to the value of the product. For example, these excess movements may occur because of lack of operator training, too much bending and lifting between batch operations, or not having supplies easily accessible for operators.

Unnecessary inventory: One of the seven forms of waste which occurs when too much material is kept on hand for the amount of product being produced or too much product is produced before it can be sold.

Value: The relationship between quality and price from the viewpoint of the manufacturer or the customer. The value equation used in this book is: value = intrinsic attributes + extrinsic characteristics + investment, i.e. the value of the product is judged by the consumer based on how much money, time, effort, and self image they have invested in purchasing it plus the benefits that the intrinsic attributes and extrinsic characteristics offer them. Customers perceive the garment to be of acceptable quality if each side of the value equation is balanced.

Vertically integrated: Manufacturers that can perform more than one part of the garment production process such as spinning yarn, dyeing it, and then knitting sweaters with it.

Waiting: One of the seven forms of waste which occurs primarily during the batch manufacturing process when materials are delayed between operations.

Waste knot: A temporary knot used on the surface of the garment to secure the end of a hand stitching thread before the stitching is done. The waste knot is later clipped off.

Wholesale: The selling of goods to retailers in larger quantities at a reduced cost with the intention that they be resold to the end user.

Yarn: Grouping of fibers in a linear form together.

Zigzag: A stitch formed by a lock stitch machine in which the needle swings from left to right while the fabric moves through the machine.

END NOTES

1. Dana Thomas. *Deluxe: How Luxury Lost Its Luster* (New York: Penguin Press, 2007).
2. Ibid.
3. Ruth Glock and Grace Kunz. *Apparel Manufacturing Sewn Product Analysis*, 4th ed. (Upper Saddle River: Pearson Prentice Hall, 2005).
4. Ibid.
5. Pietro Romano and Andrea Vinelli. "Quality Management in a Supple Chain Perspective; Strategic and Operative Choices in a Textile-Apparel Network," *International Journal of Operations and Production Management* 21, no. 4 (2001): 448.
6. Dana Thomas. *Deluxe: How Luxury Lost Its Luster* (New York: Penguin Press, 2007).
7. Ibid.
8. H. P. Scheller and G. I. Kunz. "Toward a Grounded Theory of Apparel Product Quality," *Clothing and Textiles Research Journal* 16, no. 2 (1998): 5.
9. Ruth Glock and Grace Kunz. *Apparel Manufacturing Sewn Product Analysis*, 4th ed. (Upper Saddle River, NJ: Pearson Prentice Hall, 2005).
10. Ibid.
11. Ibid.
12. Patty Brown and Janett Rice. *Ready-to-Wear Apparel Analysis.* 3d ed. (Upper Saddle River, NJ: Pearson Prentice Hall, 2000).
13. Ruth Glock and Grace Kunz. *Apparel Manufacturing Sewn Product Analysis*, 4th ed. (Upper Saddle River, NJ: Pearson Prentice Hall, 2005).
14. Ibid.
15. Patty Brown and Janett Rice. *Ready-to-Wear Apparel Analysis*. 3d ed. (Upper Saddle River, NJ: Pearson Prentice Hall, 2000).
16. "CHINA: Joseph Abboud stores to sell U.S.-made suits," July 14, 2008. Available at: just-style.com. Accessed September 3, 2009.
17. "The Story of Joseph Abboud." Available at: www.Josephabboud.com. Accessed September 16, 2009.
18. Joseph Abboud Apparel Corp. Interview. October 29, 2007.
19. Anthony Sapienza, President/COO, Joseph Abboud Mfg. Corp.
20. "Joseph Abboud Apparel Corp. Confirms Commitment to U.S. Workforce. Lean Manufacturing Techniques and Exceptional Quality Keep Factory Competitive with Overseas Labor and Allows Quick Turnaround of Fine Tailored Men's Jackets and Trousers." New York, NY, January 8, 2006. Available at: www.unitehere.org. Accessed September 5, 2009.
21. David McBride. EMS Consulting Group. Carlsbad, CA. Available at: www.emsstrategies.com/dm090203article2.html.
22. Ibid.
23. Ibid.
24. Ibid.
25. Ibid.
26. Ibid.
27. Ibid.
28. Ibid.
29. Ruth Glock and Grace Kunz. *Apparel Manufacturing Sewn Product Analysis*, 4th ed. (Upper Saddle River, NJ: Pearson Prentice Hall, 2005).
30. Ibid.
31. Ibid.
32. Dana Thomas. *Deluxe: How Luxury Lost Its Luster* (New York: Penguin Press, 2007).
33. Ibid.

INDUSTRY
CLOTHING
CONSTRUCTION
METHODS

1

Garment Manufacturing Equipment

This chapter will familiarize students with the equipment used in apparel manufacturing. Students should be able to identify every machine and tool, know how to take proper care of them, and be able to use them safely and efficiently. Eventually, the use of this equipment should be second nature to the student or designer. Students

can then move toward creating their designs with ease, as an artist does with paper, brush, or chisel, visualizing how to arrive at a certain look without hesitation. Students who are studying design, merchandising, and buying should know which apparel-construction machines a workroom should have, the capabilities of the machinery, what the machines can produce, and the attachments that are available to speed the construction process. They should also be aware of the types of laying, cutting, and pressing equipment that are available to ensure that their garments are being made with the appropriate level of quality. All fashion professionals will want to know that their products will be delivered on a timely basis. Having the right machines, including perhaps specialized automated equipment, will help ensure that customers' needs are satisfied.

APPAREL MANUFACTURING MACHINES

There are two broad categories of construction machines in the apparel indus-

try. Manual machines need an operator who manually controls the fabric positioning, the speed of sewing, and so on. These relatively simple machines perform many tasks but rely on a skilled operator for accuracy. Over half of the sewing machines in the apparel industry are manually operated. They are sometimes not as cost-effective as specialized machines because of the extra time it takes to complete a task and the greater chance of mistakes, but they can allow workers to complete a larger variety of tasks without purchasing new machines.

The other category of construction machines is automatic machines, which use computer control to perform the same operation over and over. That operation may be sewing a patch pocket on the back of a pair of jeans or sewing the flap of a welt pocket for a suit jacket. The operator of these machines simply puts the fabric into the machine and presses "go." These machines do their job very quickly and accurately and are perfect for factories that specialize in making the same garment over and over.

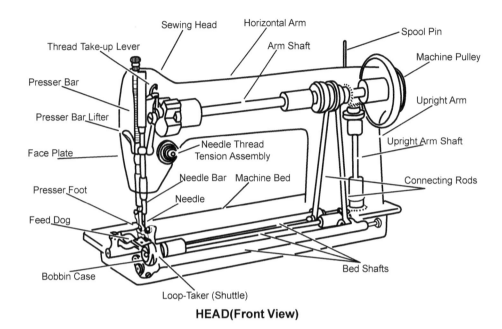

FIGURE 1.1 A basic lock stitch machine.

Sewing Head
Horizontal Arm
Thread Take-up Lever
Arm Shaft
Spool Pin
Machine Pulley
Presser Bar
Upright Arm
Presser Bar Lifter
Upright Arm Shaft
Face Plate
Needle Thread Tension Assembly
Presser Foot
Needle Bar   Machine Bed
Connecting Rods
Needle
Feed Dog
Bobbin Case
Bed Shafts
Loop-Taker (Shuttle)

HEAD(Front View)

These two categories of machines share common parts: a head or "casting," a bed, a presser foot shank and presser foot, a pressure control for the presser foot, feed "teeth" or "dogs" to feed the fabric through the machine, a needle bar and needle, a throat plate, thread guides to deliver the threads, a motor, and a control to regulate the speed at which this all happens. Let's start from the top of the machine and work our way down. You can use the diagram of a basic lockstitch machine (Figure 1.1) and a basic overlock machine (Figure 1.2) to identify these parts.

Above and behind the head of the machine are thread guides to help neatly feed the thread from the put-up (a cone, spool or tube of thread) to the machine.

From these guides, the thread goes to the threading and tension mechanism for the needle(s). The tension mechanism is responsible for feeding a certain amount of thread to the machine to create an even, durable stitch. The needle in the needle bar is threaded after the thread has passed through the thread guides and tension disk. (Needles will be discussed later.)

Below the needle is the feeding mechanism that carries the fabric through the machine. This mechanism consists of a presser foot and feed teeth or "dogs," which are below the foot. The presser foot presses the material against the feed teeth, which then move the fabric in time with the needle. On the top of the machine is a knob that controls the amount of pressure the foot uses to press the fabric against the foot. Some machines are fitted with a "dual feed" or "walking foot" that feeds the top layer of fabric at the same speed as the lower layer. The combination of needle and feed teeth with the threads produces the stitch and directly affects the stitch length. There are a variety of feed teeth, including rubber

FIGURE 1.2 A basic 3 thread overlock machine.

ones, which are more suitable for delicate fabrics. The feed teeth rise through a **feed plate** or **throat plate**, which is an integral part of supporting the fabric during sewing. Under the feed plate are mechanisms that move precisely in time with the needle to help make the stitch. These elements may be an unthreaded "spreader," a threaded bobbin with a hook on lockstitch machines, or a variety of threaded loopers or unthreaded spreaders for overlock machines. All of these parts help control the structure of the stitch the machine makes.

Around all of this is the **bed** of the machine. The bed covers the inner workings of the machine and usually a pan of oil, plus it provides a surface on which to place the fabric. Some beds are flat and flush with the surface of the table they are mounted in; some are cylindrical or shaped like a post and are above the surface of the table. Different beds are used to facilitate different sewing processes, such as sewing flat seams, the inside of a sleeve head, or a pant cuff.

Below the machine and usually attached to the table in which the machine is mounted is a **foot control** that an operator uses to regulate the speed of the machine. Obviously, the more skilled and practiced the operator is, the faster he or she can sew and maintain accuracy. There may also be a **knee lifter**, which is connected to the presser foot. Using this to lift the presser foot allows the operator to use both hands to pull out the fabric and snip threads, speeding up the sewing process.

THE WORKROOM BASICS

There are several machines that the average workroom should have to be able to construct enough of a variety of garments quickly enough to stay in business. These include a lockstitch machine (also known as a straight stitch machine) for construction tasks, an overlock machine for construction and/or edge finishing, a blind-stitch machine for hemming, plus a buttonholer and a button-sewing machine.

Lockstitch Machine

The structure of a basic lockstitch machine has hardly changed since Isaac Singer patented it in 1851. The lockstitch machine (see Figure 1.1) is the workhorse of an apparel workroom. The stitch it makes (ASTM stitch type 301) can perform a huge variety of functions, and when the machine is fitted with attachments, it can perform even more. It depends on a needle moving in a straight line to carry the thread down through the fabric, where a hook catches that thread, carrying it around the bobbin to pick up the bobbin thread. This motion locks the threads to create a stitch. The standard presser foot for this type of machine is a straight stitch foot, which has two toes and a single hole or slot in the center (see Figures 1.1 and 1.6). The machine must be kept in tune to make sure the hook arrives at the right time to avoid hitting the needle and to pick up the thread. Industrial lockstitch machines can sew at a speed of 1,500 to 3,500 stitches per minute.

The sister of the lockstitch is the zigzag machine (ASTM stitch type 304). A zigzag machine forms its stitch the same way, but the needle swings from left to right while feed teeth move the fabric. These actions produce the signature zigzag shape of the stitch. The stitch is primarily used as a decorative accent on the outside of garments or is used for applying elastic or applying trims to the surface of the fabric. The presser foot and throat plate of a zigzag machine are also different from those of a straight stitch machine. The straight stitch machine has a round hole for the needle to pass through on its way to the bobbin, whereas zigzag machines have a slot the width of the needle swing to allow the needle to pass to the bobbin mechanism.

Overlock Machine

Overlock machines (see Figure 1.2) also create a stitch that performs a variety of functions. They can be manufactured to use two, three, four, or five threads and to make a selection of stitches that always includes an overcasting stitch (stitch classes 500 and 600). They may only finish edges, or they may make a seam and finish edges. They also include a set of knives that work like a pair of scissors to trim the edge of the fabric before it is overcast. The combination of trimming, finishing, and seam-sewing greatly speeds up the construction process and produces a neat appearance that many consumers have come to take as a mark of quality. However, once a seam is sewn with an overlock, the seam allowances cannot be separated. Therefore, this stitching is not recommended for positions where allowances will need to be pressed open, such as a seam that includes a zipper.

Overlock machines, sometimes referred to as *sergers*, use one or more needles and a selection of loopers or spreaders to form stitches. Loopers are threaded; spreaders grab a loop of thread and extend it until it is caught by another thread, forming the stitch. The choice of which combination of machine parts to use depends on the function of the stitch: Are you sewing a knit or a woven fabric? Is the stitch sewing the seam or just finishing the edge? Does the stitch in a woven fabric need to be very strong, such as in the crotch of a well-made pair of dress pants, or is it more important to sew it quickly and use less thread when sewing the seam of a budget-priced camisole? (An explanation of the stitches that an overlock can perform and their most likely uses is listed in the Appendix.) As with lockstitch machines, it's extremely important that overlock machines be threaded correctly and maintained in good working order so that stitches are formed and machine parts don't run into each other.

Overlock machines will also be fitted with a variety of throat plates, depending on the stitch being formed. These plates have "tongues" that vary in dimension, from flat, fingerlike extensions to tongues the size of a sturdy pin. The larger, flatter tongues help form the wider stitches used for general seaming or overcasting heavier fabrics. Pinlike tongues are used for forming very narrow overcasting, such as rolled hems for chiffon skirts or scarves.

Blind-Stitch Machine

Blind-stitch machines (Figure 1.3) use a special mechanism to imitate a traditional hand-stitched hem that does not show on the face of the garment (stitch class 100). One thread, usually a monofilament, translucent nylon in clear or smoke color, is threaded through a curved needle. This needle works with a tiny spreader to form a line of connected loops. As the curved

FIGURE 1.3 A blind stitch machine.

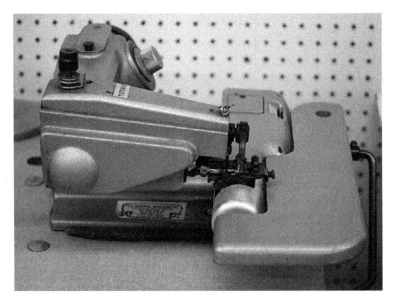

needle passes from the left to the right of the machine, it picks up a tiny bit of the fabric, securing the hem layer to the back of the garment. The idea is to pick up the smallest amount of garment fabric possible while still creating a sturdy hem. If the needle catches too much of the fabric, then the stitch will show on the face of the garment.

Instead of a presser foot lifting to press down on the fabric as it feeds through, the arm of the machine comes from below, pressing up on the fabric against a pressure plate. This plate keeps the fabric feeding smoothly and accurately to the needle so that the stitches remain consistent. Blind hemmers are used primarily for hemming all types of garments, jackets, skirts, and dress pants, from the moderate price point through designer.

Buttonhole Machine

The type of **buttonhole machine** that we will discuss uses a narrow zigzag to finish the edges of the opening. They are specialized units that can complete the stitching, trim the thread, and cut open a buttonhole, all in one operation. Fast and versatile, buttonholers can be adjusted manually or by a computer to sew a particular stitch length (density) and length of buttonhole. Whereas the previous mechanical versions of these machines may have been able to sew only one style of buttonhole, such as a keyhole, modern computerized machines can sew several styles with equal accuracy.

Button Sewer

Button sewing machines (Figure 1.4) can sew on either two- or four-hole buttons or shank buttons with amazing speed and accuracy, some as fast as 2,500 stitches per minute. As with buttonhole machines, button sewing machines are

programmable with regard to number of stitches per set of holes or shank. The operator stands at the end of a narrow bed or the front of the machine and inserts the button into a holding mechanism, which positions it exactly so that the needle will not hit the button and break it. After sewing, the machine automatically cuts the threads.

Specialized Automatic Machines

With the increase in the number of women's apparel lines being offered to consumers and the increase in production volume, the time allowed for apparel production has shortened. Buyers, merchandisers, and designers rely on manufacturers to turn garment orders around in very short amounts of time with the least amount of error possible. This has led to the computerization of many sewing tasks and to the increased usage of automated or semiautomated sewing machines. Many of these machines have been designed to work in a very efficient manner and so may not have traditional feed teeth, throat plates, presser feet, or foot controls. We've already seen how the repetitive tasks of button sewing and buttonhole making have been sped up drastically with the ability to program the details of the stitching into the machine.

FIGURE 1.4 A button sewing machine for attaching 2-and 4-hole buttons.

There are also many other tasks that have become automated with the creation of new equipment to fit those tasks. This huge category of machines includes automatic bar tackers, machines for attaching belt loops or patch pockets, machines that sew shirtfront plackets for polo shirts, and machines that will sew an entire welt pocket opening for a pair of dress pants. These machines are more complicated to maintain and are very expensive, so only factories that make the same items of apparel over and over can justify purchasing and using them.

MACHINE PARTS

Needles

The correct needle type and size for the machine you're using should be selected according to the process being sewn, thread diameter, and the characteristics of the material being sewn. Look at your machine's manual or the front of the machine to find out what system of needle you will need. As we discussed in the section about apparel machine parts, the purpose of the needle is to carry the thread down through the layers of fabric so that it can create a stitch.

Needles come in many different configurations and sizes (Figure 1.5). The size of the needle refers to the diameter of its blade portion. The shank of the needle may be round, half round, or squared off; the length of the blade changes, as will the length of the eye and the shape of the point. The length of the needle will change according to the type of machine being used. The size of the eye will change according to the type of thread being sewn with. The point will change according to the type of material being sewn. Consult the chart in the Appendix for needle types, sizes, and uses according to material and thread size.

The groove in the front of the needle is there for the thread to rest in as the needle is going through the fabric. If the needle is too small for the thread or is inserted incorrectly into the machine, the thread will have nowhere to go and will get worn or stripped. This causes thread breakage or skipped stitches or both. The scarf on the back of the needle at the eye must also be in the correct spot to allow the thread loop to be picked up by the mechanism in the bottom of the machine.

A common method for testing if the thread and the needle are compatible is to

FIGURE 1.5 Parts of a machine needle.

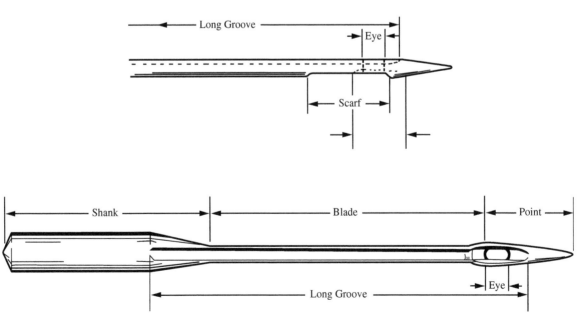

thread the needle and then hold the thread taut while tilting it at a 45-degree angle. If the needle slips down the thread under its own weight, then the needle eye is large enough. The correct-size needle will be the smallest one that works with the thread diameter. This will allow for the smallest hole possible in the fabric. If, however, the needle is so small that it breaks because the fabric is dense or many layers are being sewn, then a bigger needle size must be used.

The point of the needle must suit the type of material being sewn. There are needles for fine knits, leather, fabrics woven with microfibers, machine embroidery, and more. If the wrong point is used, the fabric yarns may be pulled, the thread may break, or large holes may appear in the fabric. Different types of needlepoints are also listed in the chart in the Appendix.

Attachments

The functions of many machines can be augmented by adding attachments to the basic unit. These attachments can be as simple as another presser foot or feed plate or can be as complex as a feeding apparatus for adding tape to a fabric's surface or for holding, feeding, and positioning elastic to be sewn to the garment's edge.

Some presser feet used on a traditional lockstitch machine that make specialized functions easier, more accurate, and less time-consuming are a left and right zipper foot, a topstitch guide foot, a gathering foot, a rolled hem foot, and a roller foot for sewing leather and vinyl. Each of these feet and the standard foot have shanks that attach to the presser foot bar with a screw. Figure 1.6 shows the basic parts of a presser foot. Different machines use shanks that are different lengths, so be sure you have the proper one for your brand of machine.

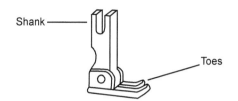

FIGURE 1.6 Parts of a presser foot.

There are a variety of guides that can apply materials to the surface or edge of fabric, such as bias binding, elastic, or twill tape. Each guide helps increase sewing accuracy, the quality of the finished product, and the speed at which the product is completed. Guides usually feed to another attachment that will fold, pleat, or stretch the material being fed. Some of these attachments are complex versions of presser feet and attach to the shank; others, such as cloth pullers and feeders, are large and must be attached to the bed of the machine or the table. Some common attachments are folders for creating lapped seams, pleaters for constructing knife or box pleats, or bias binders. If there are a large number of garments that require a certain time-consuming task to be performed, then an attachment is well worth the investment.

INDUSTRIAL PRESSING EQUIPMENT

No seam is complete until it's pressed. Depending on the type of seam, its position in the construction process, and its quality, pressing and steaming are done before or during construction or as a finishing step before the garment is presented or packaged for sale. During the construction process for a specific garment, seams and garment parts may be pressed to make it easier and more efficient to sew complete subsequent steps. This process is called *underpressing.* Although these pressing steps mean more time, effort, and money are added to the process, it can hardly be considered waste.

FIGURE 1.7 Gravity feed iron with attached bottle. Photo courtesy of Universal Sewing Supply.

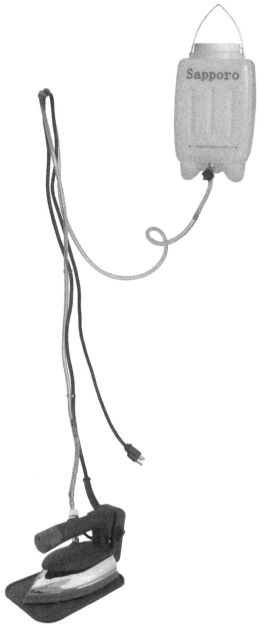

FIGURE 1.7 Gravity feed iron with attached bottle. Photo courtesy of Universal Sewing Supply.

Depending on the fabric content and weave structure, pressing will involve heat, steam, and pressure at various intensities for specific amounts of time. Irons, pressing units, and steamers all deliver these in some fashion and will be used to flatten, crease, or shape the fabric. However, it is entirely possible to overpress most fabrics. Permanent marks, fabric distortion, flattened textures, scorching, and color migration are symptoms of too-high heat or too much steam for too long. Pressing steps will be noted at the correct point during the construction steps in Chapters 3 through 11.

Industrial Irons

Industrial irons are a necessity for any workroom or factory floor. They can accomplish many tasks in many different garments because of their flexibility, and they are primarily used during the construction process. Most industrial irons are gravity fed (Figure 1.7), meaning that each iron contains its own heating unit that heats water coming from a bottle suspended above the iron. These irons vary in weight, from 2.5 to 5 pounds. More weight is intended to make the operator's job easier, because they don't have to push down on the iron themselves to achieve the necessary pressing power. Industrial irons are great for small projects and for pressing into tight or curved areas. They may frequently be fitted with a Teflon sole plate to guard against damage to sensitive fabrics.

Pressing Machines

Pressing with an iron is done on a surface called a **buck** (Figure 1.8). At home, you would call this an *ironing board*. A basic buck is shaped similarly to a home ironing board but is far more sophisticated. Often, it will have its own vacuum system to draw the steam generated by the iron through the fabric, thus drying the garment faster. There will be an additional surface to rest the iron on, sole plate down, and possibly a shelf underneath that prevent a garments from touching the floor. Additional bucks may be mounted on the board or may be on hand to press narrow shapes such as sleeves.

Other pressing machines consist of two bucks that may be shaped specifically to press certain garments such as pant legs, blouses, or jackets (Figure 1.8). When the upper buck is closed over the lower one, the garment part is sandwiched between the fabric-covered surfaces. There are also buck shapes that can be added to these machines to customize them for pressing specific parts of a garment. These bucks make the process go faster, and they create a more professional product without stressing the fabric. All of these machines have the ability to steam the garment under pressure and to dry heat with an added vacuum unit, which draws the moisture out of the garment faster to set the creases and speed the pressing process.

There are also many very sophisticated pressing machines that handle collars, shirt cuffs, pant waistbands, patch pockets, and other complicated pressing jobs by applying pressure, heat, and steam to metal blocks on which the fabric rests. Usually these machines have the capacity for the operator to work on two garment pieces at a time to speed production.

Pressing Aids

Various pressing aids exist to make pressing easier and less time-consuming and to make the end result more professional, raising the level of quality and profitability. These aids would not be used in a factory where large quantities of the same garments are made but would be found in smaller workrooms that produce a variety of higher-quality products at a slower rate or that create custom garments. The specialized pressing machines previously mentioned would substitute for these tools, achieving the same or a similar finished product.

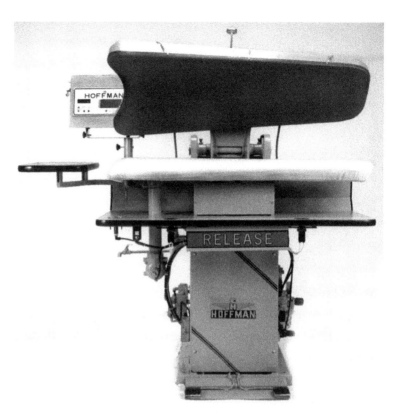

FIGURE 1.8 BCG-L4 Legger (Hoffman). Pressing machine with a buck.

The first aid, pictured in Figure 1.9, is a tailor's ham. This aid is used to form garment parts like suit collars or for pressing curved areas such as waist darts. The plaid wool side is for pressing wool fabrics; the white cotton side is for pressing items that need higher heat, such as cotton and linen.

Figure 1.10 shows a covered wood pressing board (similar to the buck shown in Figure 1.8) that can be set on another surface to press slim items such as sleeves and pant legs. Notice the board can be flipped over to use an even smaller surface.

Figure 1.11 shows a hand press pad, which can be used to form small areas that should not have the iron set directly on them, such as a puffed sleeve head.

Your hand goes inside the mitt to support the garment part while it is steamed

FIGURE 1.9 (left) Tailor's ham (B. Black and Sons).

FIGURE 1.10 (right) Covered Wood Press board (B. Black and Sons).

FIGURE 1.11 (left)
Hand Press Pad (B.
Black and Sons).

FIGURE 1.12 (right)
Point Presser and
Pounding block (B.
Black and Sons).

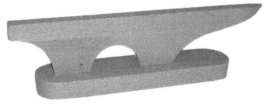

and shaped. Figure 1.12 shows a wooden point presser/clapper.

The point presser side is used to lay pointed ends such as collars over while pressing. The clapper side is used to encourage the fabric to flatten on areas like jacket facings and collars and is used to help the piece cool more quickly. A seam roll is shown in Figure 1.13. This item also has a wool side and a cotton side and functions as a very narrow surface to press a seam on when the face of the fabric would be marked if the sole plate of the iron was rested on it.

Finishing Machines

Most small workrooms and custom garment shops have a steamer of some kind to quickly freshen garments by removing wrinkles (Figure 1.14). Tap water is put into the base of the steamer, where it is heated to produce steam, which exits through the nozzle of the hose. The nozzle may have a brush attached to remove lint during the process as well.

For high-volume factories, there is a variety of specialized equipment that will finish completed garments by supporting them vertically. Some machines specialize in one style of garment, such as pants

or jackets, finishing them one at a time (Figure 1.15).

Others are large boxlike machines similar to the one in Figure 1.16, which will steam several types of garments at a time. Both types of machines are computer controlled according to the temperature, amount of steam, and timing of the procedure.

Fusing Equipment

Although the irons and pressing equipment already discussed can be used to fuse interlining before apparel construction, there are also much larger machines that are used in the factory setting (Figure 1.17). These machines can fuse many garment pieces at the same time. The pieces are loaded onto

FIGURE 1.13 (left)
Seam Roll (B. Black
and Sons).

FIGURE 1.14 (right)
J2 Standard Garment
Steamer (B. Black and
Sons).

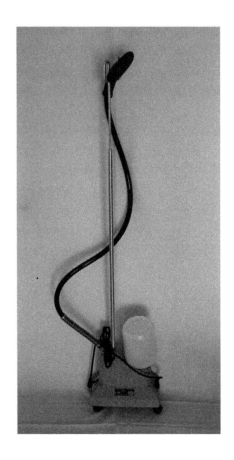

a wide belt with the interlining up, and then they pass through a tunnel with heating elements set at exactly the correct temperature for the fabric and interlining. The speed of the belt controls the fusing time and the amount of time that operators have to place the pieces to be fused onto the belt.

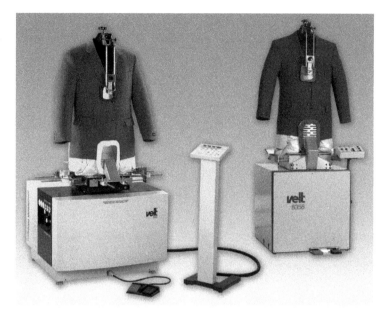

FIGURE 1.15 Form Finisher VEIT 8308 (VEIT).

CUTTING MACHINERY AND TOOLS

The fashion industry works with many different-sized operations, from large factories producing tens of thousands of units in a day to small workrooms producing fewer than a hundred. So, there are all sorts of cutting machinery and tools to suit the volume of production, the quality of the apparel being produced, and the types of materials being used. These machines and tools can be grouped into the following categories: computerized, electronic handheld, and shears and scissors. Also included in this section are other cutting tools that are found in many workrooms and factories.

Before any cutting is done, though, the pattern pieces must be made, the markers created to place the patterns on the fabric, and the fabric layup done to spread the fabric for cutting.

Computerized Cutting Equipment

To manufacture tens of thousands of units a day, a factory must be able to cut enough garment pieces. Computerized cutting systems that are connected to the marker and plotting systems streamline this process. After markers are made and the fabric layup completed, rotary or reciprocating knife cutters guided by the computer cut the fabric plies.

The cut pieces are then lifted by hand and bound with an identification tag to be taken to the construction floor. Although there are also laser, water-jet, and plasma-cutting systems, blade systems are still the most widely used for fabric.

Electronic Handheld

Fabric cutting can also be done on a smaller scale with a variety of handheld electric

FIGURE 1.16 (left) Regal Rotating Cabinet (Hoffman).

FIGURE 1.17 (right) MultiStar DX Series fusing machine (VEIT).

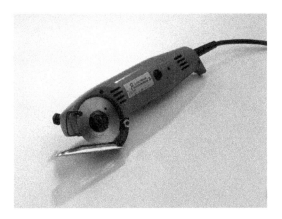

FIGURE 1.18 (above left) Eastman Chicadee Rotary Cutter.

FIGURE 1.19 (right) Eastman Blue Streak II straight knife cutter.

cutters. These cutters range from small electric rotary cutters (Figure 1.18) to large, straight knife cutters. Because the portion of the blade that engages the fabric is wide, rotary cutters or aren't suitable for thick layers of plies and tight, angular corners.

Because they are tall and narrow, straight knives (Figure 1.19) are great for cutting many plies and tight corners. If there is a section in the center of a pattern piece that needs to be removed, a hole must be cut first to insert the blade through. Also, care must be taken to ensure that the blade is at a 90-degree angle from the base plate on which the cutter rests. This is to make sure that all the plies are cut to the correct size.

Die Cutting

Factories that manufacture apparel in large quantities will often use die-cutting machines for small parts. Die cutters use a sharp-edged metal cutter that is the shape of the piece, which is forced down through the fabric to cut the layers. This process produces precisely cut shapes for areas such as pockets and collar pieces or is used to cut shapes from the center of a larger garment piece.

Shears and Scissors

Small workrooms that manufacture high-quality apparel in small quantities or custom apparel might use fabric shears to cut garment pieces. **Bent shears** have a set of blades that are angled down from the handle. This allows the blades to glide along the table surface under the fabric, producing a more accurate and less-tiring cutting motion (Figure 1.20).

Scissors are used for trimming during the construction process. The blades on scissors emerge from between the handles in a straight direction and are not meant for cutting fabric on a table (Figure 1.21).

Thread **nippers** are used to snip threads during the construction or finishing

FIGURE 1.20 (left) WISS Bent Trimmers #20, 10 inch, Inlaid.

FIGURE 1.21 (right) WISS Straight Trimmers #37, 7 inch, Inlaid.

processes. They are quicker to use and take less energy, because their spring action keeps them always open; therefore, the user doesn't need to open and close them to cut threads (Figure 1.22).

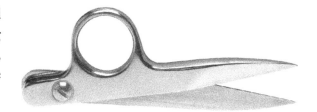

HAND TOOLS

Needles

Hand-sewing needles are still used in smaller workrooms and custom shops where hand sewing is still needed. Very little hand sewing is done in the ready-to-wear industry, because the activity is time-consuming and can be inaccurate. Hand-sewing needles are primarily chosen according to the item being sewn and the size of the thread. A number designates the needle's size, with a smaller number indicating a larger needle in length and diameter. As the number gets higher, the needle decreases in diameter and length (this is the opposite of machine needles). Three types of hand needles frequently used are betweens, long darners, and sharps. Betweens are used to make fine, short stitches. Long darners are larger and can be used for making fabric tacks to mark fabric pattern markings and for basting. Sharps can be used for hemming and hand-stitching seams.

Other Hand Tools

There are a variety of other hand tools that are necessary to maintain quality and speed during the manufacturing process. These tools are not usually used on the floor of a factory manufacturing tens of thousands of units, because the tasks they aid are usually done by automated machines. Automated machines are faster and more exact when performing these functions.

Marking tools: Marking tools such as pencils, wax cakes, powdered chalk, tracing paper and tracing wheels, and thread tackers serve to transfer markings from the pattern piece to the fabric for construction information.

Tape measure: A tape measure is helpful in many ways, including positioning pattern pieces and completing alterations on custom garments.

Clear 6-inch ruler: A clear ruler helps mark the fabric accurately for hems, button placement, and so on.

Straight pins: Straight pins temporarily align fabric pieces before sewing.

Thimble: Thimbles are used during hand stitching to protect the sewers finger while pushing the needle into the fabric.

Point turners: Point turners help produce even points when turning collars, waistbands, and so on.

Tweezers: Tweezers are helpful for removing thread jams and threading overlock machines.

Threading wires: Threading wires assist in threading overlock machines.

Screwdriver: Various sizes help with adjusting bobbin case tension and tightening screws in machines.

2

Garment Manufacturing Materials

In addition to the fashion fabrics used to create a garment, the designer or merchandiser must consider the most suitable thread, foundation fabrics, linings, trims, and closures to complete the look. Issues that affect those considerations include fashion expression, garment structure, cost, shrinkage, colorfastness, and care compatibility.

The choices made will directly affect the quality and cost of the garment.

This chapter will familiarize the designer, merchandiser, and buyer with the types of threads available for modern garment construction. We will also discuss the attributes and uses for the foundation materials that give garments their shape and contribute to durability and fashion expression. In addition, we will cover closures and trim options so that you can make informed decisions about design aesthetics, durability, care compatibility, and cost. The Appendix will include sources for these materials.

SOFT GOODS

Machine Sewing Threads

The thread you select for your garments will have a tremendous impact on your customer's opinion of your brand. Although the cost of thread is only a tiny portion of the overall production cost of any piece of apparel, many consumers mention burst seams or loose threads as a top reason for returning a purchase.

Threads can be classified in several ways, including

- the content of the thread,
- how many strands were used to make it,
- the diameter of the thread,
- the finish on the outside of the thread (Figure 2.1).

There are hundreds of different combinations of the above, but basically thread is made either of fibers, such as cotton or chopped up polyester filaments, which are spun into a strand, or of an extruded filament such as polyester. Linen and silk thread are also made but are primarily used in hand-sewing functions on custom or couture garments. Rayon thread, with its bright colors and high luster, is used primarily for machine embroidery and appliqué. Cotton thread is frequently used in the garment industry because of its sewability, meaning that it works very well in a variety of different machines under a variety of sewing circumstances without breaking. Cotton fibers accept dye well and can be made into many different-diameter

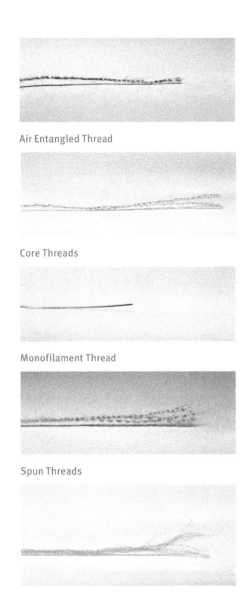

Air Entangled Thread

Core Threads

Monofilament Thread

Spun Threads

Textured Threads

so are not useful for garment seams near the body.

These synthetic monofilaments are great for hemming, because they come in smoke and clear, which blend easily. Because they are thermoplastic materials, they will melt when subjected to the needle motions of high-speed sewing machines. When sewing with these threads in an industrial setting, thread lubricants or other measures are added to cool the thread to prevent breakage.

Strands of spun fibers are called a ply. Plies are twisted together, or monofilaments may be bonded together to create thread. Thread diameter comes from many different methods of construction, but predominantly threads are made from combining plies into two-, three-, four-, or six-strand combinations; from spinning around a core of monofilament; or from bonding multiple filaments. Monofilaments have an extremely smooth finish; spun threads have a fuzzy texture that adds to their softness. There are also very loosely spun "textured" synthetic threads that are wonderful for overcasting the edges of wovens. The material is thin in the machine under tension, but when sewn over the edge of fabric, they expand to cover the fabric in a smooth, even finish, which is frequently used on rolled hems in fine fabrics.

Plies are twisted together in either an "S" direction or a "Z" direction—the "S" twist goes to the right; the "Z" twist goes to the left (Figure 2.2).

Different twists are needed to function with different sewing machines and sewing functions. The structure of the thread determines its diameter. Thread diameter is designated using two main systems for machine sewing thread: the "denier" system and the "cotton count" system. Threads in the denier system are

threads for many applications, from thick threads needed for topstitching to the thin threads used for overlocking. Thread shrinkage, causing puckered seams, can be a problem in some garments sewn with cotton if the thread quality is poor. Cotton, though, does not have the elasticity of a synthetic material such as polyester and can mildew and become weaker when wet. Combining cotton with synthetic materials can help overcome these problems. Polyester and nylon have good elasticity, but this may sometimes cause skipped stitches. They are coarse against the skin, although polyester is softer, and synthetic and are numbered higher as the diameter of the thread increases. The higher the number, the thicker the thread. The cotton count system is inverted; the higher the number, the thinner the thread.

You should also consider the finish of the thread you use for your apparel. This aspect of thread is a design choice but ultimately affects customer satisfaction. Cotton or blend threads may be left unfinished for a soft but weak thread, mercerized, or finished with glacé finish.

Mercerization is a chemical process that allows cotton fiber to accept dye more readily, resulting in brighter colors. This process also increases the strength and luster of the thread. A glacé finish coats the thread with chemicals that make it stiffer, stronger, and more resistant to abrasion. In the apparel industry, glacé threads are mainly used for basting, handwork, or sewing leather.

How to Choose the Correct Thread(s) for Your Garment

You may choose several threads for one garment, each thread performing a specific function within the garment. Use the following criteria to determine which threads to utilize:

- The garment fabric content and weight
- The expected life span of the garment
- Where the thread will be used in the garment
- What type of stitching is being done
- The performance needs of the seam
- What type of garment care will be used
- The projected budget for the garment cost

All of these criteria will affect the quality of the finished garment and hence consumer satisfaction. Remember to take into account the quality level and

FIGURE 2.2 Thread twist-spun and plied threads are twisted in one of two directions:

"S" direction or right twist is used for spinning a single strand "Z" direction or left twist for ply yarn is used when plying two yarns together.

Plying in the opposite direction from spinning keeps the yarns from separating.

retail price that the consumer desires when considering any aspect of materials for construction.

The fiber content of the thread will be influenced by the fiber content of the fabric. These should be compatible so that when the consumer is caring for the garment, the seams will not become puckered or weakened by the care method used. The thread you choose should have enough plies and be structured to maintain seam strength that lasts the life of the garment. Different positions in the garment demand different seam strengths and thread appearance, such as the back crotch seam in a pair of dress pants verses the seam attaching a cuff to a shirtsleeve. A very low price point will necessitate using an inexpensive thread to overcast seams verses the thread that might be used to create a lap-side seam in a designer signature silk blouse.

As a general rule, it is a waste of money to use a thread of a thickness or fiber that produces a seam stronger than the structure of the fabric. The seam should break before the structure of the fabric fails. It is much easier and less costly to resew a seam than try to repair a rip in the fabric. The type of seam also helps determine the type of thread used. A hem on a pair of jeans will need a thick cotton thread that coordinates with the rest of the topstitching details on the garment. The same garment needs a thin white thread for sewing the pocket bag. The content, diameter, and finish of the thread are also determined by the performance of the garment. For example, if you are designing apparel for mountain-climbing enthusiasts, you will need a strong thread of man-made fibers that are not damaged by moisture to satisfy the level of garment performance required.

The cost of the thread for your garment includes the thread that actually ends up sewing the garment together. It also includes threads clipped off from the beginning and end of the seam, thread that is ripped out when errors are corrected, thread that is used in rethreading machines after the thread has broken, and any left on the cone that is not used before it degrades and becomes unusable. Therefore, as with any material in the construction of apparel, waste is a concern. Cutting down on operator error either through training or the use of specialized machinery can help. Specialized machinery also cuts down on the amount of thread necessary for back tacking and thread holding at the beginning and end of the seams. You can also save money by correctly calculating the amount of thread needed for the numbers of units being made to avoid having overstock and by making sure that the thread is appropriate for the machine and quality level of the apparel. The cost of having a finished garment returned for poor seam quality far outstrips the investment in good-quality thread.

Remember that to sew a seam effectively, you must choose the correct needle, thread tension, and stitch length for the thread you have chosen. For example, the topstitching on a pair of jeans is often part of the label's brand image and so is usually sewn with a thick thread in an area where the thickness and density of the fabric are high. Therefore, the needle must be large enough for the thread and sturdy enough not to break. The thread tension must be balanced to create the desired, even finish on the stitching. (More information about needles is included in Chapter 1. Thread tension settings are discussed in Chapter 3.)

Foundation Materials

Hidden underneath the fashion fabric of your favorite garment will most likely be the materials that make it such a joy to wear. Foundation materials, including interlining, lining, underlining, shoulder pads, sleeve heads, elastic, and boning, create the form that gives a garment its silhouette. Whether architectural and flaring away from the body or soft and draping, some foundation material is probably contributing to the look of the garment. Foundation materials also have a direct effect on the intrinsic and extrinsic quality of the garment. They enhance its stability over time; help maintain a smooth, unwrinkled look; and contribute a great deal to fit and comfort. Foundation materials may be added to a garment to enhance the look as it hangs in the store and on the customer's shoulders and in his or her closet once it has been worn and cleaned. When customers try on the garment, their evaluation of its appearance will be based on the material, feel, and drape, as well as fit and structure. If the foundation material choices that have been made by the designer or the merchandiser, and indirectly by the buyer, meet the customer's expectations, then the apparel will be sold. If the interlining is too stiff, the shoulder pads the wrong shape, or the designer jacket not lined, the garment will stay on the rack. If fusible interlining becomes unfused or shrinks in the consumer's dryer, causing bubbling and puckering, then the garment will most certainly not meet his or her quality needs. In addition to influencing the shape of the garment, foundation materials may also provide reinforcement at areas of stress (such as buttonholes), cover the inside of the garment, add warmth, add body to a hem, or keep an area from stretching.

When you are choosing foundation materials as a whole for your garment, you should consider the following:

- Is the material compatible with the content and care of the fashion fabric, and if it is fusible, will it stay fused during garment care?
- Will the material produce the desired hand once it is inside the fashion fabric?
- Is the interlining thin enough for the fashion fabric, or will it be too bulky?
- If the material is fusible, will fusing it make the fashion fabric too stiff?
- Will the heat level and duration of fusing time that is necessary to attach the interlining damage the fabric?
- Most importantly, what is the function of the foundation material in the garment?

Interlinings

Interlinings are intended to support the fashion fabric and give it body (Figure 2.3). Some garments have no interlinings because of their extreme softness and drapes, but the rest, because of their style or design, need some inner help. Interlinings may need to be sewn in or be able to be fused using heat and moisture to melt the glue connecting the two fabrics. All interlinings should be tested for compatibility with the fashion fabric, especially with regard to shrinkage. Most interlinings will be "ready for the needle," meaning they are ready to be cut and attached to their respective garment pieces. However, a test should be conducted for hand and shrinkage with the chosen interlining during the sample sewing stage of construction to make sure that the interlining will function as intended. The interlining and other foundation materials will also be considered during costing to determine if they fit into the budget for each garment.

There are hundreds of different types of interlining for every fashion design and type of fabric. Sew-in and fusible interlinings are manufactured with three basic configurations of fibers: woven, knitted, and in "fiber webs."[1] Woven interlinings function like woven fashion fabrics. They are plain-woven of fine yarns or coarse in plain weave; have straight grain and bias directions; can shrink; are usually woven of cotton, rayon, wool, polyester, nylon, or a combination of fibers; and can ravel. Woven interlinings are great for stability in structured silhouettes and for providing a firm foundation in suits and tailored blouses.

FIGURE 2.3 A variety of interlinings.

Some knit interlinings (Figure 2.4) also share some of the characteristics of knit fabrics, such as stretch and drapeability, but some, such as weft insertion, have added characteristics for stability. Many are fusible and are wonderful for a soft hand and added strength for loosely woven fabrics without adding bulkiness. Fiber web interlinings are made of chopped synthetic fibers, which are either randomly placed, in which case they have no grain, or lined up to make a "lengthwise grain" of sorts. They are then bonded together. Fiber web interlinings are low cost, so are often found fused into lower-price-point garments that are machine washable. Because they do not ravel and are inexpensive, they may be used to firm up a low-quality fabric, making it more attractive on the rack. They may also be used to make a limp or loosely woven fabric that is difficult to handle during the construction process easier and quicker to deal with. Most fiber webs are made of man-made fibers.

Interlining is applied by either sewing it in during the construction process or fusing it onto the garment pieces before production begins. Sewing into the garment obviously takes more time, thread, and steps in the process, which all add to the garment's cost. The interlining must be correctly placed and applied so as to not distort the fabric. Woven interlinings need to have the straight of grain placed in the same straight of grain with the fashion fabric. However, they have a flexibility that fused interfacings do not have and do not come unfused later when the customer uses the garment (Figure 2.4).

There are three points during the construction process when sew-in interlining may be added to the garment:

- Before the garment pieces are sewn to anything else
- Inserted into a seam as a piece is being made
- Almost at the end of the process for stabilization, such as under a button

Fusible interlinings have a resin applied to one side, which is melted to attach

FIGURE 2.4 Knit interlining.

the interlining to the back of the fashion fabric (Figure 2.5). Care must be taken to apply and melt the resin using the proper pressure, heat, and moisture level for the right amount of time. Underfusing will allow the interlining to separate during manufacturing but most likely after the customer has purchased the garment and laundered it. Too much fusing time or too high a temperature can cause the resin to migrate through the fashion fabric to the face, melt the interlining fibers, or damage the fashion fabric. More information about the fusing process is included in Chapter 1. There is also a chart in the Appendix that gives more details on choosing the correct interlining for your fabric.

Cost factors vary depending on the type of interlining you choose. Interlinings come in many prices, with fusible, fiber web interlinings being the cheapest, and woven, sew-in, suit-weight interlinings being the most expensive. Price will also be impacted by the time needed to attach the interlining to the garment, the machinery needed to accomplish this, the energy needed to fuse or sew, and the extra quality-control steps and manpower.

Backings

Backings are materials that are found between the fashion fabric and a lining. If interlining is used, the backing will be between that and a lining. Backings provide a variety of additions to a garment, depending on the item's purpose and the type of fashion fabric it is made from. For winter coats, backings may provide an extra layer of resistance against cold and wind. For lightweight fabrics with a soft hand, a backing may enable a designer to use the fabric in a more structured look, hide construction details from showing on the outside of the garment, or improve the body and flow of a fabric. Some backings allow translucent fabrics to be used where undergarments or body parts should not show. They can also help keep a loosely woven fabric from stretching out at the seat or knee, which produces an unsightly "nose."

FIGURE 2.5 Nonwoven, nonknitted fusible interlinings.

Backings are cut from a marker like fashion fabrics and are attached to the fabric before construction begins. Then, the two layers of fabric are treated as one. Backing fabrics must be compatible according to shrinkage and care with the fashion fabric. The time, materials, and energy used to add a backing to your garment significantly increase the items' cost, so backings are rarely found in garments below the bridge price point and never at the budget level. Backings can be made of many fabric types and contents, including cotton flannel, polyester batting, wool flannel, and silk organza.

Linings

The purpose of lining a garment is to conceal construction aspects and materials such as backings, to add to the garment's durability and longevity, and to increase its beauty and value. A coat or jacket that has been constructed using methods with an eye for high quality and timeless styling may outlive the life of the lining, because the lining absorbs most of the wear and tear that an unlined jacket would endure. The coat may then be relined. Jackets may also be lined with a quilted lining to add warmth and wind resistance. Garments can be lined completely, half lined, or have only certain parts lined. Most women's suit jackets are fully lined, as are some dress pants and suit skirts. Many light skirts and pants of white, light colored, or lightweight fabrics may be fully lined to

make them more acceptable to the consumer's sense of modesty. Sporty jackets, lightweight linen spring jackets, and some dress pants may be half lined to increase wearability but reduce production costs. Some garments may have only sleeve linings to increase wearer comfort and ease in putting on the jacket. Linings may also be used to add value to the garment by adding interior details such as pockets or drawstrings.

Lining fabrics may be the same as the garment fabric, such as in the yoke of a dress shirt, or they may be some sort of slippery fabric that makes the garment easier to put on. Fabric choices include acetate, rayon, polyester and blends, and silk. Linings may be solid-colored plain weaves to coordinate with the fashion fabric, jacquard woven, a print with the designer's name or logo, or woven in a twill for added thickness and drape. They may be the same fabric as blouses that are in the same collection.

The same rules apply to selecting linings for your garment as apply to selecting interlinings and backings. Linings must be compatible with the fashion fabric according to shrinkage; care, including pressing temperature and dye migration; quality; and cost. The lining should enhance the look of the garment and not make it too stiff or hang too loosely. Most linings are made of synthetic fibers, because the yarns and the fabrics woven of those yarns are naturally slippery. Natural fibers may not be slippery and are costly. Sometimes cotton is the main lining in a garment such as a spring bomber-style jacket, which will have a polyester lining in the sleeve only. Some winter jackets may have faux fur linings to add warmth but may have a polyblend lining to save on costs and still make the jacket easy to wear.

NOTE ON INTERLINING APPLICATION

In some situations, interlining may be applied before the fabric is cut to speed up the interlining-application process. Small pieces such as cuffs and collars are frequently done this way.

Linings, of course, add to the cost of the garment, but they also add to the consumer's perception of quality. This enables the designer, merchandiser, or buyer to raise the retail price to compensate for the added cost. Linings also add to the garment's longevity, which most consumers realize. Although many designer signature lines have forgone linings to save production costs and raise their profitability, consumers still equate a lining with a certain level of investment in a long-lasting garment. The apparel professional must be sure to achieve the same level of quality with the lining as with the garment itself so that the customer's expectations are not misplaced.

Unfortunately, linings may also be used to hide poor construction techniques and poor fabric choices by manufacturers. This is of special concern to buyers when they are evaluating the quality on which their brand name depends. Problems may

FIGURE 2.6 Examples of linings.

only become evident after the customer has taken the garment home, worn it, and dry-cleaned or laundered it.

Linings are usually cut using the same grain direction of the fashion fabric, but the structure of the lining may be different from the garment. Jacket linings, for example, do not extend to the garment's front and back neck edge but only to the edge of the garment facing. They have pleats at the sleeve and bottom hems for wearing ease and at the center back. This keeps the jacket fabric from distorting

BASIC GUIDELINES FOR LAYING OUT PATTERN PIECES ON FABRICS IN PREPARATION FOR CUTTING

You may use these guidelines if you are not using marker making software. These are guidelines for general pattern placement and can be applied to basic wovens, knits, and nonwovens. They might be disregarded in certain situations, such as to conserve fabric or create a design detail:

- Pattern pieces should be laid out with the lengthwise grain of the fabric going vertically on the pattern piece and the crosswise grain going across the pattern piece.
- Selvages should not be included in the pattern area.
- Pattern pieces should not overlap.
- Pattern pieces that are identical on both sides (e.g., front of a crew-neck T-shirt) can be placed with the lengthwise fold of the fabric down the center of the pattern piece. If the pattern has been drafted as half a front, the center line of the piece is positioned on the fold.
- Multiple layers of fabric may be cut at once to save time and energy but must be firmly held in place.

at the hemlines and across the shoulders when worn. Sleeve linings may be sewn to the lining as it is constructed, before it is inserted by machine into the jacket. In better to designer signature and custom jackets, the sleeve lining is often added separately. This stabilizes the lining and keeps it from shifting away from the armhole. A full gathered or gored skirt will have a slimmer lining that is not attached to the bottom of the skirt. This allows the skirt to hang free and flow gracefully. Better-quality lined straight skirts have a crocheted tie about 2 inches long between the lining and the skirt, just above the hem at the side seams. This tie helps keep the lining from riding up when putting on the skirt and during wear.

In pants or skirts, the lining is completed separately and then attached to the garment when the waist finish is applied. If there are darts or pleats at the waist in the fashion fabric, those structural elements become unstructured tucks of the lining fabric captured by the waistband. When a waistband is being added, the inner layer of the waistband is sewn to the top of the lining, and then the lining is joined to the top of the pant waistband. If there is a zipper, then the lining may be sewn to the zipper area, and then the

entire top of the pants is finished with the waistband. If there is a waist facing, the construction order is similar. Care should be taken when creating patterns for linings, cutting them, and constructing them, because errors in these processes will result in an ill-fitting lining that can destroy the look of an otherwise attractive garment. Instructions for a lined skirt are included in Chapter 4 and for a lined jacket in Chapter 8.

Shoulder Pads and Sleeve Heads
As their name implies, shoulder pads and sleeve heads are intended to add structure to the top of the shoulder area of a jacket, dress, or blouse. The use of shoulder pads and their size are often determined by the whims of fashion taste. In the 1980s, shoulder treatments became very pronounced to achieve a masculine silhouette as women vied with men for powerful positions in the corporate world. Of course, fashion tides rise and fall, as did the sizes of shoulder pads, which gradually shrank to become almost nonexistent. A tailored jacket, however, always has some form of shoulder definition provided by a shoulder pad alone or with the addition of a sleeve head. Sleeve heads are strips of batting or batting fabric combinations that are approximately 2 inches wide but vary in length according to the garment's size. They are intended to create a smooth, structured line at the shoulder seam. Shoulder pads vary in size and shape according to the style of the garment and the look the fashion professional wishes to achieve (Figure 2.7).

Shoulder pads may be constructed of many different materials and combinations of materials, such as foam, batting, and fabric. Foam tends to be the cheapest alternative because of its impermanence. Foam degrades because of laundering,

FIGURE 2.7 Example of a shoulder pad.

dry cleaning, or just hanging on a hanger. Most foam pads appear in blouses or unlined jackets at lower price points. Other pads are made of a batting type of material layered with more wadding to create the correct shape. These pads may then be covered with a low-cost cotton fabric and stitched together to retain shape. As with fiber web interlinings, some pads are fused together after being layered to obtain the correct shape.

Many pads that will not be covered by a lining will be covered with the same fabric as the garment, if that fabric is thin enough. The cover of the pad must be compatible with the fashion fabric to avoid dye migration into the garment and shrinkage of the cover, which will cause the pad to become crushed or twisted.

Sleeve heads are inserted when the sleeve is being sewn to the shoulder of the jacket. Shoulder pads are applied by machine or by hand into the shoulder area after the garment is constructed. They will be sewn or tacked to the seam allowances. Instructions for adding shoulder pads to a lined jacket are in Chapter 8.

Boning

Boning is used to add support to tight-fitting bodices that have no other support, such as straps. Modern boning is made of stiff nylon, polyester called Rigilene, or steel, but gets its name from the original whalebone variety used in corsets from the 17th and 18th centuries.

Rigilene is very popular for the manufacturing of ready-to-wear, because it is inexpensive, machine washable, and comes in multiple widths. Boning needs to be covered because of its stiffness and sharp corners. It may come in a fabric cover that can be used to attach the boning to the garment (Figure 2.8). Or the boning may be used alone by creating a socket

---

TIP | Working with One-Way Fabrics

One-way fabrics have textures or patterns that are not the same when the fabric is viewed from opposite ends. Velvet, velveteen, corduroy, and moiré fabrics are examples of one-way textures. Print motifs that will appear to be upside down when viewed from the opposite end of the fabric are also considered to be one-way. You must make sure to lay out pattern pieces going in the same direction, generally with the motif pointed toward the top of each pattern piece. You should also lay out pattern pieces on one-way textures in the same manner to avoid having the garment look like it is made of two shades of the same color. Unless, of course, that is your intention.

---

for it from the fashion fabric or garment lining. Chapter 11 provides directions for a bustier that includes boning.

Elastic

Elastics are primarily used to draw in an opening on a garment, such as a sleeve, a waistline, or a bottom hem around the body (Figure 2.9). We depend on the elastic to stretch out to allow the body part to enter or exit the opening but then to pull back, thereby making sure the garment doesn't fall off or let cold air in. The opening must be at least the size of the largest body part, such as hips, that will pass through the opening. The consumer usually considers elastic openings to be

FIGURE 2.8 Example of grosgrain covered steel and nylon boning.

comfortable, especially at the waist area, and they have a sporty feel. Elastic is an appropriate choice with lightweight fabrics that have a soft hand. If used with thicker, fuller fabrics, the gathering forms a bulkiness that can add unwanted dimension to the area. This is especially problematic at the waist.

Elastic should be chosen using the following criteria:

- Compatibility with the fabric and its care method
- Long-lasting "snap back" qualities
- Strength and stability without bulk

Elastics always have some type of elastomeric material in them, such as rubber or polyurethane. The amount of elastomeric material will determine the strength of the elastic. Rubber is less expensive but degrades more quickly. Polyurethane is long-lasting and will withstand exposure to chlorine, dry-cleaning fluid, and detergents. Both are usually covered with another material such as cotton or poly-

ester to make a more comfortable product. They may appear on the edge of a garment such as a pair of panties or a bra, or they are found inside a fabric casing, such as on a skirt or a pair of sweatpants. The way the elastic is fabricated contributes to the strength, snap back, and crosswise firmness of the end product and what types of functions the elastic will be suitable for. Choosing the right elastic will often determine the life of the garment, because if the elastic fails, then the garment is usually discarded.

Finished elastics commonly used in garment construction come in widths as narrow as a thread or as wide as 5 inches. Elastic can be woven, knitted, braided, or come in a thin strip or a thread. Woven elastics are stiffer and do not crush as easily as braided or knitted elastics. They make great waistbands, where strength and longevity are desired. Knitted elastics are inexpensive to make and are sturdy. They do not become skinnier when stretched and have great elasticity. Braided elastics are soft in hand and crushable. They work well with soft fabrics such as flannel; in places where lighter-weight elastic is needed, such as the end of a sleeve in a jersey knit; and in garments where comfort is important. They are very stretchy, but when stretched, they do become narrower.

The way the elastic is connected to the garment will help determine how successfully the elastic does its job and how long it lasts. If the elastic is sewn through, it must not be overly stretched out when stitched or it will not be able to snap back. Usually in this circumstance, the elastic will be fed from the roll into an elastic meter, which ensures that it is stretched just the right amount for every garment before the machine sews through it. Elastic may be applied with an overlock sewn through the edge of the elastic and the fabric and then topstitched down with a straight or chain stitch. A casing should be wide enough so that the elastic can expand and contract without binding. Although a casing does add extra layers, it is a more refined treatment for an outer garment as opposed to underwear, workout wear, or sleepwear. A casing also helps the elastic last longer. Instructions for making an elastic casing are included in Chapter 4.

Trims

Trims are materials that are applied to the surface or into the seam of a garment primarily for decorative purposes. They are made from many different materials by braiding, weaving, knitting, and knotting. They vary in width from 1/8 inch to 12 inches. They may appear at a hem or another garment edge to assist in finishing that edge, in a seam to define a design detail, in the area of a garment piece to create a motif, and so forth. Trims include ribbons, fabric ruffles, piping, various kinds of cording, braids, tape, bias strips, laces, and appliqués.

Choosing trims is partly an artistic pursuit, but as with any material applied to a garment, the trim must meet the following standards:

- Must be care-compatible with the fabric
- Must not bleed or rub off dye onto the garment during cleaning
- Must not fall apart or become detached prematurely
- Must be applied in a way that does not harm the garment

Edge and Insertion Laces

Lace trims, which are made in hundreds of different varieties of fibers, fabrications, patterns, colors, and widths, can be separated into three basic categories: edge laces, insertion laces, and lace trims. Edge laces have one straight side that has a sturdy

TO APPLY EDGE LACE IN A SEAM

1. Place the straight edge of the lace facedown on the face of the garment piece; this will ensure that the face of the lace will be seen from the outside of the garment.
2. Make sure that the edge is just inside the seam line so that when the seam is sewn, the edging will not appear on the outside of the garment.
3. Glue, pin, or baste.
4. Sew the seam, then remove the basting if necessary.

TO APPLY LACE EDGE IN A SEAM (continued)

WHEN APPLYING EDGE LACE BEHIND A HEM THAT IS ALREADY FINISHED, THIS METHOD MAY SHOW FROM THE OUTSIDE OF THE GARMENT

1. Place the edge of the lace facedown on the inside of the hem, positioning the straight edge on top of the stitching that secures the hem.
2. Pin, glue, or baste the lace into position.
3. Stitch by topstitching through all layers or by hand stitching invisibly to the inside of the hem.

WHEN APPLYING EDGE LACE TO A HEM THAT IS NOT ALREADY FINISHED, THIS METHOD WILL NOT LEAVE A LINE OF STITCHING ON THE OUTSIDE OF THE GARMENT

1. Position the lace facedown on the face of the fabric so that the straight edge of the lace is even with the edge of the fabric. Stitch the lace to the hem edge using stitch 301, 401, 514, or 515.
2. Attach the hem using the method desired.

WHEN APPLYING INSERTION LACE, THIS METHOD HAS A LINE OF STITCHING ON THE OUTSIDE OF THE GARMENT

1. Use stitch 504 to finish both edges of the garment in the slot where the lace will be inserted. Press under the seam allowances to the back of the fabric and turn the fabric face side up.
2. Place the lace face side up under one pressed edge of the fabric. The straight edge of the lace should not be seen from the outside of the garment.
3. Using stitch 301, sew the lace to the fabric very near the fold through all layers.
4. Repeat with the other side of the garment and of the lace.

strip that makes the lace easier to apply and one patterned side. Edge laces may also be gathered to form a ruffle before or after they are purchased. The straight edge is applied to the back of an area such as a hem or in between layers of fabric such as at a yoke. Insertion laces have two straight sides, each of which has the same sturdy edge. They are inserted between the edges of two pieces of fabric that have already been finished or will be during the application process so that there is no fabric behind the lace. Insertion laces are commonly seen on blouses in vertical rows. Lace trims may be a variety of irregular shapes, often in floral motifs, and are applied to the surface of the garment fabric (Figure 2.10).

Braid

Braids are made in a variety of designs from a variety of materials, such as rayon, silk, cotton, polyester, or metallic. They may be made with one straight edge and one edge with a motif or two motif edges, and they are usually narrow. They may be flat or more three-dimensional. They may be plaited of several cords or woven (Figure 2.11).

Braids always serve some kind of decorative function and make a great textural accent for garment design lines, but they may also be part of a hem or other edge finish. Some braids are made to substitute for buttonholes or belt loops. They may be applied with a zipper foot, by hand, or with a braid attachment in place of a standard foot using a straight or zigzag stitch.

Piping

Piping is a cord covered with a bias strip of fabric that makes a ½-inch seam

FIGURE 2.10 Examples of lace trims.

allowance and is always applied between two layers of fabric. The covering strip must be on the bias to cover the cord smoothly, because the cord is round and piping is frequently called upon to curve. Piping may be purchased already made or custom-made from your fabric. Although solid-colored piping is used more frequently, piping of a patterned fabric is far more interesting and adds value to the garment. As with bias binding, stripes, plaids, and small patterns that coordinate

FIGURE 2.11 Examples of braids.

with the fashion fabric(s) are great coverings for piping.

When figuring the width of the bias strip to cover the piping, the diameter of the cord must be taken into account, plus an extra 1 1/8 inches for the seam allowances. A description of cutting large quantities of bias strips for industry usage is provided below, and we present a similar method for cutting smaller quantities for use in smaller workrooms or for custom apparel. A zipper foot or a piping foot may be used to apply the piping. Piping feet are chosen to accommodate a certain diameter of piping and to keep the piping snug against the left side of the needle, which makes the application quicker and more accurate. Tips for applying piping are shown in Chapter 9, "Vest Construction."

Bias Strips

Bias strips are cut on the bias of plain-woven, lightweight fabrics. Any fiber content can be used, but natural fibers such as cotton, silk, and wool work best, because they keep a crease. Because this 45-degree angle on the fabric stretches the most, it can accommodate curves smoothly when binding edges and when applied flat to the surface of the fabric.

In the garment industry, material is sewn into a tube and then a bias edge is cut into the fabric. The fabric is then put onto a slitting machine to be cut into the correct-width strips. Since the fabric has been sewn into a tube, the strip is continuous. The strips are then put up into small rolls for use at individual sewing stations. A bias binder attachment and a guide are mounted onto a lockstitch machine for the binding process. The bias binder positions the strip so that it is folded twice and ready to cover the fabric edge, which the foot also positions to make sure the binding covers the correct amount

of seam allowance. The directions for applying bias binding to cover an edge can be found in Chapter 3, in the "Hong Kong Seam Finish" section. Directions for piecing bias strips is also included in Chapter 3.

Bias binding may also be used as a design detail on top of fabric piecing seams, as in the work of designer Koos van den Akker; on top of lap seams as a decorative finish; or on a solid piece as strictly a design accent. Bias strips may also be sewn into tubes to become button loops or textural motifs, as in recent fashions by Ralph Rucci. Applying and shaping bias binding on a flat surface as a design accent is included in Chapter 9, "Vest Construction."

Ribbons

Ribbons may be made of many fibers and basically come in four different fabrications: satin, double-faced satin, grosgrain, or tapestry. Ribbons may also be printed with a design. They may range in width from 1/16 inch to 3 inches. Unlike bias, ribbons have finished edges that keep them from stretching. Therefore, they do not like to curve but can be used to stabilize while adding a decorative touch. The finishing of ribbon ends can be a concern, because they ravel so easily. Ends should be finished with a sealant or stitching so that they will last through extended wearing and cleanings. Ribbons are usually stitched with a straight stitch near the edge or a narrow zigzag. Extremely narrow ribbons up to 1/8 inch can be zigzagged over for a decorative addition.

Closures

Closures give us the ability to get into and out of fitted garments and wear them with confidence. They also provide the chance to make a decorative statement on a garment. Closures must be care-compatible with the garment and are frequently dyed or made to match. Because of the attention paid to them by the customer and the onlooker, it is essential for the garment's quality that closures be applied properly. Combinations of closures may also be used, such as the button and zipper at a waistband. Some garments call for a specific closure look, such as small, flat, four-hole buttons on men's dress shirts or metal zippers on jeans. However, in fashion, rules are made to be broken. Tiny four-hole buttons can be used to add decoration and emphasis without fastening anything. Lately, long brass jeans zippers have been visible on numerous designer signature pieces, fine ladies' dresses, and skirts. The quality, style, and appearance of closures should be carefully considered by the fashion professional to make sure that consumer expectations are met for quality, price point, and fashion statement.

Closures can be grouped into several categories, including zippers; buttons; snaps; and hooks, eyes, or loops. Of course, you should consider the look of the closures and if they will enhance your garment, but you should also consider

- how the closure fits into the performance needs of the garment,
- if the cost of the closure conforms to the garment budget,
- the material(s) the closure is made from,
- how it will be colored,
- how it will be applied,
- if it will last the life of the garment, and
- if it is care-compatible with the garment fabrics.

Zippers

Zippers are combinations of fabric with teeth or coils attached and a slider that either separates or joins the teeth or coil together (Figure 2.12).

The **zipper tape** may be made of a variety of fibers but is usually cotton or polyester. **Teeth** can be made of metal or plastic. **Coils** are always plastic. **Sliders** are always metal because of the function they must perform. They will have a **pull** attached with which to grab the slider. The pull may just be functional, or it may also serve a decorative purpose or be

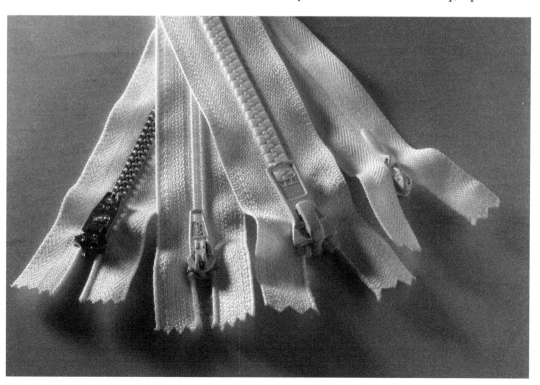

FIGURE 2.12 Assorted zippers.

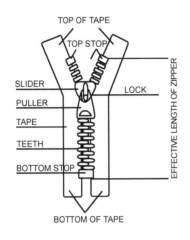

designed with the brand image or logo of the manufacturer or designer (Figure 2.13). Zippers may be nonseparating, such as an invisible zipper, or separating, such as a jacket zipper.

Separating zippers usually just separate in one direction at a time but may also have two sliders that can function independently. This gives the wearer of the garment the opportunity to unzip a longer jacket from the bottom up after the top slider has closed the front of the jacket. This makes the jacket more comfortable to wear while sitting down. Jacket sliders may also be reversible, which allows the jacket to be worn inside out. Both separating and nonseparating zippers should have a top stop to keep the slider from sliding off the top of the zipper. Nonseparating zippers will also have a bottom stop that is a metal bar attached across the teeth at the zipper's bottom. This prevents the slider from coming off the bottom of the zipper. Top stops and teeth can be removed from a metal zipper to shorten it. However, plastic zipper teeth and coils cannot be removed, because they are part of the tape. The function of stopping the slider from coming off the top of the zipper can also be accomplished by enclosing the top of the zipper in a facing or waistband seam. A thread bar tack can substitute for a bottom stop.

Nonseparating zippers can be purchased by the piece or prepared at a certain length, or manufacturers can purchase zipper by the yard, cut it to the desired length, and add their own sliders, top stops, and bottom stops. This is usually much less expensive. Separating zippers, however, must be purchased premade at the correct length because of the mechanism at the bottom of the zipper. Instructions for inserting an invisible and a lap zipper are found in Chapter 4, "Basic Straight Skirt." A fly zipper application is found in Chapter 5, "Ladies' Pant Construction." A separating zipper application is found in Chapter 7, "Fashion Jacket."

Buttons

Buttons (Figure 2.14) can be made from many materials, including plastic, metal, wood, shell, bone, or clay, and are usually round and flat, half round, or round. Novelty shapes are common, as are buttons designed specifically for brand-name garments. Many of these buttons will include a designer or manufacturer logo or name to remind the customer about the garment's brand image. In addition to the criteria listed in the introduction to this section, buttons are typically chosen with an eye toward the usual button seen on this style of garment or toward enhancing the fashion statement of the design. In jackets and overcoats, buttons may be sewn on with a clear button backer on the inside of the garment to support the button and fabric and to prevent the strain on the button from damaging the fabric.

Buttons are usually accompanied by a buttonhole but may be used strictly for decoration over a fake buttonhole, a snap, or blank fabric. Correctly sizing buttonholes is very important. If the hole is too big, the button will slip through. If it is too small, the customer will have difficulty

FIGURE 2.14 Examples of button types.

getting the button fastened. The style of the buttonhole, stitch length, and width are equally important. Delicate blouse fabrics need delicate buttonholes. Overcoats need buttonholes stitched with cording and a heavy thread. Buttonholes are most frequently made by buttonholers (as described in Chapter 1). An interlining is often inserted behind buttonholes to ensure smooth stitching and strength. Buttonholes may also be made on the edge of a garment with fabric, thread, or braid loops. Buttons on the back of bridal gowns are paired with a row of elastic loops, which makes that large number of buttons easier to handle. For women's wear, buttonholes are usually found on the garment's right side. For men's wear, buttonholes are on the left. Outerwear such as suit jackets and overcoats should have buttons that are made horizontally to allow a little bit more room for that extra layer on cold days. Horizontal buttonholes at a pant waistband will allow a bit of extra room for dessert. Blouses, vests, and so on, should have vertical buttonholes to avoid having

the button slide so far that it reveals your unmentionables. As described in Chapter 1, buttons are usually sewn on by garment manufacturing machines, but they may be sewn on by hand in designer signature apparel.

Placement of buttons is extremely important. Too many buttons will waste money, time, and materials; too few will not close the garment effectively and may lead to gaping. Button placement is particularly important on women's blouses and jackets at the bustline, where crosswise pull on the garment may be strongest. It is also important at the top of pants, because the button helps protect the top of the zipper from excess strain.

Button styles can be divided into three groups: buttons with holes, buttons with shanks, and tack buttons.

Buttons with holes may have a set of two or four. Shanks can be made of the button material—plastic, metal, and so on—or they may be attached to the button later. A shank raises the button off the garment, allowing the fabric to slip under neatly. Tack buttons consist of a hollow cap with a post for the outside of the garment and a base that looks like a metal tack for the back of the garment. They are permanently attached to the garment when the tack goes up through the fabric and connects with the button. You would usually see these metal buttons at the waistband of a pair of jeans or on a jean jacket.[2] They are extremely long-wearing. Holed buttons may have a shank formed with the thread that is being used to sew it on. Sewing on holed buttons is covered in Chapter 6, "Ladies' Blouse." Sewing on a shank button is covered in Chapter 8, "Tailored Jacket." There is also a tip on making thread shanks. Both chapters contain tips on buttonhole making.

Buttons come in a range of sizes, referred to as "lignes." Figure 2.15 shows ligne sizes and their English and metric equivalents.

Snaps

Snaps come in a great variety of styles and sizes, from tiny 1/8-inch wide to large 3/4 inch and are made of metal or plastic. They always consist of at least two parts: a post side and a socket side. The parts of the post side are attached to the under-side of the overlapping half of the garment, and the socket side is attached to the upper side of the lower layer. Sew-on snaps have holes through which thread attaches them to the fabric, and they can be sewn on by machine or by hand and can be covered with the garment fabric for a more refined look. Four-part metal snaps with caps are attached to the garment with a special tool that expands part of the snap to keep it from coming out of the fabric. These snaps have a decorative cap that can be designed specifically for the brand of the garment and can display a logo or name.

Four-part snap sizes are also expressed as lignes. If they show on the outside, snaps are generally considered to be a sporty detail. They are frequently found on sports wear such as ski jackets, wind pants, and rain gear, because they are easy and quick to use for cold, wet hands and are longer-lasting than a button and buttonhole. Plastic and metal snaps may also be mounted into a strip of twill tape for ease of insertion into garments. Instructions for sewing on a snap are included in Chapter 6, "Ladies' Blouse."

Hooks and Eyes

Hooks and eyes or loops come in a set. They range in size and are always made of metal. There are several types that basically fall into three categories: pant hooks, which have a set of prongs to attach them; skirt hooks, which use prongs or can be sewn in; and dress hooks, which are sewn in. Pant and skirt hooks are sold as a unit; dress hooks and loops are sold as units or are premounted in a strip of twill tape. They are usually black or silver colored. Some large hooks are covered with cording and are generally known as *fur hooks* because of their use in fur coats. Sew-on skirt hooks consist of two parts: the hook, which is a flat metal piece, and the eye,

FIGURE 2.15 Button ligne size equivalents.

Ligne Sizes Defined
20 Ligne = 1/2" dia. = 12.700 MM
25 Ligne = 5/8" dia. = 15.875 MM
30 Ligne = 3/4" dia. = 19.050 MM
35 Ligne = 7/8" dia. = 22.225 MM
40 Ligne = 1" dia. = 25.400 MM
45 Ligne = 1–1/8" dia. = 28.58 MM

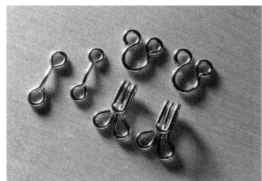

FIGURE 2.16 (left) Pant hook with prongs, sew in skirt hook, both for waistbands.

FIGURE 2.17 (right) Dress hooks, eyes and loops.

which is a flat metal bar. This type of sew-on hook can be used on pants as well. Each has a set of four holes, which are sewn through to attach them to the garment. Pant hooks have four parts: the flat metal hook and eye, plus mounting plates with prongs to attach them to the fabric (Figure 2.16).

Dress hooks and eyes are much smaller and thinner and need to be sewn on. They are for lighter-weight use where there is not much crosswise strain. The hooks can also be used with a loop. The U-shaped eye is used when the hooks are sewn onto the edge of a garment, such as at a waist facing of a skirt above an invisible zipper. The loop is used when the fabric will be overlapping, such as a garment front (Figure 2.17).

Instructions for sewing on a skirt hook are included in the waistband directions of Chapter 5, "Ladies' Pant Construction." Instructions for sewing on a dress hook and eye are included after the invisible zipper instructions in Chapter 4.

END NOTES
1. Ruth Glock and Grace Kunz. *Apparel Manufacturing Sewn Product Analysis*. 4th ed. (Upper Saddle River: Pearson Prentice Hall, 2005).
2. Ruth Glock and Grace Kunz. *Apparel Manufacturing Sewn Product Analysis*. 4th ed. (Upper Saddle River: Pearson Prentice Hall, 2005).

Seams and Seam Finishes

F ashion design emerges through the unity of fabric and seams. As a fashion professional, you will use seams to impart your own style to fabric. Proper seam choices can make the difference between successful, awe-inspiring fashion design verses just another garment. Seams hold the garment together. Seam finishes prevent the edge

of woven fabrics from raveling. Therefore, your seam and seam-finishing choices should be based on a thorough knowledge of industry garment-construction methods.

However, seams cost money. Every cut in the fabric, every stitch of thread used, and every edge finish executed represents an investment by the garment's manufacturer, not only in money, but also in time and energy. Decisions must be made with regard to quality, cost, and time that balance the vision of the designer with the cost concerns of the manufacturer, both of whom are trying to satisfy the retail customer.

Where will your seams be placed—on the straight of grain, cross grain, or bias? How many stitches per inch are right for your fabric and price point? What thread tension will ensure a smooth seam? Which seam finish represents the quality of your apparel without overinvesting in time, effort, and materials?

The purpose of this chapter is to aid the designer, merchandiser, and buyer in understanding the steps used to create seams, the quality implications of those

seams, and the cost associated with manufacturing them. The look of the seam directly contributes to the customer's initial acceptance of the garment and the brand it represents. After consumers evaluate the garment through use, the performance of the seam will affect their loyalty to the brand. Using the proper seams and machine settings will save materials, time, and labor and will preserve the reputation of your brand image as well.

HOW TO CHOOSE THE CORRECT SEAMS AND SEAM FINISHES

Before selecting the seams you will use to construct your garment, you must evaluate what you have to work with. After the garment has been designed according to the customer's needs, you must determine

- which seams and finishes will work with the structure of your garment;
- which seams will satisfy your customer's quality requirements in function, future performance, and aesthetics;

- what fabric(s) you will be constructing with;
- what thread(s) will work best with your fabric and the end use of the garment;
- what your budget is for construction;
- how many garments you're making and how much time you have to finish them;
- what machines, attachments, and needles you will need;
- what skills the workers constructing your garments must have.

The correct mixture of materials, accurately performed skills, tools, and machinery, combined with the correct seam or seam finish, will help ensure that your apparel will catch customers' attention and then convince them to open their wallet. Let's look at each of these choices in depth.

Structure of the Garment

Seams are your method of making flat fabric into a wearable shape. There are many seam choices for each position in one garment. Your job as a designer or merchandiser is to choose the seam that best fulfills the criteria we have discussed. If you are purchasing apparel, you must ensure that the seams used to make what you're buying fit your customer's needs and support your brand image. In the how-to section of this chapter, you will find recommendations for uses of each type of seam or seam finish, which will help guide you. Some questions to answer when deciding what seam or seam finish to use include the following:

- How long is the seam?
- Will the seam be visible from the inside or outside of the garment or both?
- Will the seam be covered with a facing or lining, such as at a dress neckline or in a jacket?

- Can you add value to (or cut expenses from) the garment by using a decorative form of a seam or seam finish?
- Will the seam need to be curved, straight, or both, such as in a princess seam?
- Should the seam be pressed open (such as near an invisible zipper), or should both seam allowances be pressed to one side, such as in a collar?
- Will the seam need to be easily altered, such as the seam in the center back of a pair of dress pants?
- Which seam or seam finish will be most comfortable at that location?

Function of the Seam

You will also need to know the function of the seam in the design of the garment. The ability of the seam you choose to fulfill this function depends on the following three seam characteristics: elasticity, strength, and flexibility.[1] These characteristics are determined by

- the fabric being sewn,
- the direction the seam is sewn on the fabric,
- the type of stitch being used,
- the type and dimension of the thread,
- the tension of the threads, and
- the stitch length.[2]

Elasticity

Elasticity is the amount the seam can stretch out and then quickly recover without the stitches bursting. Seams sewn on woven fabrics may not need to stretch as much as those constructing a knit garment, but with the inclusion of stretch yarns such as Lycra in many woven fabrics to improve fit and add comfort, the capacity of seams and hems to stretch and recover without bursting is an important aspect of quality construction to many consumers.

The seam must stretch to the same degree as the fabric itself.[3]

Strength

Many consumers see strength of seam as an indication of quality level in the apparel they are considering. If they can see seam "grin" (stitches showing through on the outside of a garment at the seam line), stitching that looks loose, or, worse yet, broken stitches on a blouse, they may leave that blouse right on the rack, no matter how low the price. Seams have strength in the crosswise and lengthwise directions. Strength is primarily determined by the quality of the thread, type of seam, stitch length, and thread tension. The performance of the garment is heavily impacted by the strength of the seam, but there is no point in overinvesting time or materials to create a seam that is stronger than the fabric around it. It is better to have the thread break in an overstressed seam than to damage the fabric.[4]

Flexibility

The flexibility of a seam must match the hand of the fabric. The look of the garment depends on seams that will flow and drape with the fabric so that your design statement is preserved. Comfort is also impacted by seam flexibility. Seams that are stiffer than the fabric can poke and rub the wearer, which damages not only the seam but also the brand image. The stiffness of the fabric itself, the type of thread and stitch used, and the stitch length affect the flexibility of your seam choice.

The amount of elasticity, strength, and flexibility required for the performance of the seam depends on what the function of the seam will be. Is the seam's primary function to withstand a lot of wear and tear, such as a crotch seam (which needs strength)? Or does it need to look unobtrusive, such as the seam in a translucent chiffon blouse (where it needs flexibility)? Will the seam be on the bias (where it needs elasticity), or at the shoulder seam (where it needs stability)? Tips on applying these characteristics to seam choices will be shown in this chapter.

Aesthetics

The aesthetic function of the seam will also influence your decision. The visual impact of the seam may simply be that it is neatly sewn with trimmed ends, reassuring the customer that the garment is a good investment. Or the seam may be part of the fashion appeal, which positions your garment just that little bit ahead of the competition. An added detail, such as topstitching, a contrast bias binding, piping, or a textural trim, might be the part of your design statement that convinces the retail consumer to add your garment to his or her wardrobe. Ideas for using seams as decorative detailing are included in the tip boxes throughout the chapter.

Fabric

The characteristics of the fabric you are using to construct your apparel should directly influence your choice of seam, seam finish, thread, and needle. For example, the fiber content of a polyester crepe calls for a thread that doesn't shrink, a needle that won't snag the yarns, and a stitch that will allow the fabric to drape beautifully and won't pucker at the seam.

The yarn structure of a woven fabric contributes to the ability of that fabric to hold on to the stitches making the seam. A seam sewn on a fabric such as chiffon or satin that is woven with slippery yarns may pull away from the garment, resulting in a flaw that is almost impossible to repair. A wool coating fabric with thick, fluffy yarns requires a wide seam allowance and a short stitch length to hold the seam in place. Silk shantung, which is woven with very fine yarns, should be sewn with a thread tension and small needle size that will not pucker the seam or pull the threads on the crosswise grain of the fabric. Overlocking should not be used to cover the raw edge, because it will mark the shantung during pressing.

The type of weave used to make the fabric is also a factor that you should consider. Loosely woven fabrics, such as a handwoven jacket fabric, will need special care to avoid shifting the yarns at the seam line, causing the edge of the fabric to become distorted and stretched out. A densely woven fabric with fine yarns such as microfiber needs short stitches and special needles to avoid causing pulls and puckers at the seam line; it also needs a lightweight finish to preserve the drape of the fabric.

The thickness of the fabric and the number of layers used in a seam may exclude certain finishes, because those finishes would produce a seam that is too bulky to be structurally suitable or aesthetically pleasing. Traditional flat fell and French seams look beautifully finished but involve too many layers to be appropriate for a fabric such as heavy denim or boiled wool. On the other hand, these seams are wonderful for fine shirting and translucent organza or chiffon.

In this chapter, you will find recommendations for which fabrics work well with each seam and seam finish. The Appendix contains a chart that lists seam suggestions for certain fabric types. This chart also includes sewing machine needle, stitch length, and tension tips.

Cost Considerations

As a fashion professional, you will want to select the least expensive seam and seam finish that will satisfy the needs of the fashion design and the customer while still maintaining the required quality level in performance and aesthetics. You must balance the cost implications of the seam and finish with the value of long-lasting construction and visual appeal. Generally, consumers think of garments with neatly finished edges as being of higher quality than garments with untreated edges.[5] But, as discussed in the Introduction, seams and seam finishes can no longer reliably be used as a gauge of fashion quality. Since trimming costs have become the name of the fashion game for many brands, what once were considered "cheap" seam finishes have appeared in designer garments. The fact remains, though, that the durability and performance of the garment still depends on the construction decisions made by designers, merchandisers, and buyers. Focusing too much on cost of construction and not enough on quality will damage a brand no matter how popular the name.

Time Considerations

Time, or "minutes of make," helps determine the quality of your apparel.[6] Processes such as lean manufacturing and Electronic Data Interchange have been adopted in order to have more apparel in the store exactly when the customer wants to buy it. When you're considering time in the manufacturing of your apparel, you must look at the following issues:

- The complexity of a seam or seam finish
- The number of times it must pass through a machine to be completed
- The hand, thickness, and surface texture of the material being sewn
- The type and speed of the machine being used
- The attachments or tools available to assist the worker

Making the correct choices on these construction aspects will help shorten the time necessary to complete the seam without compromising the quality level your customer expects. Also, the more accurate the workers are when sewing the seams, the less chance they will need to be redone and the more first-quality garments will be produced.

Machines, Attachments, and Tools

Having the most up-to-date, specialized sewing machines and attachments, tools, and pressing equipment available to sew and finish each step of a garment might seem to be every apparel manufacturer's dream. However, the more specialized the machines available, the more limited the types of steps and items of apparel that they can manufacture. The simple combination of a lockstitch machine, an overlock machine, a blind-stitch machine, and a buttonhole machine, plus a good heavy iron can be used to complete just about every style of apparel at every quality level imaginable. However, the worker may spend a lot of time moving from one machine to another, manipulating fabrics and trims by hand, and completing extra steps. Although in some workrooms, these machines assist workers in creating many styles of gorgeous designer ready-to-wear, in most apparel manufacturing, this is an obvious example of wasted time, motion, and materials. To remain competitive, apparel manufacturers of national brands and private labels often specialize in one style or a group of styles that require the same pieces of equipment. When sourcing, designers and merchandisers may look specifically for the factory with the right machinery to construct their apparel. This would depend on whether the production process requires specialized equipment or whether finding the lowest possible labor

costs is more important than the type of machine the construction is done with.

PARTS OF A SEAM

Before discussing how to sew the seams and seam finishes, we will identify the parts of a seam so that we know what we are talking about. We will also discuss how these parts affect the function of the seam or finish and how they affect its strength, elasticity, flexibility, and durability (Figure 3.1).

Seam Allowance

Seam allowance is the distance between the cut edge of the fabric and the line of stitching closest to the center of the garment. Various widths of seam allowance are used depending on the type of seam, the quality of the garment, the position of the seam in the garment, and the characteristics of the fabric being sewn. You should use the narrowest seam allowance possible to avoid unnecessary trimming and clipping steps, which may result from using seam allowances that are too wide in curved areas such as armholes or in enclosed, layered areas such as necklines with collars. In most apparel manufacturing, these steps would be regarded as wasted time, effort, and materials. The garment samples in each chapter are sewn using the industry standard seam allowance for the positions of the seams.

Seam-allowance decisions may begin when patterns are made for each piece of a garment. When markers are created to arrange pattern pieces on the fabric for cutting, the widths of seam allowances are taken into account to make sure that there is enough extra fabric beyond the seam line to ensure a sturdy seam with the proper finish but not so much extra fabric that it will be wasted. The width of the

FIGURE 3.1 Parts of a seam.

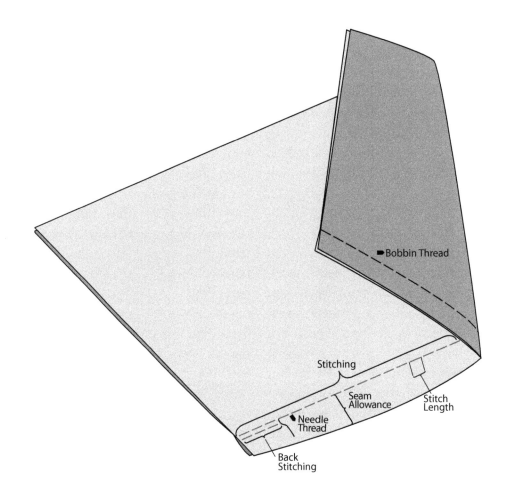

Bobbin Thread

Stitching

Seam Allowance

Stitch Length

Needle Thread

Back Stitching

seam allowances affects the strength, durability, appearance, comfort, and cost of a garment.[7]

To some consumers, wide seam allowances are still a mark of quality in better to designer ready-to-wear. In areas where alterations are frequent, such as at the waist of dressy pants, wider seam allowances are allowed as a selling point to the customer. For the same reason, extra fabric at hems is allowed (and left unhemmed) to make the pants an easier sell to taller customers. A balance must be struck between a seam allowance that is so narrow that the seam comes apart and is difficult for workers to catch all the layers of fabric when sewing and an allowance that is so wide it wastes fabric and creates extra finishing steps.[8] There are recommendations in each section for the proper seam allowances to use.

Stitches

Stitches are connections between threads created by the motion of machines. The machine you use determines the formation of the stitches. **Lockstitch** machines use needle and **bobbin** mechanisms to make the straight lines of stitching that you see on most fashions created from woven fabrics. Straight stitches can be used to hold fabrics together, apply findings such as zippers, add topstitching details, temporarily attach layers of fabric together, create decorative effects, and more. A variety of machines create variations on overlock stitches that may be used to sew seams, finish edges, secure hems, or all of these at once.

The formation of the fabric chosen to go with the stitching creates the seam. Plain seams, French seams, and flat fell seams can all be sewn with a lockstitch machine but can produce very different looks and serve different purposes because of the way the fabric is formed. Mock flat felled seams may be sewn with a safety stitch overlock, but so can the inseam of a pair of dress pants. The formation of the fabric creates two completely different results.

When setting up your lockstitch or overlock machine to create stitching, there are several settings that should be adjusted to ensure a beautifully sewn seam: stitch length, stitch width, and thread tension.

Stitch Length

Stitch length refers to the rate at which the needle carries its thread down through the fabric to join with the lower thread. The stitch length is actually controlled by the feed teeth under the presser foot. As the presser foot presses the fabric against the teeth, the teeth grab the fabric and move it at a steady pace in relation to the needle's speed. The combination of needle speed and the reach of the feed teeth produce the stitch length you have set.

Usually stitch length is expressed as stitches per inch (spi) or as stitches per centimeter (spc). It should be set according to the function of the stitch, the thread diameter, and the characteristics of the fabric. Stitch length directly impacts the manufacturer's investment in garment production. An unnecessarily short stitch length wastes time and thread. A stitch length that is too long results in poor seam performance. Incorrectly set stitch length can also ruin your fabric, causing puckers, pulled yarns perpendicular to the line of stitching, or seams that pull off the edge of the fabric. In the Appendix is a table of recommended stitch lengths for lockstitch and overlock machines for a variety of fabric types.

Stitch Width

Stitch width refers to the distance that the needle of a lockstitch machine will swing to the right and left while stitching. It also refers to the width of stitching that an overlock, a blind-stitch, or other machine produces. Lockstitch machines that have this capability produce a zigzag stitch that can be used for button sewing, bar tacking, making buttonholes, embroidery, and so on. Stitch width on these machines is adjusted according to the type of stitch, the function of the stitch, and the fabric's characteristics. Overlock machines can produce many types of seams, depending on the formation of the fabric and where the stitching appears in the garment. Blind-stitch machines are usually used for hemming and occasionally for seaming, where the majority of the stitching should not appear on the outside of the garment. Profiles of many of the machines you will encounter in the apparel industry are given in Chapter 1.

Thread Tension

Proper thread tension settings will create seams and finishes that are attractive and long-lasting, resulting in improved brand image in the eyes of the customer. Proper tension uses less thread—saving costs for the manufacturer.

Thread tension, stitch length, and stitch width should be checked on a scrap of your garment fabric before beginning any type of seam with any machine. Sew lines of stitching on the lengthwise, crosswise, and bias of the fabric to check the seam characteristics in each direction. Your seam may be perfect on the lengthwise grain but need adjustment in the crosswise or bias directions. If you notice problems with the lines of stitching, consult the troubleshooting chart in the Appendix for solutions.

Backstitching/Back Tacking

Back tacking, or sewing in place or backward for a few stitches at the beginning and end of a line of stitching or a stitching function, is frequently done when manufacturing apparel. This helps prevent a line or stitching function from coming undone. Usually, a computerized sewing machine is programmed to automatically take a certain number of tacking stitches, depending on what is being sewn—a dart, a seam, a patch pocket, topstitching, and so on. Lockstitch machines that are not computerized have a lever that the worker uses for this purpose. Some machines, such as overlock and blind-stitch machines, do not back tack. As a general rule, you should always back tack at the beginning and end of a line of stitching if you are concerned about it coming undone. If you are crossing the end of a line of stitching with another line of stitching, this will usually suffice to keep them from unraveling. Secure a seam with the fewest number of stitches to avoid wasted materials and time and to keep the stitching looking neat.

Basting

Basting (temporary sewing) by machine should be done at a needle thread tension that is 1 1/2 to 2 numbers lower than the tension used for balanced straight stitching. Use the longest stitch length available on your machine and sew the line of basting just inside the seam line for easy removal.

TYPES OF STITCHES AND SEAMS

The types of stitches included in this book are lockstitches, simple chain stitches, overlock stitches, and safety stitches. ASTM, originally known as the American Society

EXPLANATION OF STITCH NOTATIONS

The ASTM stitch notations in this and all chapters are numbered according to the following categories:

300 class—301–315: These stitches are formed with 2 or more threads which are passed through the fabric with a needle or needles to catch one bobbin thread on the bottom. Stitch 301, a single needle straight stitch is the most common. Stitch 302 creates a line of double needle topstitching, 304 is a basic zigzag which is used for satin stitching appliqués to a fabric surface and for applying lace or braid and as a decorative accent. Stitch 315 is a multistep zigzag which is great for applying elastic.

400 class—401–407: These stitches are formed by top threads interlooping with bottom threads so that the stitches are locked together. Stitch 401, a single needle safety stitch is the most common and although not stretchable, it is very strong.

500 class—501–522: These are overlock stitches that cover the edge of the seam with stitching to prevent raveling and that may also sew the seam. There are many commonly used stitches in this class, such as stitch 503, which is a two-thread overlock and is great for fine fabrics—as is stitch 504, the three-thread overlock. Stitch 515 includes a safety stitch and two-thread overlock. Stitch 516 is the same, but with a three-thread overlock. These are both great for stitches that need to be strong but are impossible to let out and do not stretch. Stitches 512 and 514 are strong, stretchable versions of the previous stitches.

for Testing and Materials, has developed a catalogue (D-6193-97 *Standard Practices for Stitches and Seams*) of standard stitch and seam forms used in the apparel industry. This ASTM guide has a wealth of material useful for making the best selection of stitches and seams for your project. Garment designers and merchandisers may use this guide to learn the exact form the fabric will take for the seams, which stitches should be used to sew it, and how many passes are required through the machine. Each stitch and seam is represented in the catalog by a diagram and a notation. The notations for each stitch and seam in this chapter are included under the name of the seam.

There are three types of seams for woven fabrics in this chapter: unfinished, self-finishing, and overlocked. There are also three seam finishes. Each seam and seam finish in this chapter has suggestions about where it can be used to advantage in your garments. The machines that sew these stitches are described in Chapter 1.

TROUBLESHOOTING

The following illustrations (Figures 3.2 to 3.13) show the most common problems encountered while sewing fabrics and how to correct them. Many problems can also be avoided by following the recommendations in the Appendix charts for thread tension, stitch length, needle type and size, and pressing temperatures. Threading diagrams for lockstitch, overlock, and blind-stitch machines are shown in the machine's manual. Properly threading your machine is also a great way to avoid stitching problems. Each illustration below includes a text box listing what may have caused the problem and how to avoid or fix it.

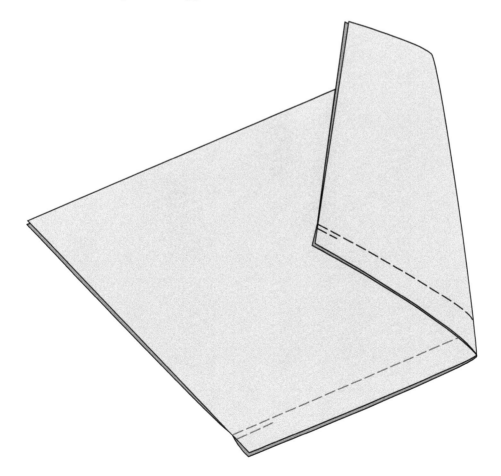

FIGURE 3.2a Balanced needle thread tension.

FIGURE 3.2b Needle thread tension too loose. Tighten needle thread tension until the joint between the threads is hidden inside the layers of fabric.

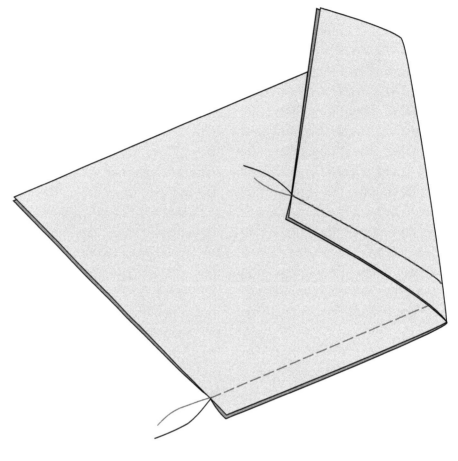

FIGURE 3.2c Needle thread tension too tight. Loosen the needle thread tension. Avoid adjusting both the needle and bobbin thread tensions because this can make the solution unneccesarily confusing.

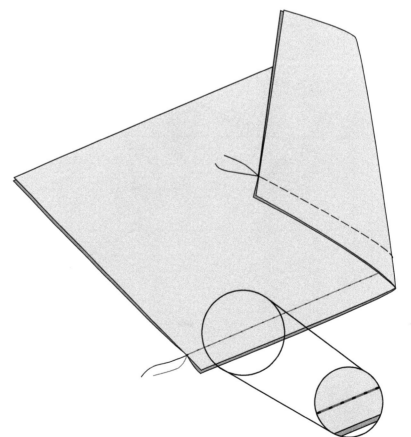

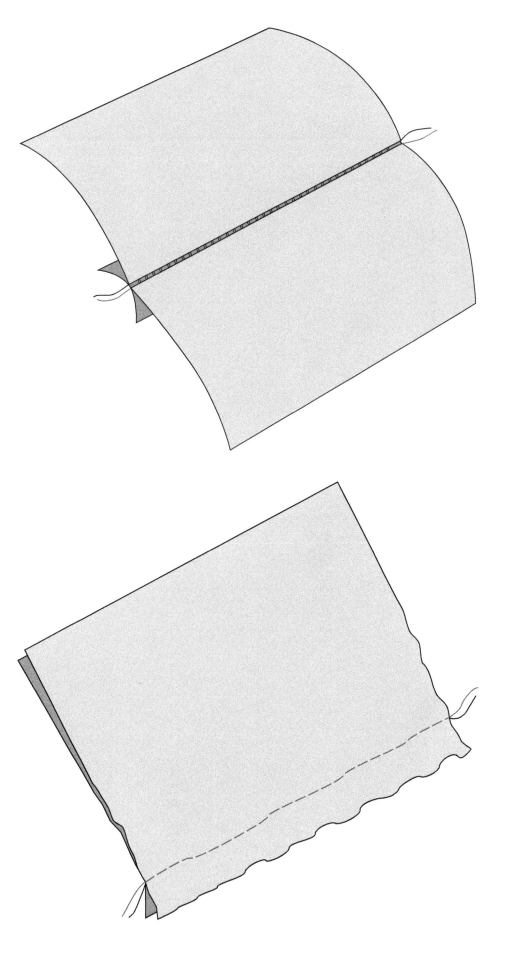

FIGURE 3.3 Seam grin. Check to make sure the machine is threaded correctly and that the needle and bobbin threads are inside the tension mechanism then tighten the needle thread tension if necessary.

FIGURE 3.4 Seam puckering. Fabric, especially light-weight, may pucker because the needle tension is too tight. Loosen the needle tension very slightly.

FIGURE 3.5 Stitch breakage. Check to make sure the machine is threaded properly, the needle is inserted correctly or replace the needle if it is bent, dull or has a burr on it.

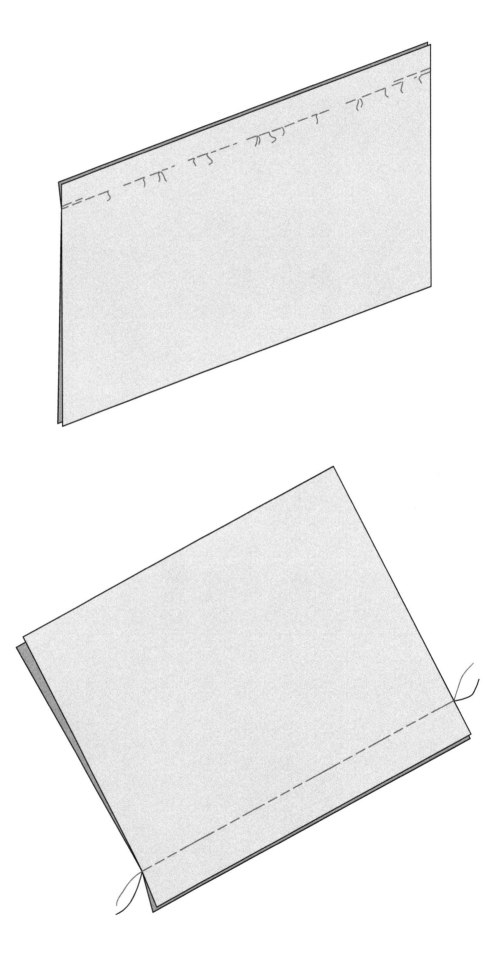

FIGURE 3.6 Skipping stitches. Check to make sure the machine is threaded correctly, the needle isn't dull, bent or inserted incorrectly. Also, when sewing a lightweight knit, make sure you are using the correct type and size of needle and the correct throat plate.

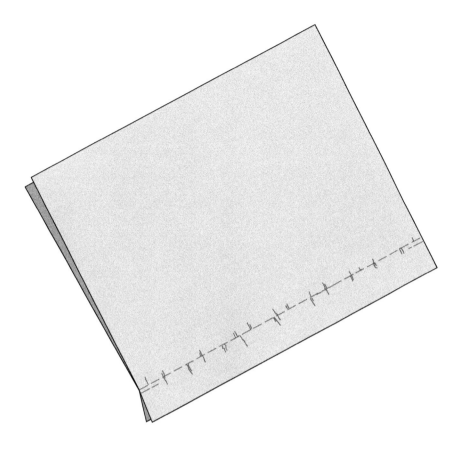

FIGURE 3.7 Snagging of fabric yarns. Check the needle to make sure it isn't dull or has a burr on it. On fabrics woven or knitted from very fine yarns, make sure you are using the correct size and type of needle.

FIGURE 3.8 Seam slippage. Make sure you are using a short stitch length and the widest seam allowance possible. Use a French seam when possible or an overlock to finish the edge.

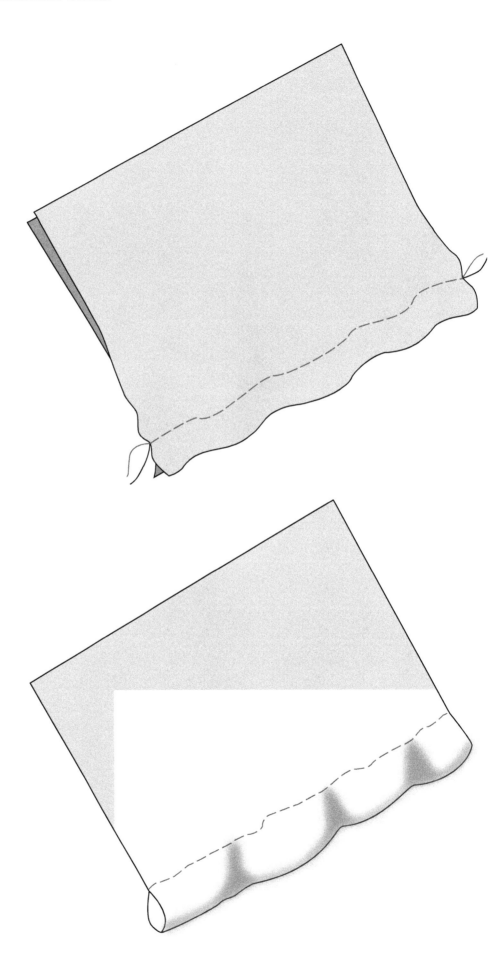

FIGURE 3.9 Stretched fabric. Avoid pullling the fabric toward yourself in front of the presser foot or away from yourself behind the foot. On thick fabrics being sewn on the bias, gently push the fabric into the toes of the presser foot as the fabric feeds.

FIGURE 3.10 Distortion of the fabric while sewing at an edge, also known as "roping." Press the edge before sewing a hem, pinning if possible. Don't pull on a bias edge while stitching.

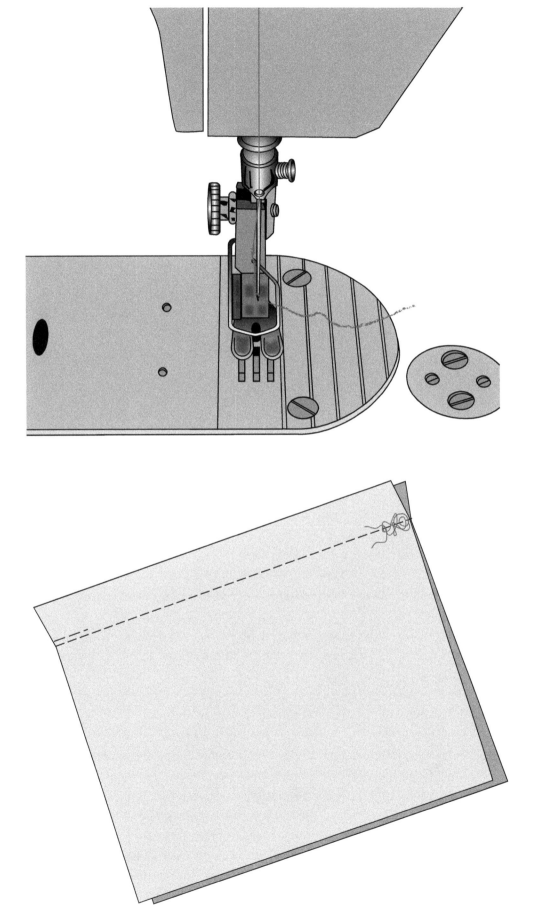

FIGURE 3.11 Frayed thread. The needle is too small for the diameter of the thread or the tickness of the fabric or the needle thread tension is too tight or you may be sewing with a damaged needle. Replace the needle and check the needle thread tension.

FIGURE 3.12 Not holding threads back at the beginning of the seam. Thread bunches on the underside of the fabric at the beginning of the seam. The threads are not being held at the beginning of the seam. Hold the bobbin and needle threads while the machine sews the first 2 or 3 stitches.

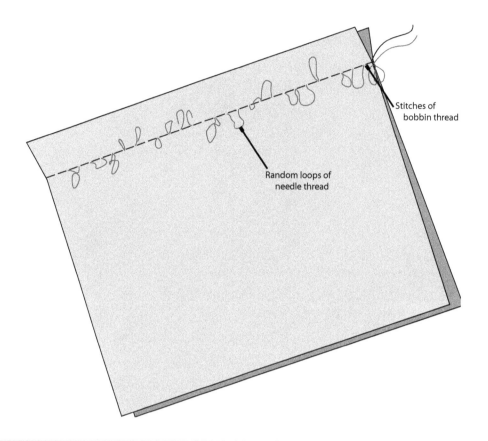

Stitches of bobbin thread

Random loops of needle thread

EXPLANATION OF ASTM SEAM TYPES

Seam types are given lettered designations in the following format (the first two letters represent the way the fabric is placed for the seam):

SS: This class uses two or more layers of fabric laid against each other in a variety of formats, often with face sides together.

LS: This class uses two or more layers of fabric lapped over each other in a variety of configurations, often with the face of one fabric against the back of another layer.

BS: This class includes seams that are bound with a folded binding.

FS: These seams have two edges that are butted against each other instead of overlapping.

OS: This class includes a variety of decorative treatments, such as topstitching, other than that which also creates a seam and raised pin tucks.

EF: Seams in this class complete a variety of tasks but are mostly used for edge finishing. This class includes stitches for hemming, making spaghetti straps, inserting elastic into hems, making belt loops, and so on.

The next, lowercase letter is simply a designation to separate one kind of seam in a class from another. The number at the end tells how many passes through a sewing machine, such as a lockstitch, overlock, or blind hemmer, is needed to complete the seam. For example, seam SSa-1 is the designation for the basic straight seam using two layers of superimposed fabric and one pass through the machine.

METHODS

Preparation for Sewing

Follow these steps before beginning a sewing session and when changing to a new fabric or thread to ensure that the seams will be well constructed and your fabric will remain undamaged. Refer to the Appendix to find the proper settings for your stitch, seam, and fabric.

1. Check to make sure your needle and bobbin mechanism are correctly threaded.
2. Check the needle thread tension.
3. Check to make sure the needle is the correct size and is in good condition.
4. Check the stitch length and width settings.
5. To confirm your choices, sew a sample on your fabric in a single layer and double layer using the settings you have chosen in the lengthwise, crosswise, and bias directions of the fabric. Using the figures presented in the "Troubleshooting" section, make corrections as needed to solve problems.

Plain Seam

ASTM Stitch Type: 301 or 401
ASTM Seam Type: SSa-1
Machine: Lockstitch
Attachments: Straight stitch foot
Machine Settings: SL 2-3, SW 0
Seam Usage: This seam is the industry standard for joining two pieces of woven fabric in any position on the garment.
Type of Fabric: Appropriate for any weight or weave of fabric
Positive: Strong; has no elasticity; has flexibility
Negative: Does not stretch
Price Point: All

TIP | Tips for sewing beautiful convex or concave curves

- Always maintain your seam allowance width.
- As the seam is sewn, you will notice that the edge begins to wander away from the seam width line on the bed of the machine.
- If the curve is shallow, you can keep the fabric edge at the seam line by gently pivoting the fabric toward the line on the machine in tiny turns. Watch the edge and the line, not the stitching.
- If the curve is tight, you may have to stop, put the needle down, pick up the presser foot, and pivot the fabric to keep your seam allowance even. Many tiny pivots will keep the curve smooth instead of a few large pivots, which end up as a bunch of disjointed angles.

Practice Exercise

1. Place two layers of fabric face-sides together under the presser foot of the machine, as shown in Figure 3.14.
2. Before starting to sew on a lockstitch machine, always hold the needle and bobbin thread or press down on them to avoid having them tangle on the bottom of the fabric.
3. Sew a seam using a ½-inch seam allowance backstitching at both ends. On the back of the fabric,

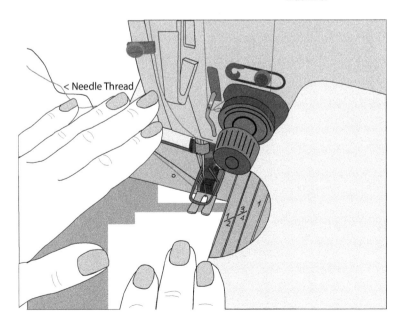

FIGURE 3.14 Correct positioning of fabric in a lockstitch machine.

< Needle Thread

TIP | Tips for sewing beautiful outside corners
In the factory, processes like this are assisted
by various computerized features on the
machine for greater accuracy and a quicker
completion.

- Always maintain your seam allowance
  width.
- When approaching the corner, slow down
  and stop when you reach the seam allowance width for the next edge (e.g., 1/2" from
  the end).
- Turn the hand wheel toward you to lower the
  needle into the fabric.
- Lift the presser foot and pivot the fabric
  until the next edge you are sewing is lined
  up with the proper seam width line on the
  bed of the machine.
- Lower the needle and begin sewing.

press the seam allowances open
(Figure 3.15).

Seam Finishes
Self-Edge Seam Finish

ASTM Stitch Type: 301
ASTM Seam Type: There is no designation for this seam, as shown here.
A similar, less-expensive finish would
be seam type SSd.
Machine: Lockstitch
Attachments: Straight stitch foot
Settings: SL 2-3, SW 0
Seam Use, Garments: Blouses and
unlined jackets for side, center back,
shoulder, and sleeve seams, skirts for
zipper or vent seams
Seam Use, Fabrics: Best for fine to
midweight fabrics that are not loosely
woven

FIGURE 3.15 Plain seam.

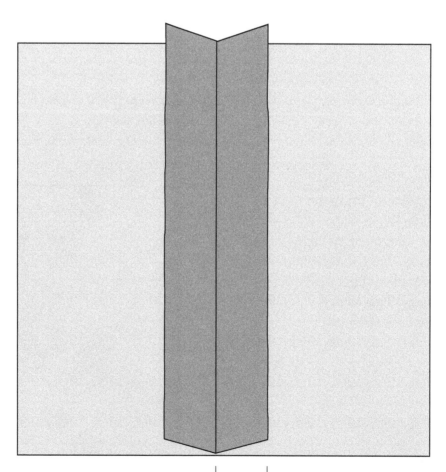

|< 1/2" >|

Positive: A simple, low-tech finish that does not need specialized equipment but that creates a high-end look; good strength; no elasticity; good flexibility

Negative: Requires three passes through the sewing machine; too bulky for many medium-weight and all heavy-weight or thick fabrics; may also produce a ridge on the face of some fabrics when pressed; flexibility is reduced when the fabric is thicker.

Price Point: Better to designer signature.

Practice Exercise

1. Sew a seam using a ½-inch seam allowance or wider.
2. Press the seam open.
3. Press each seam allowance under toward the garment so that the raw edge touches the seam line.
4. Sew through both layers of each seam allowance parallel to the original seam. Do not sew seam allowances to the garment (Figure 3.16).
5. Press again to set stitches.

Hong Kong Seam Finish

ASTM Stitch Type: 301

ASTM Seam Type: SSbh-3

Machine: Lockstitch

Attachments: Straight stitch foot. This seam finish goes much faster in only three passes when using a binding folder to fold and apply a bias strip and when using a system to feed the bias strip to the folder. The method explained here is sewn without the attachments.

Settings: SL 2-3, SW 0

Seam Use, Garments: Any area where seam allowances, facing, or waistband edges will be visible and the possibility of added bulk will not be uncomfortable

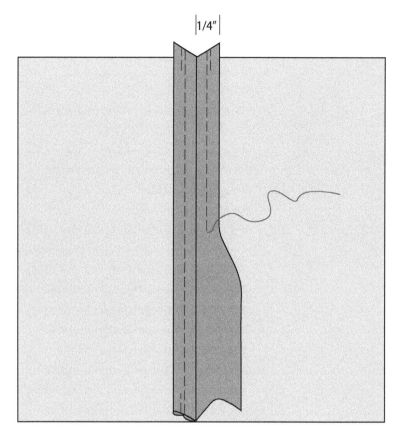

FIGURE 3.16 Self edge.

Seam Use, Fabrics: Any opaque fabric, light- to heavyweight, may be difficult on fabrics that are loosely woven or made of slippery yarns.

Positive: Strong and durable; encloses all raw edges; raises the value of the garment; can be used to coordinate garments in a line

Negative: Multiple passes through the machine and the addition of the bias strips add significantly to the cost of this seam finish and the time it takes to be completed; no elasticity: makes seam less flexible; can be bulky, especially when finishing two seam allowances together

Price Point: Budget to designer signature

Material Preparation: Bias strips should be cut of lightweight to fine fabrics, or you may use premade bias binding. The minimum width for finishing up

TIP | Tips for sewing beautiful inside corners

- Always maintain your seam allowance width.
- When approaching the corner, slow down and stop when you reach the proper seam allowance width for the next edge (e.g., 1/2" from the next edge).
- Put the needle down into the fabric and raise the presser foot.
- You have two options now:
  - If the angle is wide open, you may pull the new edge where you will be sewing so that it is in a straight line with the edge you just finished. This will form a tuck on the left of the needle, so be prepared to avoid this when continuing your seam.
  - If the angle is acute, pivot on the needle until the new edge is even with the proper seam line on the bed of the machine. Lower the presser foot and continue sewing your seam.

to a medium-weight fabric should be 1¼ inch. Thicker fabrics or finishing two fabric layers at once requires a wider bias strip.

Practice Exercise

You will be finishing the edges of two layers of fabric and then seaming the layers together.

1. Place the bias strip face-side down on the top of the face-side of the fabric seam allowance. Have raw edges even. With bias on top, stitch through the bias and fabric using a ¼-inch seam allowance (Figure 3.17).
2. Press the bias strip toward the raw edge of the fabric.
3. Fold the bias strip around the raw edge of the fabric to the back side. Fold the raw edge of the bias under so that it meets the raw edge of the fabric. Press.

FIGURE 3.17 Hong Kong step 1.

This fold should extend beyond and cover the seam line. Pin if necessary (Figure 3.18).

4. On the face of the fabric, stitch in the ditch next to the previous bias seam through the pressed bias fold on the back.
5. Repeat for other seam allowance.
6. With the face-sides of fabric together and the bias finished edges even, sew a seam using a ½-inch or wider seam allowance (Figure 3.19).
   Press seam open.

Two- or Three-Thread Overlock Seam Finish

ASTM Stitch Type: 503 or 504
ASTM Seam Type: This stitch is not recommended for seaming, because it isn't strong enough.

TIP | Tips for curving bias binding on the edges of inside and outside curves

- The bias that you use for covering fabric edges should be double fold, which has the two raw edges pressed inside to the center of the tape; then the tape is folded in half and pressed. This tape is available premade but may be custom-made as well.
- Before sewing it on, bias tape may be "taught" by steaming to conform to the shape of the curve where it will be attached. This results in a smoother finish but is a labor-intensive process that is suitable only for designer-price-point apparel.
- Stretch the center fold of the bias slightly to curve around an outside curve.
- Stretch the two folded edges slightly when curving around an inside corner.
- For very tight curves, a line of basting may be sewn by machine along the edge, which needs to be scrunched in either the center fold for an inside curve or the outer folded edges for an outside curve. The stitching may then be pulled to shrink in the edge(s).
- Frequent pinning is advisable to keep the edges under control.

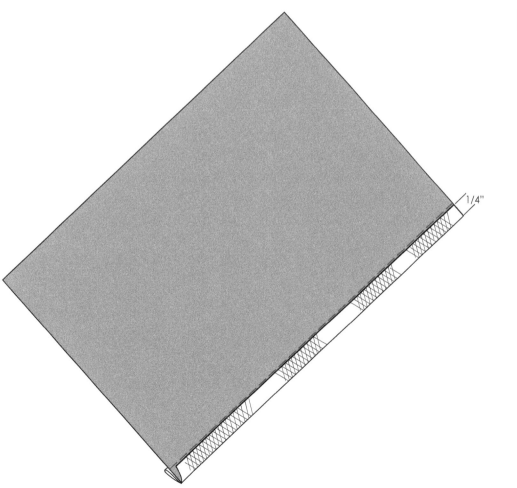

FIGURE 3.18 Hong Kong step 2.

1/4"

FIGURE 3.19 Hong Kong step 3.

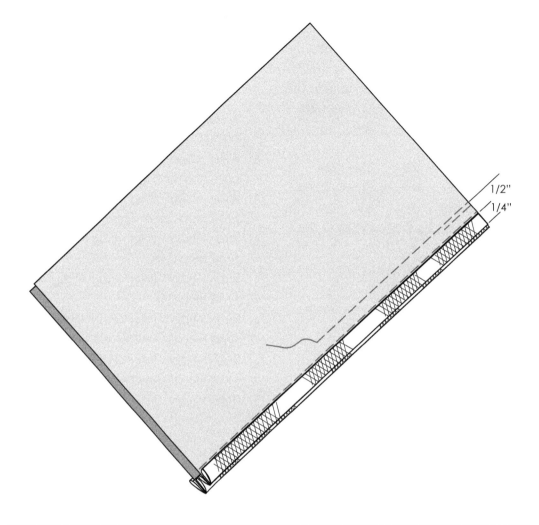

1/2"

1/4"

HOW TO SEW ENDS OF BIAS STRIPS TOGETHER TO MAKE A CONTINUOUS STRIP

In the factory, these bias strips are created from one large piece of fabric that has been seamed into a circle, then sliced into one continuous strip on a special cutting machine.

- Overlap two opposite ends of two strips of bias that are the same width, face sides together as shown below.
- Stitch between the points of the angles as shown below.

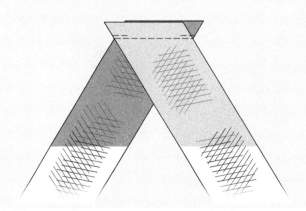

Machine: Overlock

Attachment: Standard foot

Settings: SL 2-4, SW varies according to fabric thickness

Seam Use, Garments: Any exposed seam or edge that needs a quick, clean finish

Seam Use, Fabrics: Light- to heavyweight

Positive: Lightweight; very good elasticity; strong; flexible; quick; versatile

Negative: May pull off fabrics woven with slippery yarns; may leave yarn ends showing; not suitable for sewing strong seams

Price Point: Category killer to designer signature

Practice Exercise: Gather a variety of woven fabric samples and practice finishing the edges, varying the stitch length and width using the chart in the Appendix for guidance to achieve a flat, even finish (Figure 3.20).

Self-Finishing Seams

French

ASTM Stitch Type: 301

ASTM Seam Type: SSae-2

Machine: Lockstitch

Attachments: Straight stitch foot

Settings: SL 2-3, SW 0

Seam Use, Garments: Can be used in any seam that is exposed, best in straight seams, must have a finished seam allowance of 1/8 inch or less for curved seams

Seam Use, Fabrics: Fine to lightweight fabrics, especially sheers

Positive: Strong and flexible; easy to sew; encloses all raw edges; increases the value of the garment

Negative: No elasticity; does not work with medium- to heavyweight fabrics

Price Point: Moderate to designer

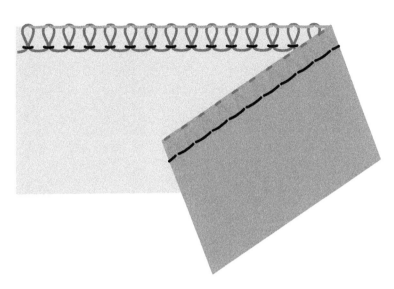

FIGURE 3.20 3-Thread overlock.

Practice Exercise

1. With fabric back sides together, sew a seam using a 1/8-inch seam allowance.
2. Press both seam allowances to one side.
3. Trim off any unraveled yarns from the fabric edges (Figure 3.21).
4. Fold fabric face-sides together, making sure that the first seam is at the edge of the fold. Press.
5. Sew again at ¼-inch seam allowance, enclosing raw edges. (Figures 3.22 and 3.23)
6. Press seam allowance to one side again to set stitches.

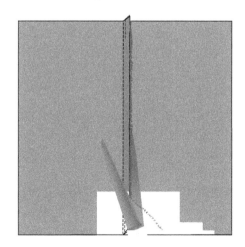

FIGURE 3.21 French steps 1, 2, & 3.

FIGURE 3.22 (left)
French steps 4, 5, & 6
backside.

FIGURE 3.23 (right)
French steps 4, 5, & 6
front side.

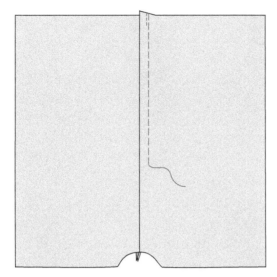

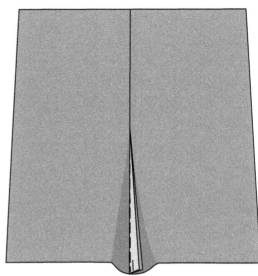

FIGURE 3.22 (left)
French steps 4, 5, & 6
backside.

FIGURE 3.23 (right)
French steps 4, 5, & 6
front side.

Lap Seams

Lap Seam Variation 1 is the classic version of this seam, sometimes known as a *flat fell*. A folder attachment is usually used to fold under the upper edge of fabric around the lower one. One row of stitching appears on the outside of the garment. The following method does not use a folder, substituting a pressing step instead.

Lap Seam Variation 1

ASTM Stitch Type: 301 or 401

ASTM Seam Type: LSc-1

Machine: Lockstitch or chain stitch

Attachments: Straight stitch foot, folder if available

Settings: SL 2-3, SW 0

Seam Use, Garments: Any exposed, straight, or slightly curved seam

Seam Use Fabrics: Light- to heavyweight fabrics

Positive: Very strong; encloses all raw edges

Negative: Can be bulky; is unsuitable for thick fabrics; no elasticity; reduces flexibility

Price Point: Category killer to designer signature

Practice Exercise

1. Press the seam allowance on one fabric edge to the face of the fabric. Press the other seam allowance to the back of the fabric (Figure 3.24).
2. Overlap the seam allowances as shown. Sew near one pressed edge through all layers, and then turn the fabric and repeat from the other end through the other pressed edge. Do not turn the fabric over (Figure 3.25).
3. Press to set stitching.

Lap Seam Variation 2

ASTM Stitch Type: 301, 401, 503, or 504

ASTM Seam Type: LSbm-3 or LSbm-4

Machine: Safety stitch, lockstitch, and overlock

Attachments: Standard foot for all machines

Settings: Overlock SL 2-4, SW varies with the thickness of the fabric, safety stitch, and Lockstitch SL 2-3

Seam Use, Garments: Any exposed seam; best for straight seams

Seam Use, Fabrics: Light- to heavyweight opaque fabrics

FIGURE 3.24 Lap seam variation 1 step 1.

Positive: Very strong; quicker finish than the traditional lap seam
Negative: Not suitable for tight curves; can be bulky; no elasticity; reduces flexibility
Price Point: Category killer to designer signature

Practice Exercise

1. Sew a seam using the lockstitch or safety stitch machine; then finish the edges together with a two- or three-thread overlock if necessary. Press the seam toward the back of the garment (Figure 3.26).

2. With the lockstitch or safety stitch machine, sew the overlocked edge of the seam allowance to the garment through all layers. You may also sew again through all layers closer to the original seam line for a topstitching detail (Figure 3.27). A quicker version of this seam is featured in Chapter 5.

Four-Thread Mock Safety Stitch
 ASTM Stitch Types: 514
 ASTM Seam Type: SSa-1
 Machine: Four-thread overlock
 Attachments: Standard foot

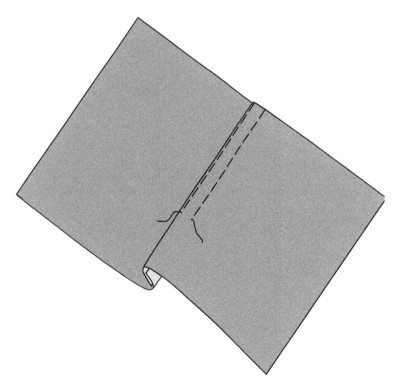

FIGURE 3.25 Lap seam variation 1 step 2 and 3.

Settings: SL 2-4, SW varies with the thickness of the fabric
Seam Use, Garments: Any exposed seam that will *not* need to be pressed open

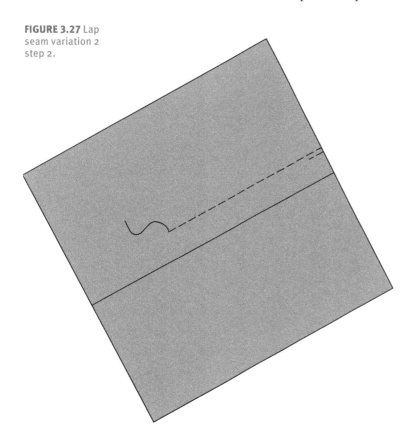

Seam Use, Fabrics: Any
Positive: Very good elasticity and flexibility
Negative: Leaves yarn ends showing; is not quite as strong as a safety stitch; may show some seam grin, unlike lockstitch and safety stitch; seam cannot be pressed open
Price Point: Any

Practice Exercise

Gather a variety of very light- to medium-weight woven fabric samples. Practice varying the stitch length and width using the chart in the Appendix while sewing through two layers of each sample. Observe the way the stitch length and width affect the look of the seams (Figure 3.28).

Five-Thread Safety Stitch

ASTM Stitch Type: 515
ASTM Seam Type: SSa-1
Machine: Five-thread safety stitch overlock
Attachments: Standard foot
Settings: SL 2-4, SW varies with the thickness of the fabric
Seam Use, Garments: Any exposed seam that will *not* need to be pressed open
Seam Use, Fabrics: Any
Positive: Very strong; good flexibility
Negative: Leaves yarn ends showing; no elasticity; seam cannot be pressed open
Price Point: Any

Practice Exercise

Gather a variety of light- to medium-weight woven fabric samples. Practice varying the stitch length and stitch width using the chart in the Appendix while sewing through two layers of each sample. Observe the way the stitch length and width affect the look of the seams (Figure 3.29).

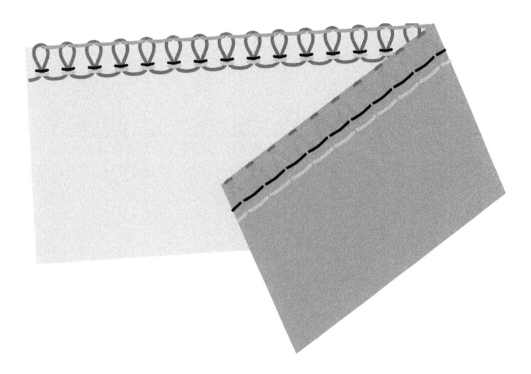

FIGURE 3.28 4-Thread mock safety stitch seam.

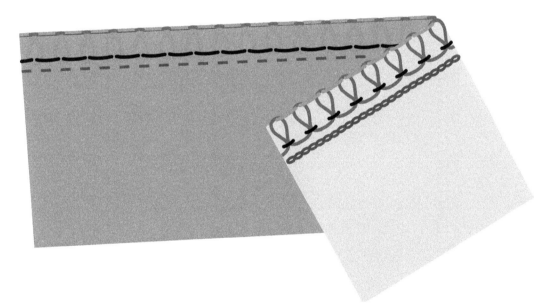

FIGURE 3.29 5-Thread safety stitch seam.

END NOTES
1. Ruth Glock and Grace Kunz. *Apparel Manufacturing Sewn Product Analysis*. 4th ed. (Upper Saddle River: Pearson Prentice Hall, 2005).
2. Ibid.
3. Ibid.
4. Ibid.
5. Patty Brown and Janett Rice Pearson. *Ready-to-Wear Apparel Analysis*. 3d ed. (Upper Saddle River: Pearson Prentice Hall, 2000).
6. Interview with Rick Motta, VP of Operations, Joseph Abboud Manufacturing Corp., 2007.
7. Patty Brown and Janett Rice Pearson. *Ready-to-Wear Apparel Analysis*. 3d ed. (Upper Saddle River: Pearson Prentice Hall, 2000).
8. Ibid.

SKIRT CONSTRUCTION ORDER

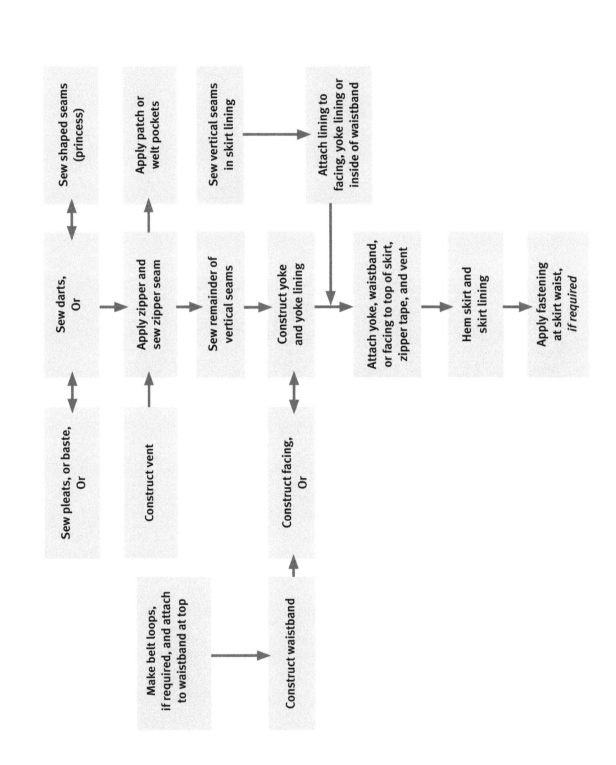

Sew shaped seams (princess)

↕

Sew darts, Or

↕

Sew pleats, or baste, Or

→ Apply zipper and sew zipper seam ← Construct vent

Apply patch or welt pockets ↑

→ Sew remainder of vertical seams

→ Construct yoke and yoke lining

↕

Construct facing, Or

Sew vertical seams in skirt lining → Attach lining to facing, yoke lining or inside of waistband

↓

→ Attach yoke, waistband, or facing to top of skirt, zipper tape, and vent → Hem skirt and skirt lining → Apply fastening at skirt waist, *if required*

Make belt loops, if required, and attach to waistband at top → Construct waistband ↑

4

Basic Straight Skirt

◇◇

S kirt hems may rise and fall, and skirt silhouettes may skim the body or balloon around it, but the skirt remains a staple of the feminine wardrobe. Skirts are used to modestly conceal or to alluringly expose. Women use skirts to express their feminine flirty side or their masculine, demand-your-attention side. In the past, the word

skirt was used as a derisive slang word to describe a woman. As a fashion professional, when a woman chooses your skirt, how will she be describing herself?

This chapter contains the construction steps for unlined casual and lined dressy straight skirts, with or without a slit for walking ease. The practice exercises are designed to be used to complete a finished skirt and are done on cut garment parts, which are shown in the illustrations. Notations are made for stitch and seam choices. Information about each method is included at the beginning of each section. The sections include

- sewing a waist dart,
- gathering to a flat waistband,
- gathering with an elastic waist,
- pleats,
- a curved and a pointed yoke,
- inserting an invisible zipper,
- constructing a lap zipper,
- sewing and attaching a lining with and without a vent,
- a waist facing,
- a straight waistband,

- a shaped waistband,
- creating a vent,
- finishing and constructing a traditional blind-stitched hem with and without a vent,
- making a rolled hem by machine and by hand, and
- attaching a dress hook and loop.

The flowchart shows the construction order for the skirts in this chapter.

◇◇

WAIST-SHAPING OPTIONS

There are a variety of shaping options to reduce the diameter needed in a skirt for the hips to fit down to the dimension for the waist. Darts and pleats create a tailored look. Gathering a skirt into a waistband creates a softer yet still tailored look. An elastic waist creates a more casual look.

Waist Dart

This type of dart is a basic shaping tool for the designer. It has one wide-open end and one point ending near the fullness of the figure (hips, bust point, etc.). It will appear vertically at the waists of skirts and pants and at the shoulder and horizontally at the bust. Three dart-point finishes are described for different price points. Pinning is recommended, but this would not happen in an industry setting.

In the industry, straight darts are marked with a hole about ½ inch in from the point of the dart on the dart shape's centerline; this is done by using a mechanical marking device or, in the case of a small workroom, tailor's chalk, which comes in different colors of wax or chalk. You may also mark your darts using a wax-free tracing paper for fabric and a tracing wheel. The lines on the sides of the darts are called *legs*.

Practice Exercises

1. Fold the fabric, face-sides together. The fold should be at the center of the open end, running through the point.
2. Pin through the markings for the legs of the dart, making sure that your pin runs through both legs of the dart.

This ensures that the dart will be the correct size when you are done.

3. Begin sewing the dart (ASTM stitch type 301) at the open end by back tacking at the beginnings of the legs and sewing down the lines to the point of the dart ending at the fold (Figure 4.1).

Finishing

1. To finish the dart, use one of the three following methods (Figure 4.2):
   a. Pull the fabric out from under the presser foot and cut the thread, leaving about 6 inches attached to the fabric. Tie a knot in the thread, using a pin inserted through the knot to hold it down onto the point of the dart. Trim the excess thread past the knot, leaving a ½-inch tail. This is the highest-quality method but is very time-consuming.
   b. Turn the fabric so that the fold is straight behind the needle, and then backstitch along the fold for five

FIGURE 4.1 Sewing an open ended straight dart.

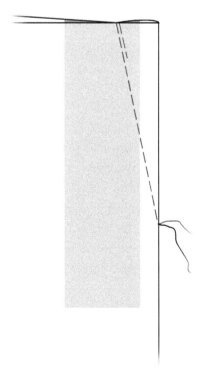

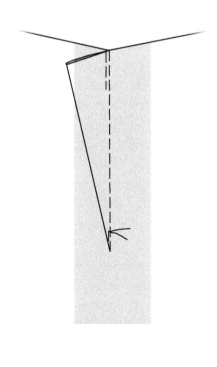

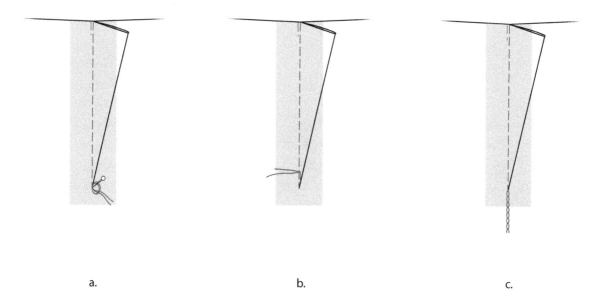

a.   b.   c.

FIGURE 4.2 Dart finishing.

or six stitches. Cut the thread close to the fold. This is a lower-quality method but is still sturdy.

c. Continue sewing beyond the end of the dart, allowing the threads to intertwine. Cut the threads about 1 inch beyond the end of the dart. This is the lowest-quality method and limits the life of the dart.

Gathering to a Flat Waistband

Traditionally, skirts are gathered into a waistband if a soft fabric such as challis, batiste, or chiffon is being used. Quite a bit of bulky fullness will be created at the waist if a stiffer, fuller fabric is used. In this case, liberal use of trimming and clipping should be used to reduce this bulk when finishing the gathered seam. This can make quite a statement if that is what the designer intends. The traditional style is called a *dirndl*. Skirts of this style can be designed to sit at the waist or lower. If they are lower, then a shaped waistband should be used instead of a straight waistband. The inside of the waistband will be finishing the seam allowance of the gathering, so there will be some trimming and clipping necessary to reduce the bulk inside the waistband.

In an industry setting, a gathering attachment on a lockstitch or safety stitch machine is used to pull the top of the skirt into soft gathers. The machine is set to gather in an exact proportion of the fabric so that the skirt is the correct dimension for the waistband length. You can get a gathering foot for your machine and use the following setting recommendations to gather your fabric, or you can use the basting method described below.

Gathering with a Gathering Foot

The following are machine setting tips for using a gathering foot:

- The longer the stitch length, the fuller the gathers will be.
- The harder the presser foot presses down, the fuller the gathers will be.
- You can also increase the volume of the gathers by increasing the needle thread tension, but too much of this can cause your thread to break.
- You can also increase the amount of gathering by putting a finger behind the gathering foot to slow the feeding of the fabric. This takes practice to get an even gather, because the effect is not regulated by the foot.

- The slicker the fabric, such as a polished cotton, the harder it will be to gather.
- The stiffer the fabric, the harder it will be to gather.
- Do a test of how full your gathers will be by taking a 1-foot-long sample of your fabric and gathering it under the foot with the settings you have. If you like the volume of fullness, then measure the strip of fabric to find out how long it is. Then multiply the length of your finished waistband by the amount that the strip is shorter than 1 foot. For example, if your 1-foot-long piece of gathered fabric becomes 6 inches long after you have gathered it, then multiply the length of your waistband by two (because the piece of fabric is now half of the 1-foot piece) to get the length of fabric you need to gather. Allow an extra foot or so of fabric to gather in case you underestimated. You can always cut some off, but you may not add any more fabric on.
- If your skirt has several sections, in order to achieve the length to equal the waistband length, sew those sections together before using the gathering foot.

If your fabric does not work with the gathering foot and you have *a lot* of time on your hands, you can use the following gathering method. This method is too time-consuming to be used anywhere but in a custom or couture setting.

HOW TO MAKE A CUSTOM RUFFLE OUT OF FABRIC ON THE STRAIGHT GRAIN OR ON THE BIAS USING A PLEATER ATTACHMENT ON A LOCKSTITCH MACHINE.

1. Cut a sample strip of your fabric that is at least a yard long and is the width of your finished ruffle. Make sure you note the length of the strip. If you are making a ruffle with a fold at the edge, you must make the strip twice as wide as the ruffle. Remember to add to the width for the seam allowance. Fold the strip face-sides out.
2. Set the stitch length on your machine to 3.
3. Set the pleater to the number of pleats per stitch and the depth (bite) of pleat that you think you will need for your finished ruffle. Consult the directions with the pleater to adjust these settings.
4. Sew a sample run of your ruffle, adjusting the stitch length, bite, and number of pleats per stitch until you achieve the desired amount of pleating. You may need to baste, overlock, or pin the raw edges together to keep them feeding smoothly.
5. Measure the completed sample and multiply the length to cut the desired strip length for your finished ruffle. You may have to piece fabric strips, especially if you are using bias strips, in order to get the desired finished length. For example, if your strip measured 24 inches at the beginning and 12 inches at the end, you will need a strip twice the length of your finished ruffle. Add 12 inches or so at the end in case you underestimated. You can easily cut some off.

Gathering with Gathering Threads

1. Sew the sections of the skirt together if needed.
2. Select a heavier-weight thread such as topstitching and a larger needle if your fabric can withstand that needle size. If not, use a standard needle and thread for the fabric. The heavier thread makes it easier to gather.
3. Set your machine to baste (longest stitch length), and loosen your needle thread tension about 1½ numbers.
4. Sew two rows of gathering stitches, one within the seam allowance and one just outside the seam allowance in the body of the skirt.
5. Break the stitching at all seam lines, and start again to lessen the strain on the thread and fabric when completing the next step.
6. Pull the bobbin threads to gather the fabric, taking care to apportion the gathers evenly around the skirt. Dividing the skirt into quarter sections will help with this task (Figure 4.3).
7. After sewing the gathered layer to another layer of fabric, pull out the bobbin threads and then the needle threads before pressing your seam.

Practice Exercises

1. Cut five or six lengths of muslin or other lightweight cotton fabric that are 1 inch on the crosswise grain by 12 inches on the lengthwise grain, and cut one piece that is 6 inches square.
2. If you have a gathering foot, practice gathering the strips, changing the settings and techniques as explained above. Record your settings by writing them on the fabric, and then compare your findings to see how the settings affected the amount of gathering.

FIGURE 4.3 Attaching gathered fabric to flat fabric.

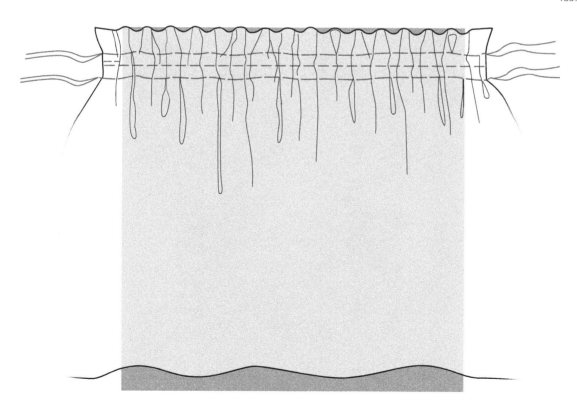

3. After resetting your machine to the basting settings, try the gathering thread method on another of the foot-long pieces. Gather the piece to 6 inches in length, and then reset your machine for a traditional lockstitch (ASTM stitch type 301). Sew the gathered piece to the 6-inch square.

Pleats

Pleats are a more tailored method for taking the fullness out of a skirt waist. They tend to go in and out of fashion but always make an interesting design detail when used together or alone. Pleats come in three forms: knife, box, and inverted box. The three forms are shown in Figure 4.4.

Pleat Forms

Box pleats are more flattering in the front of a garment, because they point outward, away from the center front of the skirt. Inverted box pleats have the opposite effect. Pleats that touch each other produce more thickness, which can be a concern, depending on the thickness of the fabric.

There are industrial pleating machines, or pleaters, that can be attached to lockstitch machines to pleat fabrics in a set pattern and to a set fold dimension,

FIGURE 4.4 Pleat forms.

Knife Pleat

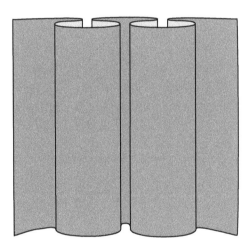

Box Pleat

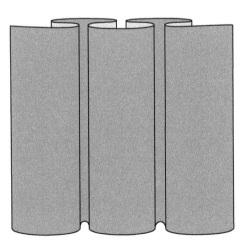

Inverted Box Pleat

greatly speeding up the process and eliminating the possibility of most operator errors.

Stitching

The machine stitches down the pleats as they are made, either just to the pleated strip itself or to another layer of flat fabric such as a waistband. The amount of fabric needed to equal the length of the waistband will be calculated before the pleating occurs. Extra fabric is often allowed to prevent the fabric from being too short.

Because pleats usually start right at the garment's waist, if they are not being made by an attachment, they are marked with notches or clips in the seam allowance of the fabric at the points where the folds occur. The operators are trained to know which ways the pleats are to be folded, because they are doing the same folds over and over. They will stitch a line of stitching through the pleats to hold them in preparation for another operation.

Practice Exercises

If you have a pleater attachment for your lockstitch machine, read the instructions on how to mount it on your machine, set it correctly, and position the fabric properly in the pleater. If you are using a knife pleater, do not pull the fabric toward you because that will jam the pleater blade, bend it, and possibly rip your fabric. Cut several lengths of fabric several feet long by 3 to 4 inches wide. Experiment with the pleater, changing the settings according to how large the pleat is and how many times the pleater makes a pleat.

Yokes

A skirt yoke is a garment piece that starts at the waist or right below and extends to the hip area. It is often lined with the same fabric as the outside. The skirt yoke is shaped to the angles of the female form above the hip and takes the place of other shaping such as darts or pleats but without extra seaming or folding. The lower edge of the yoke where it joins the skirt is a wonderful place to make a design statement because of its position at a wide part of the body and because of the transition between the yoke and the skirt. This s eam can be symmetrical or asymmetrical, curved, or angled, and it can have added ruffles or piping. Below you will find methods for attaching a skirt to symmetrically curved and pointed yokes.

Most yokes are closed with a zipper at the left side seam or the center back. If the zipper is at the left side seam, then sew the yoke sections and skirt sections together at all other seams. If your closure is at the center back, then sew all other seams. The yoke and skirt should still be two separate pieces. If your zipper extends into the skirt area below the yoke, you will have to sew the yoke to the skirt first and then complete your zipper. If the closure area does not extend below the yoke's bottom, you may finish the zipper area first, sew all the skirt seams so that the skirt forms a circle, and then join the circle of the yoke to the circle of the skirt. Either way, follow the steps below to join the skirt and the yoke.

Seaming Curved Yokes to Skirts

Your yoke will be a convex curve, and the skirt will be a concave curve.

1. Stay stitch the skirt's top edge to prevent it from stretching while you sew it to the yoke (ASTM stitch type 301).
2. Match the center points of the yoke front and back to the center points of the skirt with face-sides together and pin.

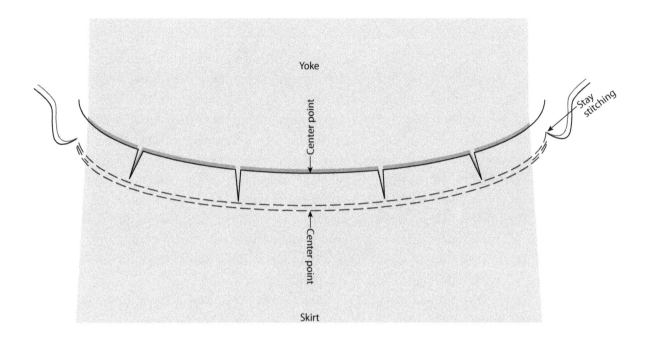

FIGURE 4.5 Attaching a curved yoke to a skirt.

3. Match the seams of the yoke to the seams of the skirt face-sides together and pin.
4. Match the remainder of the yoke to the skirt face-sides together, making sure the cut edges of the seam allowances are even. You must pull up the concave edge of the skirt to match the convex curve of the yoke. You may pin this before you sew, or you may sew it while encouraging the edges to stay even with your fingers (ASTM stitch type 301, seam type SSa-1; Figure 4.5).
5. Press the seam allowances up into the yoke.

Seaming Pointed Yokes to Skirts
The yoke will have a point at the center front and back, and the skirt will have an indentation at the centers.

1. Stay stitch the top of the skirt to prevent it from stretching while sewing it to the yoke (ASTM stitch type 301).

2. Pin the center points of the yoke to the centers of the skirt with face-sides together.
3. Pin the vertical seams of the yoke (such as the side seams) to those of the skirt face-sides together.
4. At the seam line, align the cut edges of the skirt with the cut edges of the yoke. A fold will form at the skirt's center at the point of the yoke. Clip the skirt from the cut edge to the stay stitching; this allows it to relax so that you can line up the skirt's edges with the yoke. Two pins on either side of this clip will help.
5. Insert your needle at the center point, and sew from this center point along the straight edge, making sure to back tack at the beginning of this stitching (ASTM stitch type 301, seam type SSa-1). Start the stitching on the other side of the point, making sure that you're not leaving a gap between the starting points. Not stitching across the points will prevent a pucker from forming (Figure 4.6).

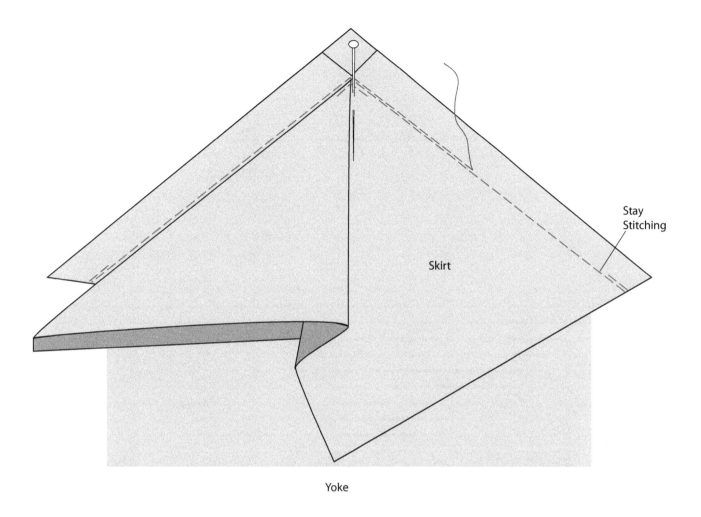

Stay
Stitching

Skirt

Yoke

Finishing Yoke Linings

A yoke lining is usually made from the outer fabric, but don't miss an opportunity to make a design statement or increase the value of your skirt in the customer's eyes by being ordinary. Why not choose a contrast fabric of the same weight? Or if your outer fabric is heavier, choose an inner fabric that is lighter to remove some of the bulkiness in the seams, creating a smoother finish. Just make sure that the fabrics are care-compatible and that the dyes will not bleed on each other.

1. Sew the same vertical seams in the lining as the outer yoke.
2. Finish the lower edges of the lining by turning under the seam allowance and pressing or by using one of the seam finishes detailed in Chapter 3. The Hong Kong finish (ASTM stitch type 301, seam type BSc or BSf) makes a nice surprise on the inside of the garment. The serged edge (ASTM stitch type 504) is a quicker finish but can be viewed as being lower quality.
3. For either yoke treatment, sew the yoke linings to the top of the yokes, face-sides together (ASTM stitch type 301, seam type SSa-1). Make sure that the raw edges of your zipper opening are aligned with each other. The lining should cover the zipper.
4. Now sew the lining edges down over the zipper tapes just inside the zipper stitching on both sides of the zipper (ASTM stitch type 301, seam type

FIGURE 4.6 Attaching a pointed yoke to a skirt.

SSa-1). Clip off the corner of the zipper tape to reduce the bulk there.

5. Turn the lining inside the skirt to the back of the yoke.

6. Stitch the lining to the yoke, covering the lower seam allowance where the skirt is sewn to the yoke using stitch type 301 and seam LSf over the lining's folded edge (Figure 4.7). If you have finished the lower edge of the yoke lining with an overlock or a

FIGURE 4.7 Attaching the yoke lining.

Hong Kong finish, use seam LSf but do not turn under the finished layer. This treatment is easier, depending on the type of equipment you have on hand.

ZIPPER APPLICATIONS
Invisible Zipper Application
An invisible zipper is the industry standard now for skirts and some pant designs at

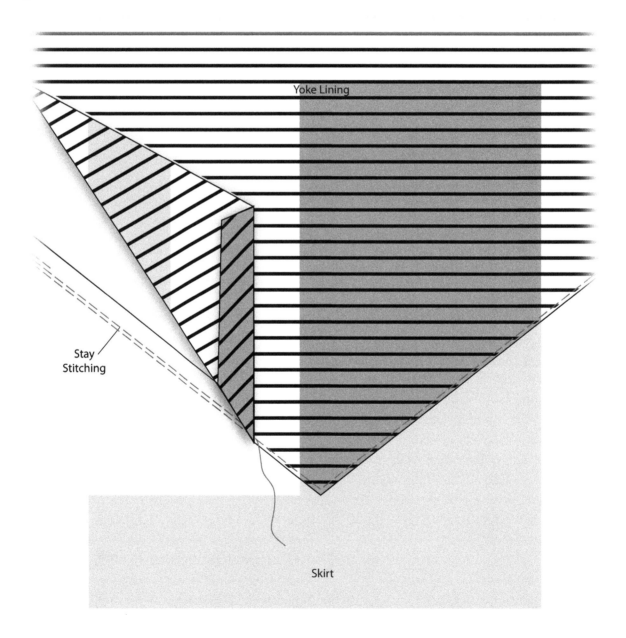

any price point. It is most often used with a facing finishing the top of the garment because of the ease of sewing the facing down to the zipper tape, but it may also be used with a straight or shaped waistband. The value of an invisible zipper is that no part of the zipper or any stitching shows on the outside of the completed garment. In the industry, an invisible zipper foot would be used to position the zipper coil correctly. A standard ½-inch seam allowance is used, because the zipper tape is ½-inch wide. Pinning may be used, but this would not happen in an industry setting.

This application assumes you will be using a conventional zipper foot on a straight stitch machine. Which foot you use will depend on whether you sew down the left or the right side of the zipper first. You will use the foot that has the cutout for the needle on the side where the zipper coil will be when you're sewing. You can use this method either for a back-seam application or a side seam using a ½-inch seam allowance. Since the side seam will be curved, make sure to follow the edge of the fabric, maintaining your ½-foot seam allowance when positioning the zipper.

Practice Exercise

1. Finish the edges of the zipper seam using one of the seam finishes from Chapter 3. The standard is usually ASTM stitch type 504.
2. Unzip the zipper completely. Unroll both coils on each edge of the tape, and press them to keep them open.
3. Align the open zipper facedown on the face of the fabric. Remember to apply the following three requirements before sewing the sides of

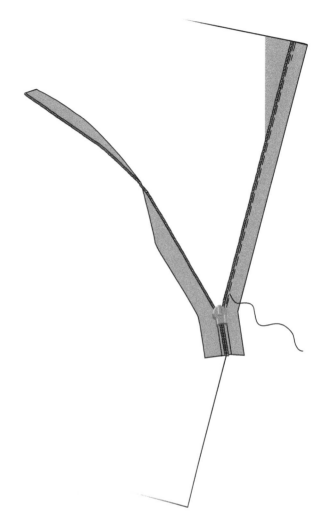

FIGURE 4.8 Preparing to sew an invisible zipper.

the zipper to the face of the fabric (Figure 4.8):

a. The coil of the zipper must be lined up on the seam line.
b. The edge of the zipper tape must be next to the fabric's edge.
c. The zipper must be face-side down on the face of the fabric.
d. The top end of the zipper must be toward and even with the top edge of the garment.

4. With the fabric face-side up and the zipper's top toward the back of your machine, line up the zipper coil next to the hole in the foot. You must guide the zipper close to the needle, making sure that you don't sew too close (makes the zipper impossible to zip) or too far

away (makes the zipper visible) from the coil.

5. Sew down the zipper (ASTM stitch type 301) toward the pull as far as possible, then backstitch. You may need to move the pull out of the way at some point. If so, just put your needle down into the fabric to keep your place. You will have to stop before reaching the pull.

6. Align the other side of the zipper, following the rules above. Sew by switching to the other zipper foot.

7. Zip up the zipper, and admire your lovely work.

8. Attach the zipper foot with the hole on the right. Turn the fabric, back side facing you, and align the fabric edges together, including the seam below the zipper.

9. Begin sewing down to the bottom of the seam (or to the top of the vent) by starting four stitches above the bottom of your previous lines of stitching and one or two yarns into the garment to the left of that stitching. Be careful not to catch the end of the

zipper tape in the stitching (ASTM stitch type 301, seam type SSa-1) (Figure 4.9).

10. Press the seam open.

Lap Zippers

Lap zippers are frequently used on side seams, because the overlap of the fabric from front over back covers the zipper very effectively, giving a smooth finish. You may also see them at the center back of a dressy skirt or pant. The seam allowance for sewing this zipper is ¾ inch. Anything narrower makes a cleanly finished zipper application impossible. There will be topstitching on the outside of the garment, so matching thread is a must. A conventional nylon skirt zipper is used in this application. You will want to have one that is about 2 inches longer than the desired finished length.

You will need a conventional zipper foot on a lockstitch machine. Which foot you use depends on which side of the fabric overlaps the other. For a zipper in the left side seam of a skirt, which is what we will be practicing, you will need to use the left foot, meaning the foot that will be on the needle's left side when you are stitching.

FIGURE 4.9 Completion of invisble zipper seam.

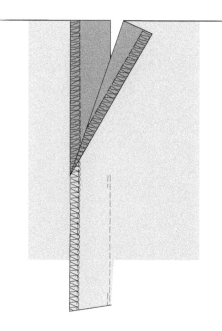

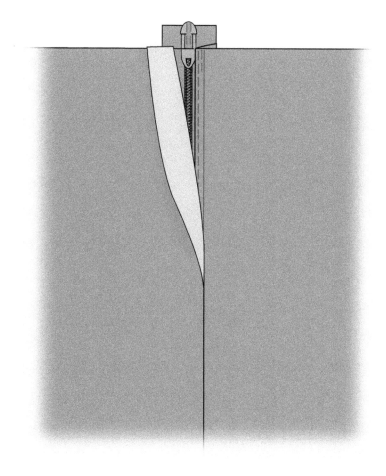

Practice Exercise

1. Prepare the seam where the zipper will be applied by finishing the edges. An overlock finish, ASTM seam type 504 is a good, quick choice. Take care not to cut off any of the seam allowance.

2. Place both layers of the skirt face-sides together, having the finished edges even.

3. Start sewing using a conventional straight stitch foot from the notch for the bottom of the zipper opening down to the bottom of the garment (ASTM stitch type 301). The bottom stop of the zipper should not show when the zipper insertion is completed.

4. Press open the seam allowances along the entire length of the seam, including the unsewn section where the zipper goes, making sure that you maintain the ¾-inch seam allowance width in this area (Figure 4.10).

5. Turn the skirt face-side up and place the zipper, pull-side up, under the right-hand seam allowance with the pull just above the top of the garment.

6. Nudge over the seam allowance until the zipper coil is a generous 1/8 inch in toward the left side of the seam from the pressed seam line (Figure 4.11). You are doing this so that the left seam allowance will cover the zipper coil and the stitching. Pin the zipper under the folded seam allowance so that the fold is close to the zipper coil, but not so close that the pull can't go up and down the zipper.

7. Attach your left zipper foot and sew close to the fold from the bottom to the top of the zipper, taking care not to catch the other seam allowance in the stitching.

8. Place the fabric down so that the left front overlaps the zipper and the stitching. Pin, making sure to catch the zipper tape, and keep the fabric as flat as possible.

FIGURE 4.10 (left) Preparing the fabric to sew a lap seam zipper.

FIGURE 4.11 (above) Pinning the zipper under the right side.

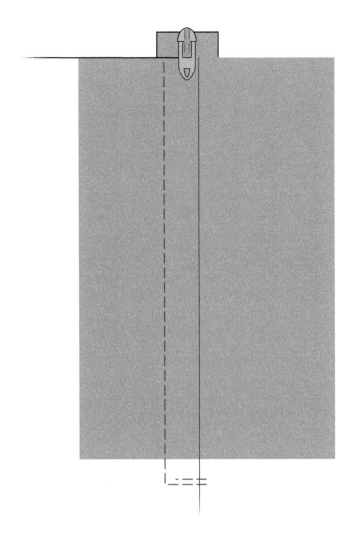

FIGURE 4.12 Sewing the left side of the stitching.

9. Sew down the left side of the zipper through all the layers, turning at the bottom just where your seam stitching ended, and sew across the zipper to the end of the stitching (Figure 4.12). Back tack.

WAIST FINISHES

Facing

A facing is a strip of fabric that invisibly finishes an edge of the garment by being turned inside at the stitching line. The facing will take the shape of the garment edge. It may appear at a waist, neck edge, armhole, jacket front, and many other places, including in place of a hem when the bottom of the garment is shaped.

Facings are usually 2 to 3 inches wide but may be wider in more expensive apparel or narrower at lower price points. A narrower facing may creep to the outside of the garment. Wider facings in higher-priced garments will be tacked to the garment where it covers points that will not show from the outside, such as a dart or a seam allowance. They are usually made of the same fabric as the garment but may be made into a design accent by using a patterned or contrast fabric. The facing, as a contrast, may also be turned to the outside of the garment with the addition of some trim, such as bias binding or fringing. The basic technique shown in this section is suitable for all waist, neckline, and armhole finishes that are not connected together (as in an all-in-one facing) and for jacket facings that are not connected to a lining. It can also be used for hems on skirts, pants, or jackets, and so on, where the hem is shaped in a design such as a scallop.

Waist Facing Application with an Invisible Zipper and No Lining

1. Prepare the facing by applying interlining, then sewing the front and back pieces together at both side seams for a back zipper or at the right side seam for a side zipper. Note: Most side seam zippers appear in the left side seam of a skirt or pant, so the right seam is sewn closed (ASTM stitch type 301, seam type SSa-1).

2. Consult the edge-finishing choices detailed in Chapter 3 for finishing the lower edge of the facing, or skip to the section on attaching the lining.

3. With the skirt face-side out, pin the side(s) seams and center front (and back) of the facing face-side to the skirt, keeping the top edges even and the ends of the facing even with the seam allowances next to the zipper tape. Be sure to fold the seam allowances out away from the skirt when pinning them to the ends of the facing (Figure 4.13).
Stitch the facing and the skirt together, starting at the top corner at the zipper's end and sewing across the facing to the zipper's other end (ASTM stitch type 301, seam type SSa-1.

4. Attach your zipper foot and sew down the facing from the upper edge to the lower edge just inside the stitching, which attaches the zipper to the skirt on both ends. Be sure to back tack the seams (Figure 4.14).

5. Trim the corners next to the zipper tape.

6. Press the seam and facing away from the top of the skirt, turning the facing to the back side of the skirt at the corners.

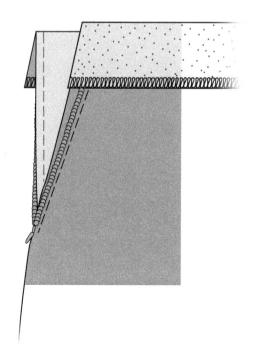

FIGURE 4.13 (left) Positioning the facing on the waist of the skirt.

FIGURE 4.14 (right) Sewing the facing end to the skirt.

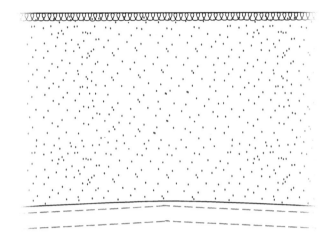

7. Understitch the facing as far as possible, back tacking at the ends of the stitching (Figure 4.15).

One-Piece Straight Waistband

Straight waistbands are best used on skirts and pants that sit right at the waist. Waistbands that sit much below that will need to be shaped to fit the curve of the hip. Waistbands that sit higher will need to be shaped to the torso. Straight waistbands are usually made of a continuous fabric band cut along the lengthwise grain. They sometimes include the selvage edge on the inside of the garment to reduce bulk at the waist seam and to save a step in finishing the band. Waistbands can range from skinny bands that snugly cover the top of the skirt to bands that are 1½ inches wide. Wider bands may need to be shaped at the side seam to not bind the wearer. Some straight waistbands do have a seam at the side of the garment, depending on the order of construction.

Waistbands usually have a button, hook, or snap closure but may also include the top portion of an invisible zipper extending up from the skirt. Waistbands are most frequently found with lap and fly zippers at any price point and any quality level. What's inside the waistband, such as interlining or lack thereof, and how the inside of the band is finished are frequently good indicators of garment quality. Interlining in a straight waistband is a must no matter how narrow to firm up the fabric and help it last through crosswise stress.

The waistband should be the length of the top of the skirt, including the edges of the zipper application, and it should have an area of tab for a hook or button (designer's choice; perhaps about 2 inches), a ¼-inch seam allowance on both ends, and the width of twice the finished width plus a ½-inch seam allowance on both sides. For example, a skirt with a waist circumference of 30 inches would have a waistband length of 33½ inches (30 inches + 1 inch for zipper overlap + 2 inches for a tab + ½-inch seam allowance). The width for a band that is 1 inch finished in width should be 3 inches cut (2 inches + 1-inch seam allowance for both sides). This application is just as good-looking on a pair of pants.

Straight Waistband with a Lap Zipper and No Lining

1. The skirt should have the waist shaping and zipper application done.
2. The interlining should be applied to the back side of the waistband fabric. If you didn't cut the waistband out using one of the selvages as one long edge, you will finish the other long edge of the waistband with an overlock or Hong Kong (ASTM seam type SSbh-d).

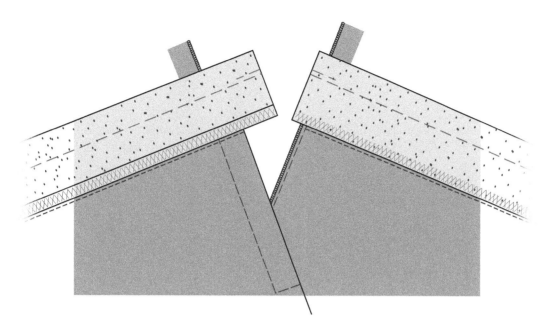

FIGURE 4.16 Attaching a straight waistband to the top of a skirt.

3. You may want to stay stitch the top of the skirt if it is not gathered or pleated to prevent it from stretching while you are sewing on the band.

4. Turn the skirt face-side out and open the zipper.

5. Match the unfinished long edge of the band face-side down to the top of the skirt, keeping the long edge even with the top of the skirt. The ends of the band should extend ¼ inch beyond the edges of the zipper area on the underlay and 2¼ inches beyond the zipper's edge on the overlap. Pin where necessary. Sew the entire length of the band to the skirt, taking up a ¼-inch seam allowance (ASTM stitch type 301, seam type SSa-1; Figure 4.16).

6. Press the band and seam allowance up away from the skirt.

7. Fold the band in half lengthwise so that the seam line on the finished long side matches the seam between the band and skirt. The band should extend below the seam by ½ inch.

8. Sew the tab on the overlap side, taking up ¼-inch seam allowance across the end and ½ inch along the lower edge.

9. Before turning the tab face-side out, trim off the seam allowance in the tab area as shown (Figure 4.17). Press. The seam allowance on the band's inside edges will gradually taper into the inside of the tab. The same will occur on the other end.

10. Also, sew across the underlap end of the band, taking up a ¼-inch seam

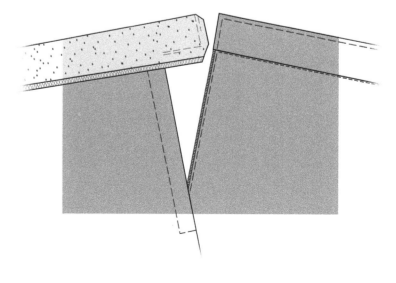

FIGURE 4.17 Sewing the ends of the waistband.

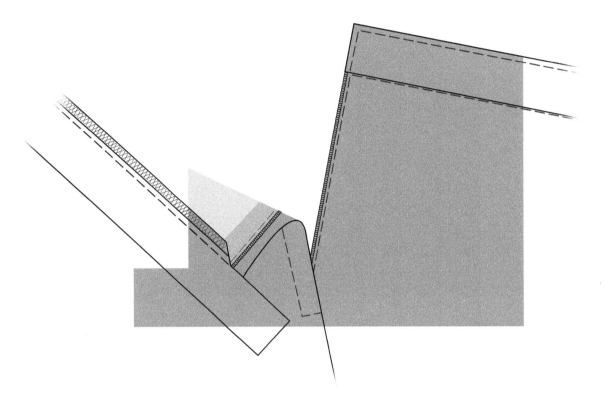

FIGURE 4.18 Sewing the inner edge of the waistband to the skirt.

allowance. This stitching should end right at the skirt's edge. ASTM stitch type 301, seam type SSa-1). Trim this end and press it.

11. Pin the finished long edge to the rest of the band, making sure the seam line is on top of the ditch.

12. On the face of the fabric, sew the finished edge in the ditch at the edge of the band, back tacking at both ends (Figure 4.18).

13. Add a horizontal buttonhole to the overlap end of the tab and button or the skirt hook. The end of the buttonhole should be at least half a button width away from the end of the band to prevent the button from extending past the end of the tab when buttoned.

Shaped Waistband

A shaped band is used when the top of the skirt or pant is below the waist. The shaped band conforms better to the silhouette of the hips and tummy. It will need to be in pieces. This waist treatment can be used with any zipper application at any price point. Where the opening is depends on the placement of the zipper, left seam, center back, or front, but this band will always have at least three parts. Let's say that our band is for a fly zipper in the front of the skirt. The three pieces would then be a back, a left side, and a right side. When drafting the skirt pattern, you may want to make an extension for a closure on one of the bands to overlap for a closure. You will have six pieces altogether, three for the outside of the band and three for the inside. Interlining should be attached to the bands before application, and the skirt should have all waist-shaping done and zipper application completed. The lower edge of each band will be convex; the top of the skirt will be slightly concave. You will want to stay stitch the skirt's top edge to prevent it from stretching out while attaching it to the band. Finish the lower edge of one band with an overlock or Hong Kong seam finish (ASTM stitch type 504, or seam type BSc; Figure 4.19).

Shaped Band for a Skirt with No Lining

1. Sew the side seams of the band together to make two bands, the inner and outer. Press the seams open. Finish the lower, convex edge of one band using the methods described above.
2. Turn the skirt face-side out and pin the lower, convex edge of one band face-side down to the top of the skirt, clipping the skirt to the stay stitching line if necessary to allow it to conform to the band. You must keep the raw edges of the skirt top even with the raw edge of the band.
3. Sew the band to the skirt (ASTM stitch type 301).
4. With face-sides together, sew the concave edges and ends of both bands together. Trim the corners, turn

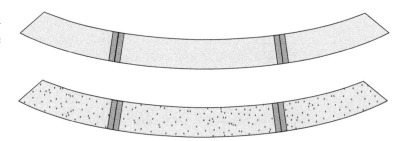

the bands face-side out, and press (Figure 4.20).

5. Pin the lower, finished convex edge of the inner band over the seam line of the outer band. Stitch in the ditch of the seam between the waistband and the skirt to attach the inner band to the skirt.
6. Add your closure to the band.

Vents

There are many different ways to add a vent into a skirt for walking ease or as a design detail. The pattern will be designed with the correct shaping for this area, which usually includes an extension

FIGURE 4.19 The pieces of a shaped band for a skirt waist.

FIGURE 4.20 Atttaching a shaped band to a skirt.

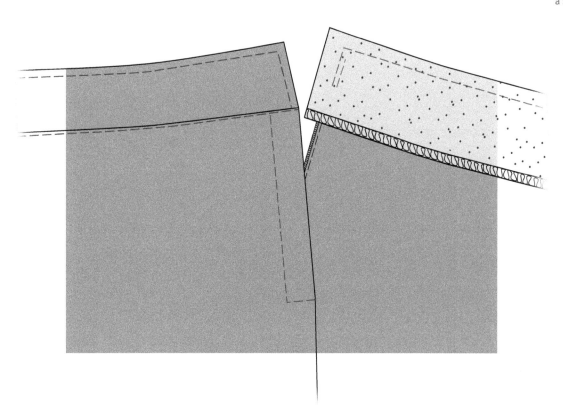

that is about 1½ to 2 inches wider than the seam allowance. Vents can appear in any vertical seam on a straight skirt near the hem, but the treatment would be the same. The following basic vent design can be completed with and without a lining. Both are explained.

Creating a Vent for a Skirt with No Lining

1. Finish the edges of the vent seam allowance with ASTM stitch type 504). The hem may also be finished at the same time or may be left for finishing while being hemmed with seam tape for example.

2. Sew the seam above the vent to the top of the vent extension seam allowance (ASTM stitch type 301, ASTM seam type SSa-1). Press the extensions toward the skirt at the seam line. Note: A quality touch here would be to add a length of fusible interlining onto the vent extension extending from the hemline to the top of the vent and past the seam line by ¼ inch into the skirt. This helps the vent edge keep its crease and resist wear.

3. Miter the hem and vent extension at the corner using the following method:
   * Press both hems up along the hemline, overlapping them.
   * Fold out the hems to see the pressed lines in the shape of an (Figure 4.21a).

FIGURE 4.21 Mitering at the corner of a vent and hem.

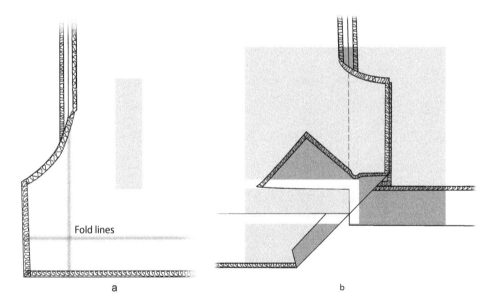

Fold lines

a   b

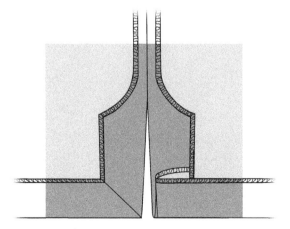

c

- Fold up the corner toward the skirt on the point of the X, matching the pressed lines.
- Press across the fold and then fold the hems up. Two new 45-degree diagonal folds should form; press these new folds.
- Open out the hem and trim away the point about ½ inch inside the corner. (You may avoid this step by drafting the pattern with the corner removed so that it is replaced with a ½-inch seam allowance, and then sew a seam here and trim the point to reduce bulk.) (Figure 4.21b)
- Refold the hem and vent, invisibly stitch the finished edges down using a blind hem (ASTM stitch type 101) or a hand catch stitch (ASTM stitch type 204). (Figure 4.21c)

Sewing and Finishing a Vent for a Lined Skirt

The process for making a vent when the skirt is to be lined is the same as the above up to the point of mitering the corner. The hem is not completed until the lining has been sewn to the vent. (See the following section on how to sew a lining to a vent.)

LININGS

The use of linings in the fashion industry has declined in recent years because of the significant extra expense a lining represents. Some top designers have opted out of linings in garments that we never would have dreamed of seeing unlined even 20 years ago. On the opposite end of the price spectrum, budget stores may have jackets below 30 dollars that are lined to cover flaws in fabric choices or construction. And skirts seem to be consistently lined so that women no longer have to depend on slips to keep their skirts from riding up while they walk and to give a clean look when paired with a suit jacket. There are still many relatively invisible corners that can be cut to save time, materials, and, of course, money. Some we will mention in this section. We will first discuss how to construct a lining and then how to attach it with an invisible zipper, with two different waist finishes and with and without a vent.

Constructing the Lining with a Waist Facing, an Invisible Zipper, and No Vent

The lining application shown here is a basic design that includes being attached to a facing and an opening for the invisible zipper. It is applied completely by machine without hand stitching, which takes a lot of time and is unlikely to appear in ready-to-wear. The skirt should be completed up to the point of adding the facing, which is sewn to the lining before the entire facing/lining piece is sewn to the skirt. This lining application may also be used on finished pants with a facing at the waist.

1. Construct the lining, sewing the same vertical seams that were sewn on the skirt, leaving the zipper seam open (ASTM stitch type 516, ASTM seam type SSa-1 or ASTM stitch type 301 or 401 plus 504 and ASTM seam type SSa-2). Press the seams.
2. Finish the edges of the lining at the zipper seam using ASTM stitch type 504 or another suitable finish. (This step may be omitted to save costs.)
3. Sew the top of the lining to the bottom of the facing (ASTM stitch type 301, ASTM seam type SSa-1). Press the seam open to reduce bulk.

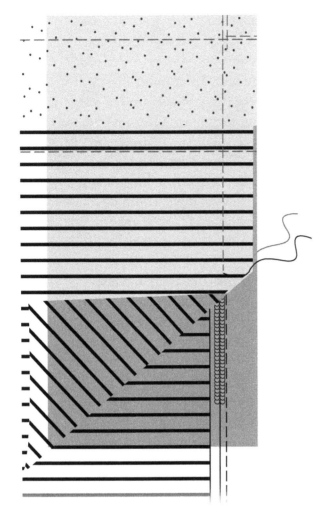

FIGURE 4.22 Sewing the lining to the zipper area.

Attaching the Lining without a Vent
(ASTM stitch type 301, ASTM seam type SSa-1)

1. Pin the seam allowances of the lining/ facing zipper seam face-side down to

the back side of the skirt zipper seam, from the top of the zipper seam to just below the zipper.

2. Sew the lining to the zipper tape/ skirt seam allowance just inside the seam line, back tacking just above the end of the zipper (ASTM stitch type 301, ASTM seam type SSa-1; Figure 4.22).

3. Starting just above the end of the last stitching, back tack and then sew the remainder of the seam down to the bottom of the skirt (ASTM stitch type 301, ASTM seam type SSa-1). Press the seam open.

Note: To speed this process at a slightly lower quality level, do not finish the seam allowances of the lining; sew the unfinished seam allowances to the zipper, and then use ASTM stitch type 516 to sew the seam below the zipper area. Press the seam to one side.

Lining a Skirt with a Vent

The lining for a vent is pictured in Figure 4.23. This application can also line a vent that does not have a zipper above it—for example, in the front of a skirt.

1. The first steps in lining a skirt with a vent are to prepare the lining to the

FIGURE 4.23 A skirt with a vent and it's lining.

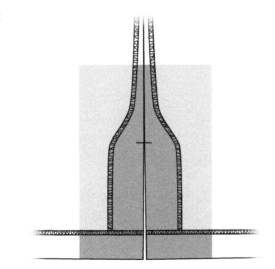

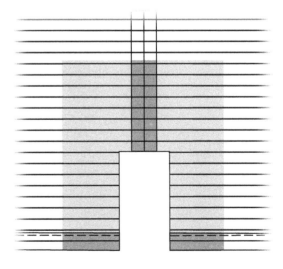

point where the seam below the zipper is sewn. Instead of sewing this seam down to the bottom of the lining, it must be sewn only to ¾ to 1 inch above the top of the skirt vent area. The lining should not extend beyond this point. It is not necessary to finish the edges of the lining, because they will be completely covered. In order for this application to work, you must clip the seam allowance into the corners of the lining. Do not clip past the seam line.

2. Hem the lining using one of the techniques listed in the following section on hemming. If you are adding hem tape to the skirt hem or finishing it with an overlock, it would be easier to do that now.

3. Place the face-side of the lining down to the face-side of the vent extension. The top edge of the lining seam allowance should be toward the zipper, and the side raw edges of the lining should be even with those of the side of the skirt vent.

4. Sew the lining across the top of the vent extensions, starting from the seam to the lining corner and then down along the side of the vent. Notice the positioning of the lining in Figure 4.24. Make sure that the vent and hem of the skirt are unfolded so that you are not sewing through the skirt.

5. Sew the other side of the lining to the vent. Do not sew across the zipper seam.

6. Turn the skirt back side out and press the seam of the lining with the tip of the iron.

7. Hem the skirt using the techniques in the following section.

HEMS

Hems are finishes for garment lower edges, such as on skirts, pants, jackets,

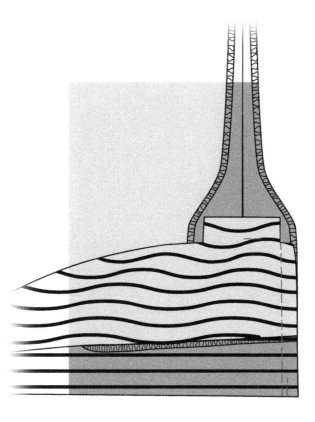

FIGURE 4.24 Positioning and sewing the lining to the vent.

and blouses. Standard hems can range from 1/8 inch in width to 2 inches. Moderate to designer signature labels often have wider hems, which create a smoother look, hang flatter, and wear longer than a cheaper, narrower hem. If the hem width is wide and the skirt or pant is slightly flared, then the hem may need to be eased into the circumference of the skirt. This is usually done by the operator, who blind hems the garment by gently encouraging tiny tucks to form in the hem. Care must be taken to keep the top of the hem on the straight of grain with the pants so that folds do not form at the hem's lower edge. If the skirt or pants are very flared, then the edge of the hem must be eased into the garment or a narrow hem must be used. This requires a lot of time and energy and is usually done only on custom-made garments. Type and width of hem are determined by these criteria:

- Style of garment
- Design choices
- Cost of fabric, time, and other materials (such as hem tape or interlining) needed to execute the hem
- Whether the hem is straight or curved and how curved it is
- If the hem is combined with a vent such as on a jacket sleeve or skirt
- How the hem will be attached to the garment (such as topstitching or blind hemming)
- The equipment available
- Allowances for possible alterations done later, such as in better overcoats

Hems on designer signature, bridge, and some better dress pants are left undone so that the hem may be custom-ized to the consumer's preferences and height. Not hemming the pants makes complimentary alterations easier for the store's staff to execute. A narrow rolled hem is included in Chapter 6, "Ladies' Blouse." A ½-inch-wide topstitched hem is included in Chapter 5, "Ladies' Pant Construction." A narrow, budget-rolled hem treatment for a curved skirt hem is included in this chapter. The basic hem below is for a skirt without a vent and its lining and a skirt with a lining and a vent. If the skirt is being hemmed or altered for an individual, you must mark the hem before proceeding with these instructions. If the hem is being made on the factory floor, then the hem is sewn where marked by the manufacturer.

HEMMING OPTIONS BY MACHINE AND HAND

The choice of how a garment is hemmed affects the customer's perception of quality and, of course, the cost of making the garment. Any costs that can be saved should be balanced with the style of the garment, customer expectations, and look. As a general rule, straight and slightly flared dressy pants and skirts should have a hem allowance of at least 1¼ inches. Curved hems should be narrow to create a smooth look and not interfere with the flow of the garment. Also, hems can be turned to the outside for a decorative effect, or the hem may be both secured and emphasized with a row of lace, braid, ribbon, or another contrast fabric. The upper edge of a garment hem, which is turned to the inside, can be finished in several different ways, including using an overlock stitch (ASTM stitch type 504) and hem tape and being turned under 1/8 to ¼ inch. All of these finishes are included below. Also included are several methods of keeping the hem in place via hand catch stitching, blind hemming by machine, and topstitching.

Hand Catch Stitch

This method requires the upper edge of the garment hem to be finished first. It is used exclusively for hems in dressy garments and is an extremely expensive treatment, usually done only on very high-end custom apparel.

See Figure 4.25 for the formation of the stitch (ASTM stitch type 204). Only one strand of thread should be used with a small needle such as a between, which will allow you to pick up only one or two of the yarns in the garment above the hem. Each stitch in the garment above the hem should only be ¼ to 3/8 inch from the next. When you have hemmed about 6 to 8 inches of the hem, you should start a new length of thread. That way, if the customer catches his or her toe in the stitching of the hem, only one section of stitching will need to be replaced. If you use your right hand to stitch, start the stitching on the hem to your left. If you are left handed, start from your right.

Practice Exercise

1. Cut a section of muslin that is 10 inches square.

2. Finish one side of it by overlocking it or pressing under ¼ inch of the raw edge.
3. Press up 1¼ inches of this side.
4. Thread a needle with a thread that matches your fabric or is slightly darker. Knot the end of the thread and begin stitching until you have hemmed the entire edge. Finish your stitching by taking a few tiny stitches in the hem edge and then burying your thread end and clipping it off.

Machine Blind-Stitch Hem

A blind-stitch machine hems using a needle and a spreader to form stitches that look like crocheting (ASTM stitch type 103). Each time the curved needle swings to the right, it picks up a tiny bit of the fabric being hemmed to secure the hem to the garment's body. In a small workroom or alterations shop, clear or smoke-colored monofilament nylon or polyester thread is used to stitch the hem, because this thread will match practically any color of fabric so the machine does not need to be rethreaded each time a new color of fabric is sewn. In a factory where large numbers of the same garment are made, blind-stitch machines will be threaded with thread

FIGURE 4.25 Hand catch stitch.

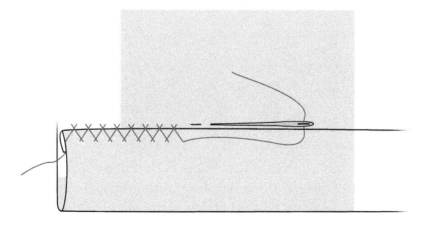

that matches the garments. Some blind-stitch machines will be fitted into a table for hemming long lengths of open fabric; others have a cylindrical arm to allow for hemming of narrower openings such as pants. These machines also have settings for the thread tension and the bite of the needle. These should be adjusted according to the thickness of your fabric.

Practice Exercise

We have included a separate practice exercise here, because a blind-stitch machine may be new to you, and it takes a bit of getting used to. It is best to do a sample of your fabric anyway, just like with a lock-stitch or overlock machine, to get the settings correct. The seam designation for a traditional blind hem is EFm-1.

1. Cut a length of suit-weight fabric such as wool or linen that is 12 inches long by 8 inches wide. Sew the 8-inch-long sides together so that the fabric forms a circle. Press this seam open. Finish one long edge of the fabric with an overlock. Press this edge up to a 1¼-inch hem.
2. Lower the feed mechanism and lay the fabric with the hem side up over the bed of the machine, having the hem edge lined up with the hem guide and the needle lined up with the bottom of the hem to your right.
3. Stitch the hem, starting at the seam. When you arrive at where the stitching began, sew just over the beginning of the stitching and then remove the needle from the fabric before taking the fabric out of the machine. Clip the threads.

Skirt Hem with a Lining and No Vent

These steps assume that the skirt hem edge has already been finished with tape or with ASTM stitch type 504.

1. Hem the lining using the method detailed in Chapter 5. Keep in mind that while a narrow hem does save fabric, a wider hem is a mark of quality, because it will be flatter and hang more smoothly. The hem of lining should be about 1 inch shorter than the skirt so that it slightly overlaps the top edge of the skirt hem, covering the stitching that secures the hem. This will also prevent it from showing on the outside when the garment is being worn.
2. Hem the skirt using the catch stitch or blind hem methods previously described.

Skirt Hem with a Lining and a Vent

The top of the skirt hem should be finished with tape or with a 504 overlock. The lining hem was already finished before it was sewn to the edge of the vent.

1. Fold up the skirt hem face-sides together on the hemline next to the seam sewing the vent and the vent lining together. You should be covering the lining with the folded hem.
2. Sew the hem end to the vent's side and then clip the seam allowance to the seam line just above the hem's edge. Turn the hem to the inside of the garment and press.
3. Fold the seam in toward the skirt on the fold line for the vent, and tack it down to the hem with a few hand stitches or by machine. Do not sew through to the outside of the skirt (Figure 4.26).
4. Blind stitch or hand catch stitch the skirt hem to secure it.

Hand-Rolled Hem

A hand-rolled hem is another very costly finish for lightweight and sheer fabrics.

FIGURE 4.26 Folding in the vent and tacking it to the hem.

The hand version is featured below. It can be imitated by using a roll hem foot on a lockstitch machine. There are various sizes of these feet to work with different weights of fabric and to produce different hem widths—but never anything wider than 1/8 inch on anything heavier than a shirting fabric. Although these produce a structure that is like that of a hand-rolled hem, you will get a row of straight stitching on the outside of the garment, which may or may not be suitable. There are also other versions of rolled hems, such as a Merrow hem done with a machine that functions like an overlock, and a version done on a zigzag machine, which is featured in a text box in this chapter.

Practice Exercise

1. Mark the hem to the correct length. Do not trim the hem.
2. Sew a line of stitching with a lockstitch machine that is 1/8 inch outside the marked hem. This stitching serves as both a stabilizing force for the edge and a line to sew on to make sure the stitching is even. You will need to use a short stitch length to sew on the single layer of your fabric if it is sheer. It is important to make sure that the fabric doesn't pucker while it is being stitched. If the edge of the fabric is curved, take care not to stretch the edge of the fabric while doing this line of stitching.
3. Carefully trim the excess fabric off 1/8 inch below the line of stitching, taking care to maintain this width.
4. Thread a fine short needle, such as a between, with a single strand of lightweight thread that matches the fabric. Take a tiny stitch on the line of machine stitching to start leaving a thread tail that will be rolled inside the hem.
5. Begin hand stitching using a slip stitch, rolling the fabric up so that the line of machine stitching ends up on the inner folded edge and the raw edge of the fabric is enclosed inside

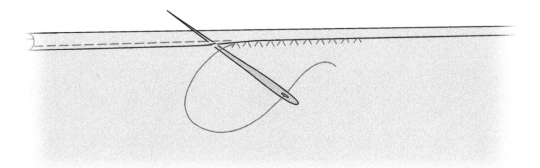

FIGURE 4.27 Hand rolling a narrow hem.

the seam (Figure 4.27). To finish your thread, take two tiny stitches in the line of machine stitching and bury the thread end inside the rolled fabric.

Narrow Topstitched Hem

The steps to complete this hem are detailed in Chapter 5. For skirts, this technique works well on ruffles at the hem and on casual skirts with a slightly curved hem.

WAIST FASTENINGS FOR SKIRTS

Dress Hook and Eye

This application works for any situation where the hook and loop will be at the garment's edge, such as on a pant, dress, or blouse. Here it is positioned at the top of the invisible zipper to take some of the strain off the zipper and prevent unexpected openings.

1. Mark the position of the hook with a pin. The holes of the hook should be on the inside of the facing so that the end of the hook lines up with the end of the facing.
2. Sew through the holes neatly, using a waste knot to fasten the end of the thread as shown in Figure 4.28.
3. Line up the loop with the hook so that the loop just extends beyond the end

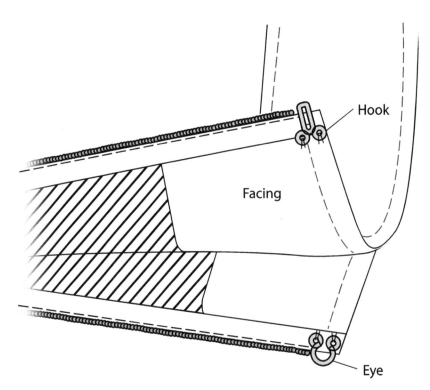

FIGURE 4.28 Sewing a hook and eye above an invisible zipper.

Hook

Facing

Eye

of the facing, and sew down neatly using the stitching configuration shown below.

Skirt Hook and Eye

A skirt hook may be sewn on or attached by having its prongs bent before the waistband is sewn to the skirt. This step is done by machine when manufacturing any quantity of garments or by hand for custom apparel or as an alteration. Figure 4.29 shows the correct configuration of stitching for each piece of the fastening. Make sure to sew the hook part on the overlap of the band and the loop on the underlap.

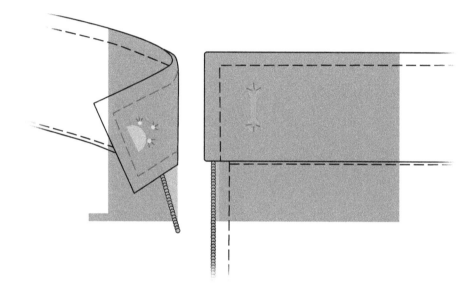

FIGURE 4.29 Sewing on a skirt hook and eye.

JEAN STYLE PANT CONSTRUCTION ORDER

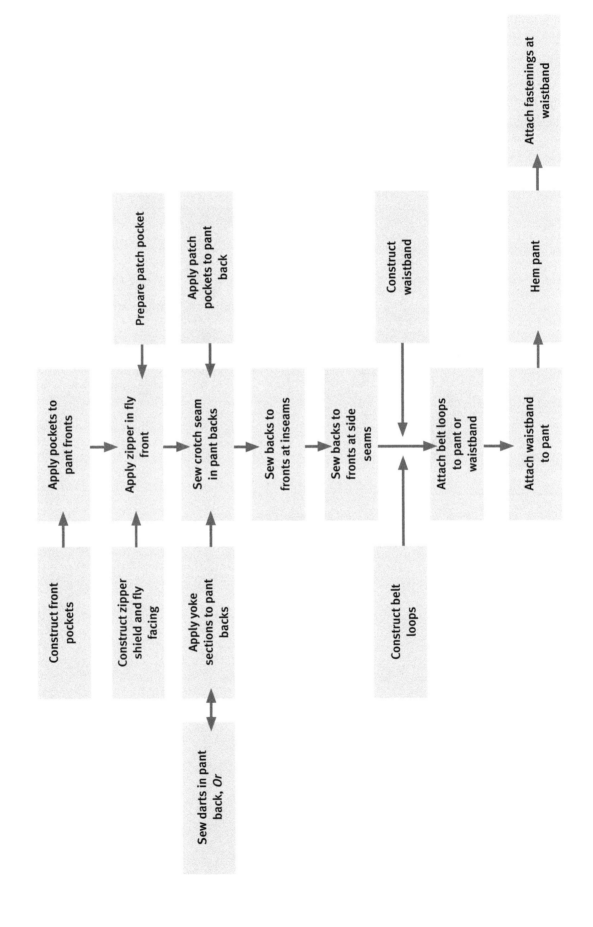

5

Ladies' Pant Construction

The phrase "who wears the pants in the family" is no longer the gender-loaded qualifier of familial leadership that it used to be. But where did this phrase come from? In Western culture, the wearing of pants by women in public was not considered decent until the 1890s. Women who wore pants were simply trying to free themselves

of garments such as corsets that were damaging their health. Many men and women thought these apparel revolutionaries were challenging the position of men in society as the source of all the knowledge that capitalism depended on. Suffragettes in the United States—such as Amelia Bloomer, for whom the gathered-at-the-ankle style of pants that she wore in public under her skirt was named—were partly responsible for this shift in the freedom of women's dress. Now women wear pants as a basic and accepted style for any social situation. Who will your pants liberate?

In this chapter, you will practice constructing a

- fundamental fly zipper,
- elastic waist,
- belt loops,
- patch pocket,
- jean-style front pocket,
- inseam pocket, and
- topstitched hem.

You will also practice basic pant-seaming techniques. Combined with the invisible

zipper, waist treatments, and hemming techniques in Chapter 4, you can create a variety of pant styles.

Fly Zippers

Fly zippers may be found at every price point, from designer signature to category killer. The construction details may be very similar. Usually the fabric and finishing details are all that is changed.

Unlike blouses and jackets, there is no set format for which side of the garment overlaps the other at the fly in women's wear. You will have established that during pattern drafting. This pant assumes the traditional direction of right over left. If your pant differs, just reverse the directions.

Although the structure of a fly zipper is very similar among manufacturers from one pant to another, the length of the opening varies with the height of the waistband. The fly facing will echo the topstitching on the outside of a fly zipper, because it is under that topstitching. The facing should be about ½ to ¾ inch wider than the topstitching will be. Also, the dimensions of the fly underlap will change depending on design aesthetic and price point of the pant. Frequently, the higher the retail cost of the pant, the wider the fly underlap. Also, a lower-retail-price pant will have a fly facing extending off the left front of the pant instead of a separate facing. This does save time, materials, and money but is not as sturdy as the application below. The parts of a pant fly front are pictured in Figure 5.1.

1. Apply fusible interlining to the fly facing and the seam allowance of the left side of the zipper area (see Figure 5.1).
2. Use ASTM stitch type 504 to finish the edges of the seam allowances between the waistline and the inseam of both pant fronts. Also, fold the fly facing in half and finish the curved edges together with the same stitch.

3. Sew the pant fronts together from the inseam to the bottom of the fly facing using ASTM stitch 301 and seam type SSa-1. Back tack and press the seam open.
4. Construct the fly underlap by folding it face-sides together and sewing the lower end. Turn it face-sides out, press it, and then finish the open side together with ASTM stitch type 504. Leave the top open (see Figure 5.1).
5. Place the fly facing front-side down on the right front, straight edges even. Sew the facing to the pant front; press the seam allowances toward the facing, and then understitch the facing (Figure 5.2).
6. Turn the zipper face-side down onto the facing so that the coil is ½ inch inside the line of understitching and so the top of the zipper is even with

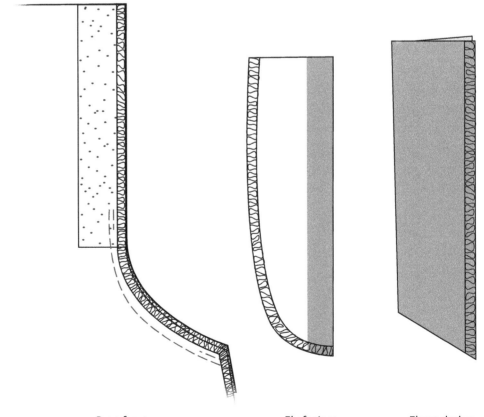

FIGURE 5.1 Pant fly zipper pieces.

Pant fronts   Fly facing   Fly underlap

Understitching

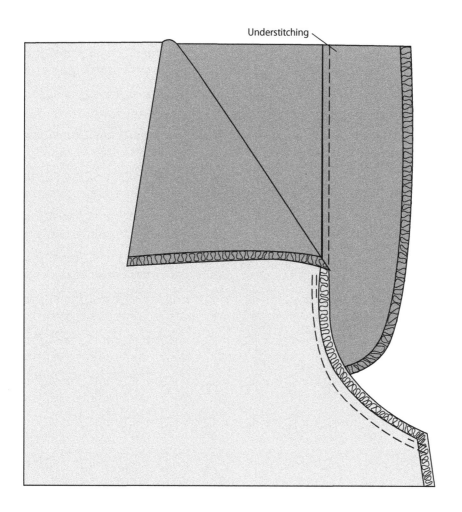

FIGURE 5.2 Sewing the fly facing.

FIGURE 5.3 Sewing the zipper to the facing.

the top of the facing (Figure 5.3). Stitch the zipper to the facing near the coil. You may include another row of stitching near the outer edge of the zipper tape to add more strength to the application.

7. Lay the other half of the zipper face-side down on the left seam line of the pant front, and pin. Lay the finished straight edges of the fly underlap on top of the zipper so that all the edges are even. Sew the pant front, zipper, and underlap together near the zipper's coil. Flip the pant face-side up and extend the underlap toward the pant's right side. Press and then edge stitch the zipper next to the pressed edge (Figure 5.4).

8. Zip up the zipper and carefully arrange the right pant front over

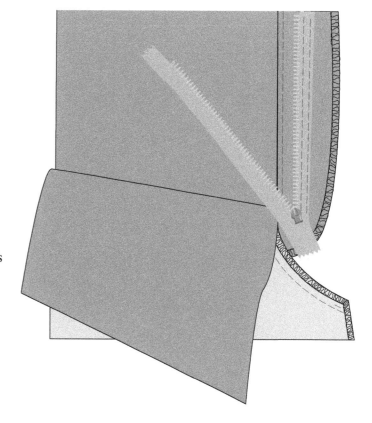

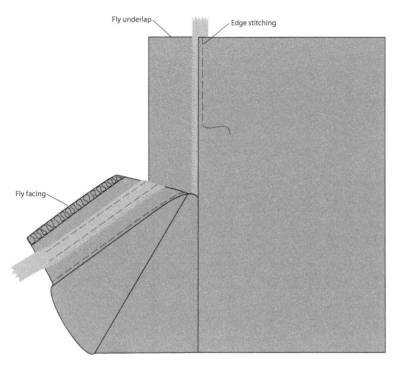

FIGURE 5.4 Sewing the zipper to the underlap.

the left, making sure that the fly underlap is not under the facing. Pin the right front close to the zipper. Topstitch the right front facing to the

pant, following the line of the facing; make sure to stop at the crotch seam and back tack (Figure 5.5).

9. By machine, tack the underlap to the facing at the lower edges near the end of the zipper. Do not sew to the pant.

Inseam Pockets

Inseam pockets have openings on the side seam of the pant. They may also appear vertically in the side seams of skirts and jackets and in the princess seams of tailored ladies' jackets. It is important to keep the pocket fabric as lightweight as possible because of the sensitivity of bulk at the hip area. If the pant is at all fitted at the hip, then a side seam pocket must be kept very slim. It is also important that the pant fit the figure without the pocket gaping. In our example, there are four pocket pieces, two for the pant fronts and two for the back. This pocket can be made

FIGURE 5.5 Final fly topstitching.

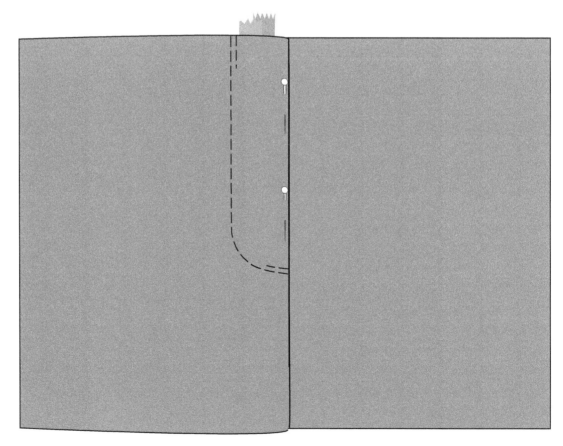

with or without an extension off the side seam of the pant where the pocket will be. If there is no extension, then there is a better chance of seeing the pocket fabric when the pant is worn. An extension of the pant fabric prevents this from happening.

1. Attach the pocket bag pieces to the side seam extensions using ASTM stitch type 516 if the pant is not lined or using stitch type 301 if the pant is lined.
2. Press the pocket bag sections away from the pant (Figure 5.6).
3. Place the front and back of the pants face-sides together, making sure that the pocket bags are aligned.
4. Stitch from the top of the pant down to the opening of the pocket. Turn and stitch around the pocket bag and up to the side of the pant. Turn again and stitch down the side of the pant to the hem (Figure 5.7).
5. Press the pocket bags toward the center front of the pant. On the face of the pant, you may want to edge stitch the pocket bag to the pant front at the opening. Take care not to stitch through to the back side of the pocket, which would close the opening (Figure 5.8).

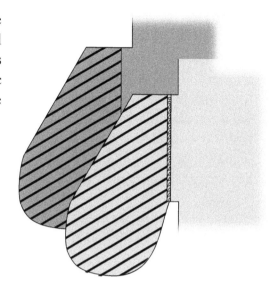

FIGURE 5.6 Sewing pocket bag to front and back pant outseams.

Jean-Style Front Pocket

Depending on the thickness of your fabric and how you have drafted your pattern, you may use only the pant fabric for your front pockets, or you may substitute a cotton or polycotton pocketing fabric or garment lining for the inside pocket bag, which is covered by the fashion fabric. The pocket shown here is made only of the garment fabric and consists of two pieces, the pocket

FIGURE 5.7 (left) Sewing pant outseam and pocket bag together.

FIGURE 5.8 (right) Topstitching front of inseam pocket opening.

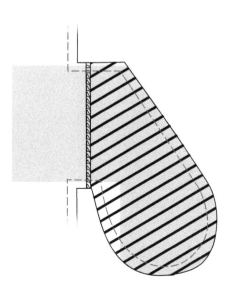

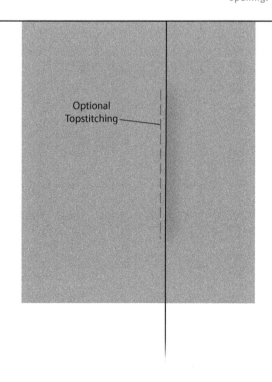

Optional Topstitching

front and the pocket back, which also make up part of the pant front.

1. Lay the pocket back onto the pocket front, matching the outer curved edges and placing the face-sides of the pocket front and pocket back together (Figure 5.9).
2. Sew along the outer curved edge. ASTM stitch type 514 is a good choice for a one-pass, clean, sturdy finish without a lot of thickness. Stitch type 301 or 401 may be used if the garment is to be lined.
3. Match the upper curved edge of the pocket front to the curved area of the pant front with the face-sides of the fabric together (Figure 5.10).
4. Sew the pocket to the upper edge of the pant using a ¼-inch seam allowance, making sure not to stretch the fabric. Press the seam open, taking care not to crease the fabric.

FIGURE 5.9 (left) Sewing pocket back to pocket front.

FIGURE 5.10 (right) Sewing pocket front to pant front.

5. Fold the pocket to the inside of the pant front, press the edge, and then topstitch through all layers at the pocket opening.

Unlined Patch Pocket without a Facing

The patch pocket on a pair of jeans has become a signature part of a brand image for a company or designer. The designs made with embroideries, jewels, trims, and crystals are trademarked as brand statements. In garment factories that produce thousands of pairs of the same design of jeans, one-pocket sewing machines will take the cut denim blank with its design, press it, position it, and then stitch it down. These are highly specialized machines, so we are going to use a lockstitch machine to create ours.

Practice Exercise

1. Press the hem under at the top of the pocket and then stitch. The narrow topstitched hem (shown at the end of this chapter in Figure 5.16) is a standard finish here.
2. Press under the remainder of the seam allowances on the pocket, using a metal template if available (Figure 5.11).
3. Position the pocket, and stitch down the side, across the bottom, and up

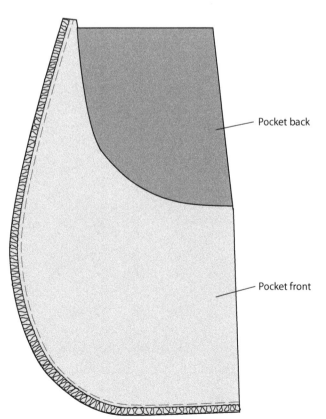

Pocket back

Pocket front

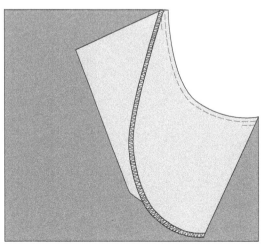

the other side; make sure to back tack at both ends over the edge of the pocket onto the pant back (ASTM stitch type 301 or 401, seam type LSd-1). Reinforce the pocket corners with a thread bar tack or a rivet for added strength.

Belt Loops

Belt loops, also known as *carriers*, can be made any width and can be attached in any position at the waist, with or without a waistband. Generally, they appear on pants with a fly zipper, two on each side within 2 or 3 inches of the front closure. There are two more at the side seams and then one or two at center back. You may add more than these, change up the width, or cross them over each other, and so on. When attaching them to the pant, it saves time and money to enclose one end in either the top waist seam or in the seam that attaches the waistband to the pant. In the method below, we will attach the loops to the pant before sewing on a straight waistband. The full instructions for this waistband are in Chapter 4.

In the garment factory, there are cover stitch machines that will execute a seam in a strip of fabric to make belt loops while finishing the edges and adding two rows of topstitching to the face of the loop. No turning is required. Other machines will take the belt-loop segment, position it on the fabric, and hold it there while it is stitched down using a bar tack. We, on the other hand, will create a belt loop using the following method.

1. Cut a fabric strip that is twice the finished width of your belt loop plus ½ inch for a seam allowance. The minimum width for a belt loop should be 3/8 inches finished. The length

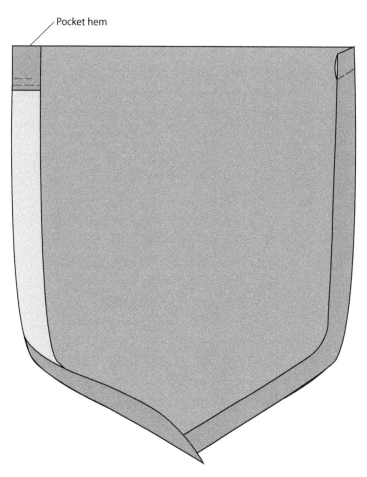

Pocket hem

FIGURE 5.11 Pressing an unlined patch pocket around a template.

of the strip should equal the number of belt loops in your design times the length of each belt loop. The length of each loop should equal the width of the waistband plus at least 1 inch extra to sew down to the band's other edge. For example, for five loops that are each 1¼ inch wide (3/8 inches wide finished) and 2 inches long (1 inch long finished), you will need a strip that is 1¼ inches wide by 10 inches long. You can add ½ inch or so extra to avoid shorting yourself.

2. Position the strip face-sides together, and sew down the long side of the strip. Using a bodkin or loop turner, turn the strip face-side out and press so that the seam is centered on one side of the strip, not at the edge. Topstitch along both long edges of the strip.

3. Measure carefully and cut the strip in sections that are the length of the loops.

4. Position the belt loops face-side down at the waist of the pant, making sure that one end is even with the fabric's raw edge. Pin to temporarily secure (Figure 5.12).

5. After completing the waistband, you may attach the belt loops to the top of the band using the following method:
   - Position the belt loop as shown in Figure 5.13 and zigzag or straight stitch (ASTM stitch type 304 or 301) over the raw end of the loop.
   - Move the belt loop up toward the top of the pant, and sew again above the first sewing, through all layers.

Sewing the Inseam and Outseam

This section is intended to help with seam choices and to prepare for the attachment of a waist finish such as a band. The first step is to sew or finish sewing the crotch seam. Choices include seam type SSa-2 with stitch type 301 or 401 and finishing with stitch type 504. This seam can generally be found in pants at a higher price point than budget and is able to be altered if the waist needs to be taken in or let out. A less-expensive alternative is seam type SSa-1 with stitch type 516, but since the seam allowances are sewn together here, the seam cannot be altered.

Inseam

For comfort, this area needs to be low on bulky layers, so a lightweight seam and finish are called for. Seam type SSa-2 with stitch type 301 or 401 and finishing with stitch type 504 is a good choice. At a lower price point and slightly less comfortable is seam type SSa-1 with stitch type 516.

1. Position the pant front face-side down on the corresponding pant back for each leg.
2. Sew the inseam from the top of the pants down to the hem on both legs. Press the seams.

Outseam

The seam and stitch type that you use for the outseam depends on the look you want for your design and on the price point of your garment. It also depends on whether you have an inseam pocket there.

1. Match the front to the back at the outseam, face-sides together on each leg. Carefully position the front pocket so that it lies flat and all edges are even before sewing.
2. Sew the outseam from the top of each leg to the bottom. For outseams with an inseam pocket sewn into the

FIGURE 5.12 Positioning belt loops to be sewn under the waistband.

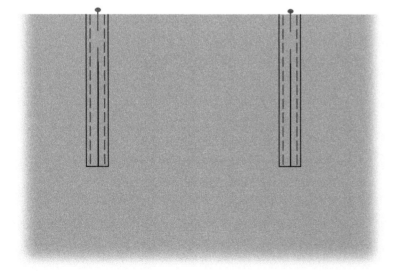

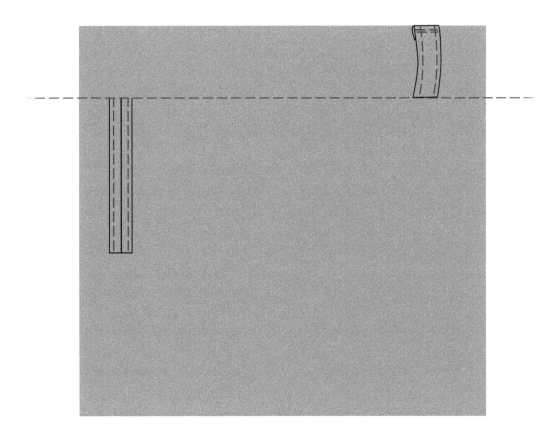

side seam, a good choice is seam type SSa-2 with stitch type 301 or 401 and finishing with stitch type 504. Seam type SSa-1 with stitch type 516 also works, as does seam type SSa-2 with stitch type 516. An extra run of 301 or 401 makes a mock lap seam that is a quick, sturdy finish for seams that have no pocket and for garments where an extra row of topstitching on the outside of the item will make an interesting design detail.

Gathered Waist with Elastic or Drawstring

A gathered waist is a decidedly casual look done best in a soft fabric. Because of its comfort, an elastic or drawstring waist is frequently found in lounge wear, pajamas, or apparel that is geared toward strenuous activity. However, the casing and drawstring application detailed below

can be done in many different spots on many styles. Try a drawstring casing at the neck of a cotton gauze blouse for a peasant look or near the end of a sleeve for a romantic touch. The same technique can be used to add elastic to the cuff of a pair of wind pants or the wrist of a lining for a winter coat.

A gathered waist can be made with an added casing or an extension of the pant waist. Both edges are folded over to the inside and then topstitched down to make a casing for the elastic or drawstring to travel through. The width of the casing depends on the width of the elastic. The casing must be wide enough to allow the elastic to travel through without binding but must be narrow enough to not be baggy. For example, if you are using 1-inch-wide elastic, your casing should be at least 2½ inches wide—1 inch for each side of the elastic, ¼ inch to turn under at the bottom edge, and an extra ¼ inch to give the elastic room to move.

A drawstring casing is usually narrow. However, the folded-over section at the top of the waist may be wider, with two rows of straight stitching added to make the narrow slot for the drawstring. In the factory, a special folder attachment on a lockstitch machine will make the necessary folds. A simple casing is explained below.

For Elastic

1. Press under ¼ inch of the raw edge of the casing to the back side of the fabric.
2. Fold the casing over and press on the fold line. Pin if necessary.
3. Edge stitch next to the lower, pressed edge, leaving a section undone in the back of the garment through which to insert the elastic (ASTM stitch type 301 or 401).
4. Insert the elastic, then overlap and sew the ends together; be careful not to twist the elastic. Sew the opening closed (Figure 5.14).

For a Drawstring

1. Make one or two buttonholes in the center front of the inside of the casing before folding it over.
2. Fold over the casing and stitch down as before. You may want to add two more rows of stitching to make the slot for the drawstring narrower.
3. Insert the drawstring into the casing, making sure to knot the ends to prevent it from coming out of the casing (Figure 5.15).

Hemming

The hem included in this chapter is the standard for a casual pant in denim

FIGURE 5.14 Inserting elastic into a casing.

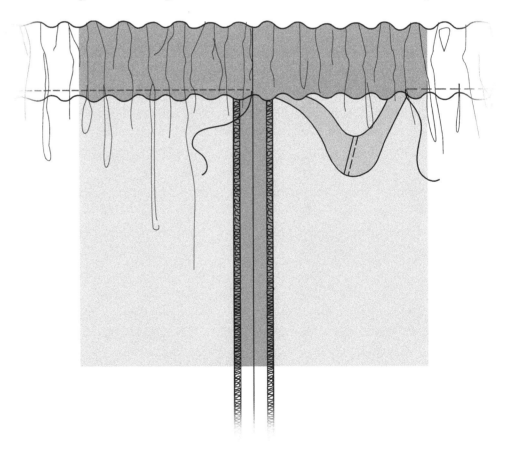

or other sturdy fabric. The standard wide hem for dressy pants and skirts secured with a catch stitch or a blind hemstitch is detailed in Chapter 4. A narrow, rolled hem that could be used for a palazzo pant of chiffon is also listed in Chapter 4.

Narrow/Topstitched Hem

1. Press up ½ inch at the bottom of each pant leg twice, taking up 1 inch for the hem (Figure 5.16). Use seam type EFb-1, stitchtype 301.
2. Topstitch close to the top fold.
3. Press again to set stitches.

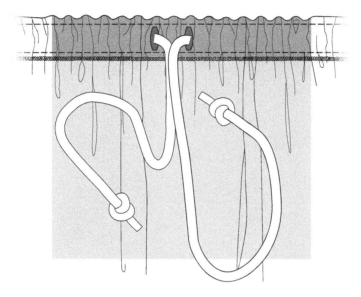

FIGURE 5.15 Inserting a drawstring into a casing.

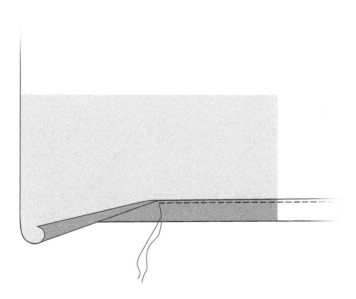

FIGURE 5.16 Top-stitched hem.

BLOUSE CONSTRUCTION

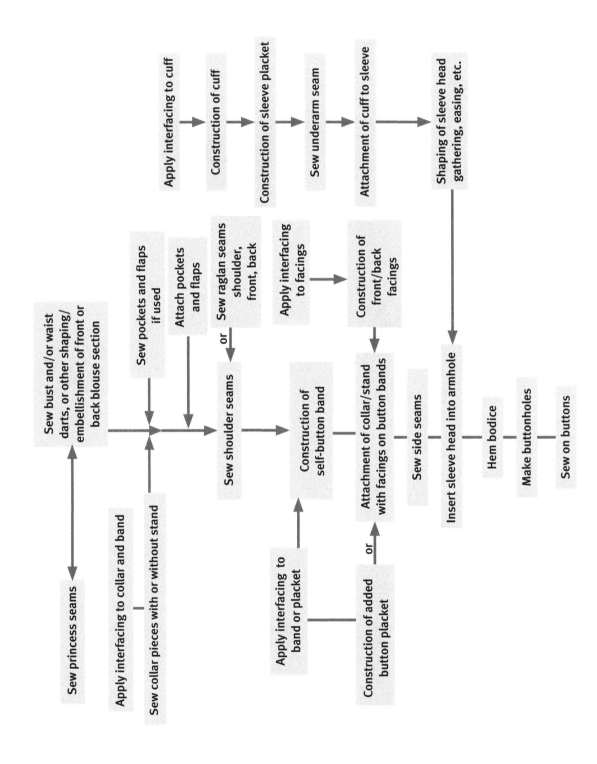

Sew princess seams

Sew bust and/or waist darts, or other shaping/embellishment of front or back blouse section

Apply interfacing to collar and band

Sew collar pieces with or without stand

Sew pockets and flaps if used

Attach pockets and flaps

Sew raglan seams shoulder, front, back

or

Sew shoulder seams

Apply interfacing to facings

Construction of front/back facings

Construction of self-button band

Attachment of collar/stand with facings on button bands

Sew side seams

Insert sleeve head into armhole

Hem bodice

Make buttonholes

Sew on buttons

Apply interfacing to band or placket

Construction of added button placket

or

Apply interfacing to cuff

Construction of cuff

Construction of sleeve placket

Sew underarm seam

Attachment of cuff to sleeve

Shaping of sleeve head gathering, easing, etc.

6

Ladies' Blouse

W hether frilly or tailored, a lady's blouse is an expression of how a woman feels at any given time in a certain situation. Endless possibilities for design make this garment a dream for the designer, merchandiser, or buyer who has something to say to his or her client about fashion. What texture will grace the front of the blouse—tucks, ruffles,

embroidery? What will the sleeve length be—three-quarter length finished with a tailored cuff or a tiny cap of flirty chiffon petals? What will you say with the collar? Are you seeing a trend toward a high, military style or soft layers of lace? What is *your* statement, and how will you express it?

In this chapter, all of the folding tasks and sandwiching of fabric layers in between other layers, such as at the collar band/neckline seam or the cuff/sleeve seam, may be done entirely by machine in the industry setting. Elaborate folding attachments and specialized machines position the fabric layers and pieces precisely so that the entire process is completed in minutes with little operator error. The following techniques imitate those machines and can be used in a small workroom or custom sewing studio.

In this chapter, you will learn to construct

- bust darts;
- princess seams;
- fold-over, two-layer, and concealed button plackets;

- collars with a stand;
- patch pockets with facing;
- buttonholes;
- lap plackets on a sleeve; and
- basic buttoned cuffs.

You will also learn how to set in a sleeve and sew on buttons. The content in Chapter 7, "Fashion Jacket," can help add to your repertoire of garment pieces with which to design your blouse.

BUST-SHAPING OPTIONS

In loose-fitting woven blouses, there is no need for shaping at the bust to tailor the garment to the figure. If you want a more fitted look, you will need a dart, a combination of darts, or a princess seam to shape the fabric. In this section, we will discuss constructing bust darts, waist darts, and princess seams.

Bust Darts

Bust darts are marked and sewn using the same methods described in Chapter 4, "Basic Straight Skirt." Care must be taken hipline. If the dart ends above the hipline, it may taper but will not end in a point. Follow the tips below to sew either kind of dart.

1. You will sew an open-ended waist dart using the same steps as a bust dart or the waist dart on a skirt. Use the appropriate finishing method for the price point of your garment.
2. Make a double-ended waist dart by sewing two single-pointed darts, as shown in Figure 6.1.

Princess Seaming

A princess seam sculpts the garment to the shape of the waist and bustline for the bodice front and the waist and shoulder blade for the back. It substitutes for the bust and waist darts while adding a flattering, vertical design line. Because of the way they are drafted, the garment pieces that form a princess seam have one convex side and one concave side. For a buttoned blouse, the pieces will be two center fronts, two side fronts, two side backs, and one center back, as shown in Figure 6.2.

Create your princess seam using the following steps:

1. Stay stitch the concave edge of the bodice pieces just inside the seam line (ASTM stitch type 301).
2. Pin together one center front of the blouse to a side front piece and face-sides, matching the top and bottom edges at the pieces. Continue pinning toward the curved area. There should be a notch at the bust point on both pieces. Match those notches to make sure the pieces are aligned. Clip the concave side if necessary so that the raw edges of the seam allowance will conform to the convex side. The two seam

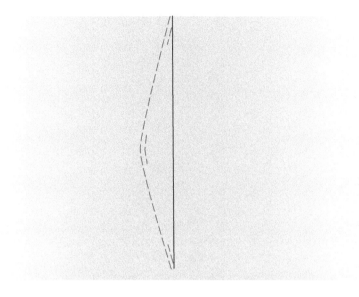

FIGURE 6.1 Sewing a double ended waist dart.

to sew the bust points accurately so that they match. Choose the appropriate finishing method for your price point. Always press horizontal darts down toward the bottom of the garment.

A waist dart can have one point or two depending on how long the garment is. A waist dart may be used on a blouse, dress, vest, or jacket. If the garment extends down to the hip area, then it will have a point near the bustline and one near the

FIGURE 6.2 Pieces of a garment that make up a princess seam.

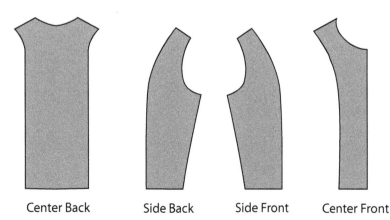

Center Back   Side Back   Side Front   Center Front

allowances must be kept even (Figure 6.3).

3. Stitch the two sides of the seam together (ASTM stitch type 301, seam type SSa-1), making sure to maintain the bust curve and to avoid sewing a tuck of extra fabric into the seam. The concave side must be slightly stretched to meet the convex side.

4. Press the seam open on the back side of the fabric using a tailor's ham. If the garment is to be lined, no further finishing of the seam is necessary.

5. If there is a facing on the garment that extends to the princess line, you can press both seam allowances toward the center of the garment so that they will be under the facing edge.

6. If the garment is not lined, then a three-thread overlock can be used to finish the pressed open allowances (seam type SSa-2, with stitch type 301 or 401 and 504). On a lightweight fabric, such as a fine, plain woven cotton, use a lightweight thread so that the stitching doesn't show through to the outside if the fit is tight.

7. If it fits into your design, topstitching the seam allowance to the garment makes a nice addition to accent the seam's vertical line while also finishing the seam allowances.

◇◇

BUTTON PLACKETS

The look of the button placket on your blouse, the feel of the fabric, and the way the buttonholes are stitched are often indicators of garment quality to consumers. They must interact with this area of the garment as soon as they try it on in the store and will continue to interact with it as they

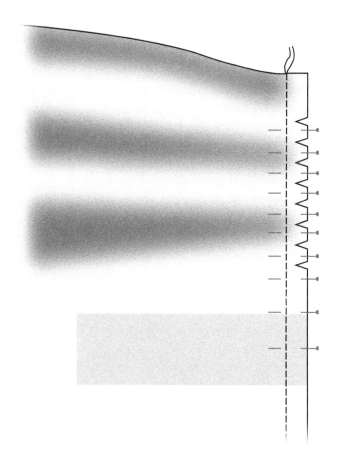

FIGURE 6.3 Sewing the front princess seams.

use the garment day to day. The choices you make here, as in many other parts of the garment, are crucial to maintaining the quality of your brand image. The following techniques for a basic fold-over band appear at many price points and will contribute to an appropriate quality image. In women's wear, the right front will overlap the left, so the buttonholes will be on the front's right-hand side.

Fold-Over Button Band

This fold-over button band may be made with or without interlining. The appropriate interlining can add to hanger appeal and to the feel of the band, and it can help the band maintain its form longer. To make a fold-over band, there should be a horizontal extension going past the center front line, which is twice the width of the finished band. This type of band may be used on either side of the bodice.

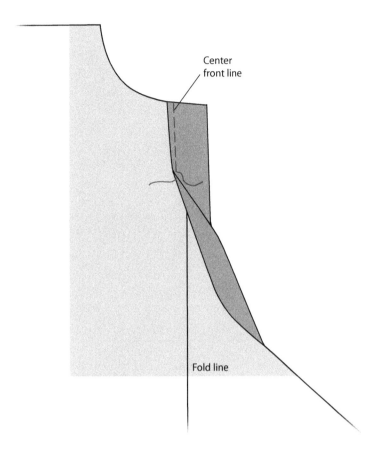

Fold line

FIGURE 6.4 Folding and stitching a basic button placket.

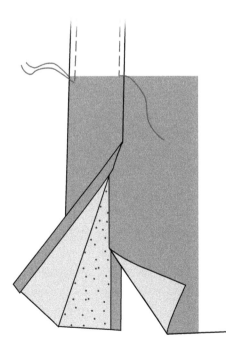

FIGURE 6.5 Two layer button placket.

inner folded edge (ASTM stitch type 301 or 401; Figure 6.4).

Two-Layer Button Placket

This two-layer placket can be made sturdier by adding another interlined fabric on the inside. This fabric could be a less-expensive material to save on costs. When applied by the correct machines, it could be a faster application as well. This placket can be matched with a fold-over placket on the left side.

1. Turn the band to the inside of the blouse, turning under the outer edge so that it touches the fold on the inside. From the face of the fabric, topstitch through all layers at the

1. Cut two bands the length of the blouse front by the desired width of the band plus at least ½ inch for seam allowances on both edges. This band will extend ½ inch past the front edge of the blouse. Apply interlining to the back side of one of the pieces to make the inner band. This inside band may be cut out of an inexpensive fabric that coordinates with the fashion fabric. It will show on the outside of the garment at the neck when the buttons are fastened.
2. Sandwich the right side of the blouse face-side up inside the two layers of the bands, as shown in Figure 6.5. Pin if necessary.
3. With the face-side of the blouse up, stitch through all of the layers using ASTM stitch type 301 or 401, starting with the band's inner edge (see Figure 6.5). Then repeat the operation with the outer edge of the band.

Concealed Button Placket

A concealed button placket speaks of quality and exclusivity. However, it is an expensive addition, because it uses extra fabric up to three times the width of the finished band. The left side of the bodice can compensate for this by using

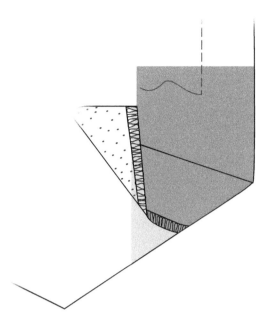

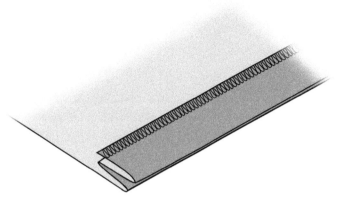

a simple band with interlining folded under once with an overlocked inner edge (Figure 6.6). Construct the button plackets as follows.

The Right Side

1. Apply interlining to the inner half of the band. Overlock the outer fabric edge (ASTM stitch type 503 or 504).
2. Press the button band as shown in Figure 6.7.
3. Carefully align the serged edge and the second fold under the stitching line, and pin.
4. With the face of the fabric up, stitch through the outside layer, the folded layers, and the overlocked edge (ASTM stitch type 301 or 401). Press to set the stitches. Note: It is easier to make the buttonholes in the front band now instead of waiting until the ends are finished at the collar and the bottom hem.

COLLAR WITH STAND

Constructing the Collar

1. Apply interlining to one of the collar pieces. Place the two collar pieces

face-sides together and stitch using the following method (Figure 6.8).

- Sew across one end, back tacking at both ends (ASTM stitch type 301, seam type SSa-1).
- Turn the collar and sew across the outer edge, back tacking at both ends.
- Sew across the other end, back tacking at both ends.
  Press the seam to one side as far into the corner as possible before turning the collar face-side out. An ironing board with a point-pressing end will help with this maneuver.

2. Turn the collar face-side out and re-press the collar with the stitching line at the edge.
3. Topstitch the sewn edges of the collar.

Adding the Stand

1. Apply interlining to one of the collar stand pieces.
2. Sandwich the collar between the collar stand pieces, taking care to use the

FIGURE 6.6 (left) Pressing the left side button hole placket.

FIGURE 6.7 (right) Placing the layers of the concealed placket before stitching.

FIGURE 6.8 Stitching the collar pieces.

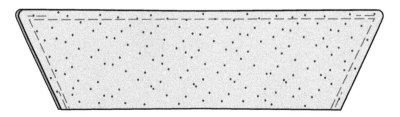

ALTERNATIVE BUTTON LOOPS ON A TWO-LAYER BUTTON PLACKET

Creating decorative button loops on the front of a blouse, jacket, or coat has a striking effect. You may use premade coordinating ribbon, braid, or cording. You may also create your own loop material out of a bias-covered round cord or flat bias strip by sewing a narrow tube of bias from ¾ inch to 1½ inches wide, using seam type SSa-1 and stitch type 301. The material should be sufficiently long to make enough loops for all of your buttons. Make sure to allow enough so that the loops can easily make it around the buttons without being so loose that the buttons will slip out. The loops may all be sewn on as one long length on the outside of the garment as a design detail or may be separated into sections and sewn into the seam of a two-layer button placket.

correct edges of the stand, and pin (Figure 6.9).

3. Stitch the stand seam, taking care to sew the ends accurately so that they match (ASTM stitch type 301). Press the seam on the face of the fabric, gently pulling the stand pieces away from the collar. Edge stitch the seam in the stand.

4. Press the seam allowance of the interlined edge of the stand to the back of the fabric (the inside of the stand). Topstitch this layer to the stand through the center of the seam allowance, taking care not to stitch it to the other side of the stand (Figure 6.10).

FIGURE 6.9 (left) Positioning the collar stand on the collar.

FIGURE 6.10 (right) Stitching the stand seam allowance to the stand.

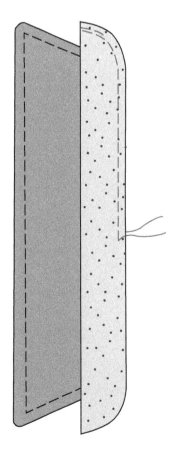

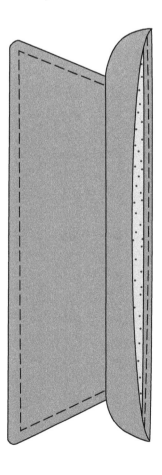

Preparing the Neckline to Add the Collar

1. If your blouse does not feature a yoke, continue to step 2. Construct the front and back yokes if they are part of the blouse design. See Chapter 7, "Fashion Jacket," for instructions on sewing a yoke.

2. Place the front of the bodice facedown on the face of the back at the shoulder seam. Stitch and finish this seam. Options for this seam include seam style SSa-2 using stitch type 301 or 401 and 504 to finish the seam edges, or seam SSa-1 using stitch type 514. Press the seams.

3. Stay stitch the neck edge, sewing over the tops of the neck bands to secure them for attaching the collar (ASTM stitch type 301).

Applying the Stand to the Neckline

During the application of many collar units, applying the stand to the neckline would be accomplished in only one or two steps with a specialized machine manufactured for the sole purpose of doing this task. Provided all of the collars, bands, and necklines are made the same, the manufacturer will be able to accommodate a variety of fabrics and blouse designs quickly and efficiently with little operator error. This style of application can be seen at price points from designer signature down to budget.

1. Pin the lower edge of only the uninterlined side of the stand to the face of the fabric at the garment neck edge; make sure to align the center back of the stand with the center back of the bodice, and make sure the folded edges of the button plackets are aligned with

the seam line at each end of the stand (Figure 6.11).

2. Stitch the neckline using stitch type 301 or 401 and seam type SSa-1. While stitching, make sure that the seam allowance of the neckline, which is concave, stays even with the straight or slightly convex edge of the collar stand. You may need to snip the neck edge to the stay stitching to make this work (see Figure 6.11). Press the seam allowance up into the stand.

3. Carefully pin the remaining, interlined layer of the collar stand to the inside of the neckline, covering the previous line of stitching.

4. On the outside of the blouse, stitch in the ditch between the stand and the garment's neck edge, catching the edge of the stand in the stitching. Press the seam.

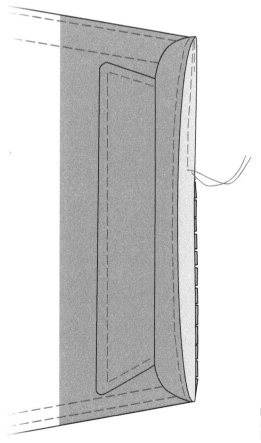

FIGURE 6.11 Stitching the stand to the blouse neckline.

CONSTRUCTING AND APPLYING A PATCH POCKET WITH FACING

1. If the fabric is loosely woven, you may want to apply interlining to the entire pocket inside.
2. Finish the pocket's seam allowance edges with stitch type 504. You may choose to finish the lower edge of the facing only if you are using two rows of topstitching to attach the pocket.
3. Fold the facing to the face-side of the fabric on the fold line (Figure 6.12).
4. Sew down each side of the facing (ASTM stitch type 301), beginning at the fold toward the facing lower edge and taking up the allowed seam allowance. Trim off the upper corners at the fold if necessary (see Figure 6.12).
5. Turn the facing to the inside of the pocket and press the fold line.
6. Continue pressing the seam allowance under around the entire pocket. Miter the corners or consult the directions for pressing under curved edges.
7. Pin the pocket in place on the bodice at the markings.
8. Stitch around the pocket edges, beginning and ending at the top fold;

FIGURE 6.12 Completing the facing on the pocket.

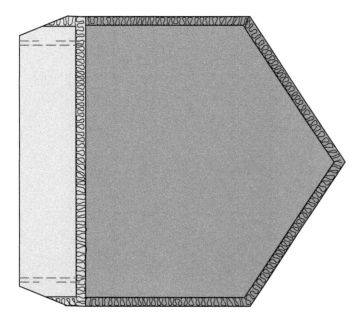

make sure to start on the bodice fabric (ASTM stitch type 301 or 401, seam type LSd-1). If using only one row of stitching to secure the pocket, make sure that row is no more than 1/8 inch from the pressed edge.

BUTTONHOLE OPTIONS

A square-ended buttonhole consist of two parts: the bar tacks across the ends and the legs. When considering the creation of your buttonholes, take into account your fabric and the stitch length and width that are appropriate for the fabric. Usually, the thinner the fabric, the narrower the leg and the more dense the stitching. Buttonhole bands should be interlined to avoid puckering of the fabric when stitching the hole and to improve the look of the front of the blouse as it is being worn.

Buttonholes on blouses are always vertical, with the exception of a buttonhole on a collar stand. Vertical buttonholes help keep the blouse closed when being worn. The horizontal buttonhole at the collar is usually more a matter of tradition, because this button is seldom fastened. Buttonholes should be at least one to one-half the width of the button away from the edge of the band to prevent the button from extending past the edge when fastened and to ensure that the hole will not tear out of the fabric. On custom blouses, a button is positioned precisely at the customer's bust level.

For manufacturing, the button at the bodice level is placed according to the fit model so that every same-size blouse is alike. Follow the instructions for your buttonholer to stitch the buttonholes on your blouse.

SEWING ON BUTTONS

Buttons will be sewn on the left side for women's wear. Mark each button placement carefully so that both sides of the blouse will align when buttoned. If you do not have a professional button-sewing machine, you may follow the steps below to use a zigzag machine to apply two- or four- hole buttons. You must be able to lower the feed teeth on your machine and have a button-sewing foot to hold the buttons in place while stitching. For each garment, you should stitch a sample to check the settings for the stitch width with your particular button.

1. Mark the locations of your button placement. An easy way to do this is to pin the right button band over the left, taking care to align the edges accurately.
2. Using a fabric-marking pen or pencil, make a mark in the center of each buttonhole.
3. Place the fabric on the bed of the machine with the mark centered under the foot. Place the button under the foot on top of the mark. Set your stitch length to 0 and your stitch width to 3.
4. Carefully lower the needle by hand to make sure the button is aligned properly, and then continue stitching to complete at least four cycles of stitching through both holes.
5. For a quick finish, set the stitch width to 0 and then stitch a few stitches into one hole of the button. Clip the threads close to the button. This finish imitates what a commercial button-sewing machine would do.
6. Use the following technique for a more expensive finish that eliminates the frustration of buttons that drop off after one wearing. Pull out at least 6 inches of thread before cutting. Pull the needle thread down to the back of the fabric, tie in an overhand knot, and bury the ends between the fabric layers.

SEWING THE SIDE SEAMS

Before hemming the blouse, you must sew the side seams. If you are setting in a sleeve, as in this blouse, you will need to sew the side seam first. If you are attaching a sleeve flat to a dropped armhole, as in the jacket in Chapter 7, you will apply the sleeve first and then sew the underarm and side seams together.

There are several options here for stitch and seam type. Which one you use depends on your fabric, the level of quality your customer and brand image require, the retail price point of your blouse, and what type of machinery you have available to you. Options for the side seam of your blouse are listed below, with their stitch and seam notations and their pros and cons.

> **French seam—seam type SSae, stitch type 301:** Has a high-quality look and creates a terrific finish on sheer fabrics but is labor-intensive
> **Lap seam (also known as** *single-needle tailoring*)**—seam type LSc-1 or LSc-2, stitch type 301 or 401:** Traditional look, viewed as high quality, and quick to execute with the right attachments
> **Mock lap seam—seam type LSq-2, stitch types 516 and 301 or 401:** Quick to execute and can be seen as poorer quality but appears at many price points
> **Overlocked seam—seam type SSa-1, stitch type 516:** Very quick, has an image of low quality, seen in moderate to category-killer price points.

HEMMING

If you are setting in a sleeve, you will create the hem before setting in the sleeve. If you are adding a sleeve to a dropped-shoulder look, then the hem is done after the sleeve.

A rolled hem by machine or by hand is the basic hem for a blouse that results in the least amount of bulk when tucking it in, as described in Chapter 4 (seam type EFb-1). The usual hem width using a rolled hem foot is ¼ inch. You may also overlock the lower edge of the blouse and then topstitch through it with stitch type 301 or 401.

This takes less fabric but is seen as a lower-quality finish. It may also have a tendency on curved edges to flip toward the outside of the garment.

PREPARING THE SLEEVE

In the fashion-manufacturing process, sleeves are prepared at the same time as bodices on a separate line or by separate operators in a lean manufacturing pod. That way, the bodice and the sleeve are completed at the same time so that they can be attached quickly.

The sleeve in this chapter is called a *set-in sleeve*, because the armhole is formed first. The underarm seam is sewn, and then the cuff is added to the sleeve. The circle of the sleeve head is attached to the armhole. Chapter 7 contains instructions for a drop-shoulder sleeve application.

Most sleeves for women's woven fabric blouses will contain a placket of some kind to finish the opening that allows the hand to get through, to secure the cuff tightly around the wrist to achieve a blousing effect, and to prevent the sleeve from falling down. There are many different types of plackets to use; some are more expensive to make, because they use more fabrics and more steps. In this section of the chapter, we will make a simple lap placket. A more complex, tailored placket often found in men's dress shirts is included in Chapter 7.

Lap Placket

A lap placket uses a slim strip of fabric, often cut on the bias to finish the edge of a slit in the back of the sleeve. The slit averages around 3 inches in length. The strip should be at least 1¼ inches wide and twice the length of the slit plus an extra inch or two for ease of application. In the industry, this slit would be bound with a binder attachment on a lockstitch machine. The precut binding strip would be applied from a continuous length on a roll, so just the right amount would be used to avoid expensive waste. We will imitate that application with the following steps.

1. With the sleeve flat and face-side up, place the face-side of the strip down on the fabric, centering it on the slit. Using a ¼-inch seam allowance, stitch the strip to the slit's edge (ASTM stitch type 301, seam type BSg or BSo), pulling the slit's sides into a straight line and maneuvering the edges so that they stay even with the strip's straight edge. Note that at the middle point of the slit, the sleeve fabric will form a fold. Make sure not to stitch this fold into the seam. You can accomplish this by stitching almost to the point, putting your needle down, and then moving the fold behind the needle (Figure 6.13).
2. Press the strip away from the sleeve, and then press the unsewn edge under so that it touches the edges of the other seam allowance (Figure 6.14).
3. Fold the pressed edge over the first seam line and pin.
4. Turn the fabric over and stitch in the ditch where the lap meets the sleeve, taking care to catch the lower fold. Press the strip.
5. From the back side of the fabric, fold the strip in half at the midpoint, making sure that both sides of the strip are lined

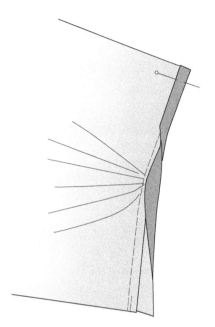

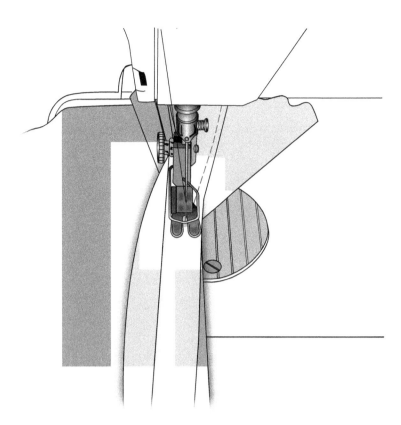

up. Sew a diagonal line of stitching from the seam to the fold. This bit of stitching keeps the lap from showing on the outside of the sleeve (Figure 6.15).

6. In preparation for sewing on the cuff, fold the end of the lap toward the front of the sleeve under to the inside of the sleeve (see Figure 6.15). Pin it temporarily. When you are attaching the cuff, the other end of the lap will extend out to the cuff's end. Before adding the cuff, you must also prepare the end of the sleeve by creating any pleats, darts, gathers, or other shaping.

Cuff

A blouse cuff is another area where having the right specialized machine on the factory floor cuts a many-stepped process down to something that takes a few minutes. However, without that machine, you can use the following steps to achieve a high-quality result. You should have two cuff pieces for each sleeve.

1. Interlining should be applied to one side of the cuff.
2. On the side that is interlined, press under the seam allowance and stitch it

down to the cuff through the middle of the allowance (ASTM stitch type 301; Figure 6.16).

3. Place the cuff's face-sides together and stitch around the outer edges and side (ASTM stitch type 301, seam type SSa-1; see Figure 6.16). Trim the corners off if necessary, and then turn the cuff face-side out.

FIGURE 6.13 (right) Sewing the strip to the slit in a lap placket.

FIGURE 6.14 (left) Pressing the strip before sewing the other side.

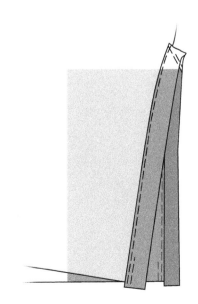

FIGURE 6.15 Diagonal stitching at the point of the lap.

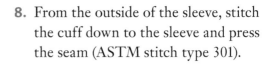

TIP | Tips on easing

Easing occurs when a slightly longer layer is reduced in length to fit a shorter layer. Easing may appear at the sleeve cap, the waist of a pair of pants or a skirt, or under the bust area for the purposes of shaping. Use the same technique to achieve easing as with gathering; however, less fullness is pulled in than for gathering, so no visible "gathers" should appear on the fabric, either inside or outside the seam line. If gathers appear, then the easing has not been apportioned properly—too much fabric has been left in one spot, so it should be spread out over a larger area.

4. Press the cuff, making sure that the seam line remains on the edge of the cuff.
5. Place the cuff with the uninterlined side facedown on the back side (inside) of the sleeve, making sure that the seam allowance edges are even along the sleeve's bottom and that the lap ends are inside the cuff's edge (Figure 6.17). Sew across the cuff (ASTM stitch type 301, seam type SSa-1).
6. Press the cuff away from the sleeve, pressing the seam allowance toward the cuff.
7. Pin the interlined side of the cuff down over the seam allowance and previous line of stitching on the outside of the sleeve.

FIGURE 6.16 (left)
Stitching the cuff.

FIGURE 6.17 (right)
Sewing the cuff to the end of the sleeve.

8. From the outside of the sleeve, stitch the cuff down to the sleeve and press the seam (ASTM stitch type 301).

Set-in Sleeve Insertion

Fullness exists at the cap of a set-in sleeve, because the shoulder and arm need it to be able to move comfortably. The fullness amount can range from just enough for comfort to huge extensions. This fullness needs to be taken in somehow so you can connect the sleeve to the armhole. A variety of techniques can be used to do this, including gathering, pleating, and pin-tucking. Gathering is the most common method and may range in amount from easing to a full-blown puff.

The gathering is there to accommodate the shape of the shoulder, which is softly and shallowly sloped in the back and sharply curved in at the front. No fullness is needed below the slope of the back and the ball of the shoulder joint in front, so the sleeve should be flat there. A basic set-in sleeve without a pronounced puff should have a bit more fullness in the front than in the back to match the body's shape. The seam between the armhole and the sleeve head can be sewn with many

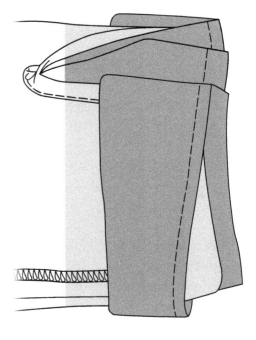

different combinations. Some of the most popular are the following:

- Seam type SSa-1 with seam type BSc, also known as a *Hong Kong finish* (see Chapter 3 for instructions); high to moderate price point, more labor-intensive
- Seam type SSA-2 with stitch type 301 or 401 and an overlock finish, stitch type 504; requires two passes through the machines but may be perceived as cheap; bridge to budget price point
- Seam type SSA-1 with stitch type 516; very inexpensive to manufacture, as it requires only one pass but may be perceived as being cheap; better to category-killer price point
- Seam type LSq-2, stitch types 516 and 301 or 401; used to make a mock lap seam; better quality but the overlocking still shows

1. At this point, the underarm seam should be sewn and the cuff application or hem completed.
2. Use the same gathering technique that is described in Chapter 4 to prepare the sleeve head for insertion into the armhole.
3. Turn the bodice inside out and the sleeve face-side out.
4. Insert the sleeve into the armhole, making sure to match the markings for the back of the sleeve to the back of the bodice and to match the front markings to the front of the bodice. Pin the center of the sleeve head to the shoulder seam, and pin the underarm seam of the sleeve to the side seam of the bodice.
5. Pin upward toward the sleeve head, keeping the fabric of the sleeve flat below the slope of the shoulder and keeping the edges of the seam allowances on the bodice and sleeve even (Figure 6.18).
6. At the top of the sleeve, pull the gathering threads to place the fullness carefully to suit the shape your garment requires (a little easing or a large puff, etc.), and pin in place. For a lot of fullness, as in a puff sleeve, make sure that the fullness is evenly apportioned over the top of the sleeve (see Figure 6.18).
7. Place the sleeve under the presser foot so that the sleeve is on top. Sew the sleeve into the armhole using the method you have chosen, taking care to not stitch unwanted parts of the sleeve into the seam (Figure 6.19). Be sure to sew over where you started the machine and back tack if needed.

FIGURE 6.18 (left) Pinning the sleeve into the armhole.

FIGURE 6.19 (right) Sewing the sleeve into the armhole.

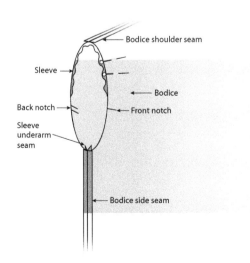

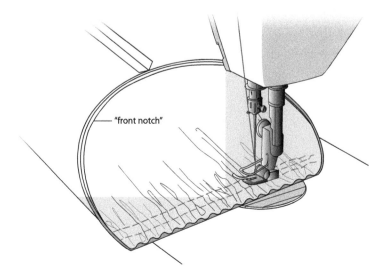

LADIES' FASHION JACKET CONSTRUCTION

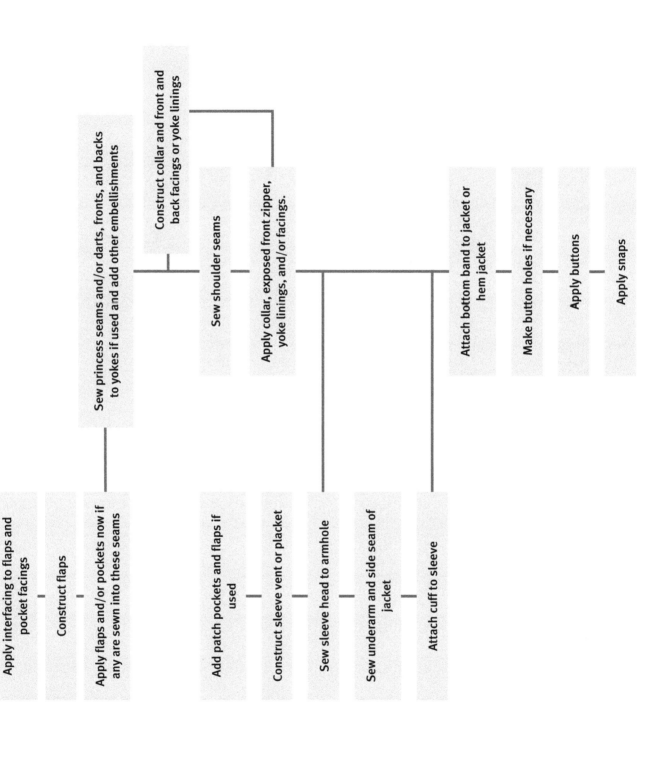

Apply interfacing to flaps and pocket facings

Construct flaps

Apply flaps and/or pockets now if any are sewn into these seams

Sew princess seams and/or darts, fronts, and backs to yokes if used and add other embellishments

Construct collar and front and back facings or yoke linings

Sew shoulder seams

Apply collar, exposed front zipper, yoke linings, and/or facings.

Add patch pockets and flaps if used

Construct sleeve vent or placket

Sew sleeve head to armhole

Sew underarm and side seam of jacket

Attach cuff to sleeve

Attach bottom band to jacket or hem jacket

Make button holes if necessary

Apply buttons

Apply snaps

Fashion Jacket

A sporty jacket is the perfect accessory to throw on when heading out for a weekend getaway on a cool spring morning or to dinner at the corner restaurant on a weekday evening. A great jacket can be dressed up or down and makes a versatile layering piece.

In this chapter, you will find

- a convertible collar;
- an inverted patch pocket with a flap;
- a centered, separating zipper;
- a drop sleeve;
- a tailored sleeve placket; and
- a jacket waistband.

This chapter, plus the content in Chapter 6, "Ladies' Blouse," can help customize your design. A lap seam is standard for many of the seams in this jacket style. They can be found in Chapter 3 as ASTM seam type LSc-1 using ASTM stitch type 301 or 401. A very common variation on this seam is ASTM seam type LSbm-2, which uses ASTM stitch type 516 and 301 or 401.

back would be LSbp-2, in which both layers of the yoke are joined to the jacket back simultaneously using stitch type 301 or 401. The same stitch is used for a line of topstitching after the seam is pressed. Our version is below.

1. Lay down one section of the yoke back face-side up. Lay the lower section of the shirt back face-side down on top and the second section of the yoke face-side down on top of the back. Make sure all the seam allowances are even. Stitch all sections together using stitch type 301 or 401 and seam type LSbp-2.
2. Press the seam, pulling the outer yoke section away from the lower back, and topstitch through all three layers. Press the inner yoke section over the seam (Figure 7.1).

YOKES

Jacket Back

A traditional shirt and jacket back will include a yoke section, which is self-lined. At the factory, the seam type used to connect the yoke to the bottom of the jacket

Jacket Front

Patch Pocket with Flap

For our jacket front, we are adding a patch pocket style that is commonly seen on jean jackets but can be added to any

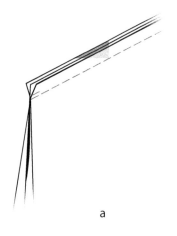

FIGURE 7.1 Placement of sections and seaming of back yoke.

a

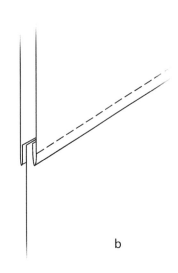

FIGURE 7.2 Pieces of a front yoke pocket.

b

garment with a front yoke; with slight adjustments, it can also be added to any other seam, such as a princess seam or side seam on a jacket or even a yoke on a skirt. The pocket and flap are added to the front before the yoke is sewn on. The pieces of this application are pictured in Figure 7.2.

1. Snip the lower jacket front at the pocket facing section down to the seam line.
2. Place the pocket facing face-side down on the face of the jacket's lower front, between the snips. Stitch the pocket facing to the top edge of the lower jacket front from snip to snip (ASTM stitch type 301, seam type SSa-1). Press the seam allowances and the facing up away from the jacket; then fold the facing to the inside of the pocket and press again, making sure the seam is at the edge of the pocket. Topstitch the top of the facing (Figure 7.3).
3. Place the flap pieces face-sides together and stitch the sides and across the end (ASTM stitch type 301,

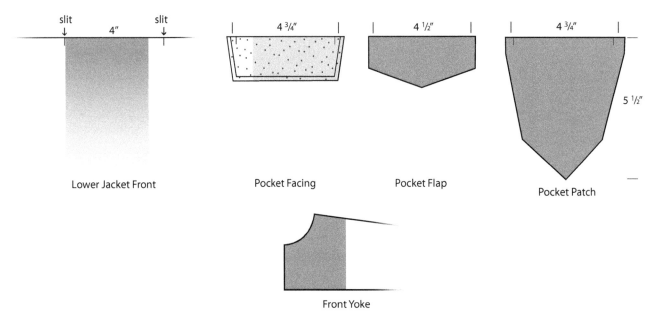

slit   4″   slit

Lower Jacket Front

4 ³/₄″

Pocket Facing

4 ¹/₂″

Pocket Flap

4 ³/₄″

5 ¹/₂″

Pocket Patch

Front Yoke

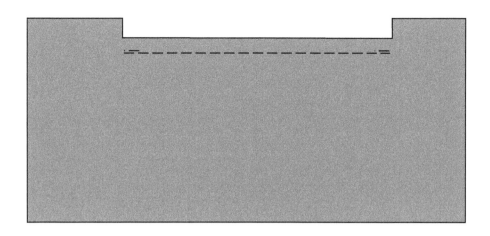

FIGURE 7.3 Creating the pocket facing.

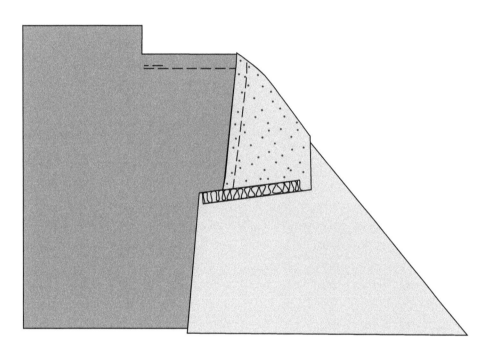

seam type SSa-1). Turn face-side out and press, making sure that the seam is at the edge. Topstitch one or two rows around the sewn edges of the flap.

4. The machine makes a buttonhole at the center of the flap at least ½ inch of the button width up from the point.

ALTERNATIVE DECORATIVE SEAM FINISH

A Hong Kong finish can be a decorative addition to casual, unlined jackets. The binding fabric can be made to coordinate with the pocket; with the inside layers of cuffs or collars; with sleeve linings if those are part of the jacket; or with other garments in a line such as blouses or pants. For a quicker, lower-cost alternative, finish both layers of the seam together with one Hong Kong binding. Topstitch through the seam allowances and the jacket just to the inside of the binding to add an extra design detail to the outside of the jacket.

FIGURE 7.4 Position-
ing the pocket flap on
the yoke and finishing
the edges.

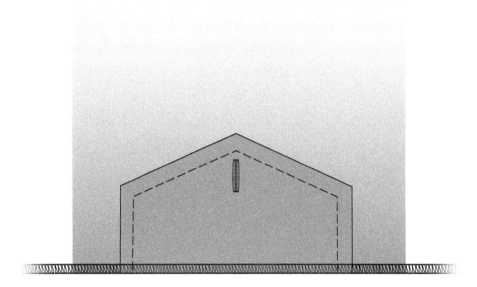

5. Place the flap face-side down on the front yoke at the pocket position, and pin in place. Overlock the pocket flap to the bottom edge of the yoke while finishing the edge using stitch type 504 (Figure 7.4).
6. Overlock all four edges of the pocket patch (ASTM stitch type 503 or 504).
7. Position the pocket patch face-side up under the jacket's lower front, between the clips. The face of the pocket patch will be against the back of the jacket

FIGURE 7.5 Position-
ing and sewing the
pocket patch onto the
lower front.

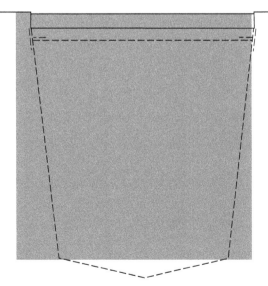

fabric. The top of the pocket patch should be even with the seam allowance of the jacket front. Pin in place if necessary (Figure 7.5).
8. Topstitch through the jacket front and pocket patch (see Figure 7.5).
9. Place the yoke face-side down on the jacket's lower front, making sure all of the seam allowances are even. Check that the pocket flap is lined up with the faced pocket opening and that the flap is extending down over the pocket opening. Finally, check that the faced opening is out of the way of the seam so that you won't sew the pocket closed by mistake.
10. Stitch across the seam using stitch type 301 or 401. Press the seam allowances up toward the yoke.
11. From the face of the fabric, stitch another row of stitch type 301 through the seam allowances.
12. Sew a bar tack or a short section of straight stitching at the upper corners of the pocket on the lower front just below the seam line to reinforce this area (Figure 7.6).

CONVERTIBLE COLLAR

The name *convertible collar* describes the ability of this garment part to either lie flat against the shoulders or flip up around the neck. This collar has no stand, so it is a simple, easy-to-create neck treatment. This collar may extend to the edge of the jacket front or may end an inch or two from the edge on each side for a lapel effect. It can be applied with or without a neck facing. When applied with a back neck facing, the seam allowance could be as little as ¼ inch. If there is no back neck facing, the seam allowance on the collar should be at least ½ inch to allow it to finish the neck edge. If you have only a front facing, it will extend just to the shoulder line. We explain both treatments.

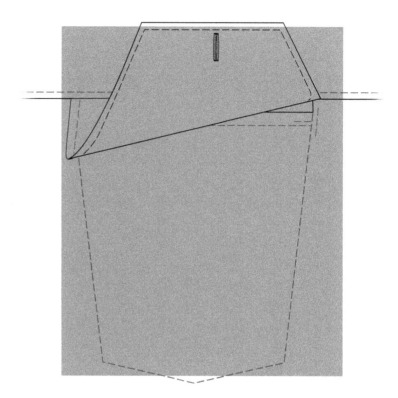

1. Sew the shoulder seams of the jacket (and the yoke lining if there is one; stitch type 301, seam type SSa-1).
2. Apply interlining to one of the collar pieces.
3. Place the collar pieces face-sides together and pin if necessary. Stitch the collar pieces together as follows:
   - Sew across one end, back tacking at both ends
   - Turn the collar and sew across the outer edge, back tacking at both ends
   - Sew across the other end, back tacking at both ends

   Press the seam to one side as far into the corner as possible before turning the collar face-side out. An ironing board with a point-pressing end will help with this maneuver.
4. Turn the collar face-side out, taking care at the corners, and re-press the collar with the stitching line at the edge.

5. Stay stitch the neck edge of the jacket in the seam allowance.
6. Center the collar with the non-interlined side down on the face of the jacket fabric. There are instructions below for either using or not using a back neck facing. Follow the instruction that applies to you.

FIGURE 7.6 The finished pocket.

Back Neck Facing

1. Pin both sides of the collar to the neck edge, making sure that the collar and neck edges stay even. You may need to clip the neck edge to the stay stitching so that it can meet the collar.

No Back Neck Facing

1. Clip the interlined edge of the collar at the shoulder line.
2. Pin the noninterlined edge and both edges from the shoulder line to the end of the collar to the neck of the

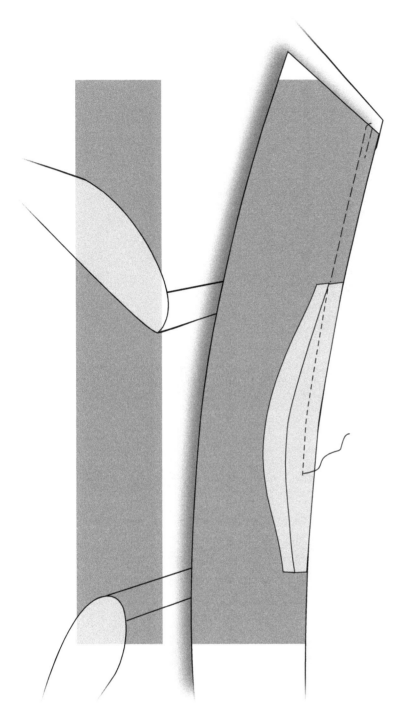

This stiffness can help the bodice lie in a more flattering way and can provide a stabilized area for a closure, such as a buttonhole. The lower ends of the front facings will be finished by the jacket hem. Facings are meant to be inconspicuous but can serve as an interesting surprise when the interior of the bodice is seen. The seam between the facing and the garment is also a great place to apply piping. Chapter 4, "Basic Straight Skirt"; Chapter 8, "Tailored Jacket"; and Chapter 10, "Ladies' Jumper with All-in-One Facing" also contain information on facings. As with those garments, you should make a bodice facing that is shaped appropriately for the curves of the edges and that is wide enough to prevent it from creeping to the outside. Understitching and topstitching help prevent this.

1. Apply interlining to the back sides of both facings.
2. Continue following the instructions below for a back neck facing or a front facing only.

With a Collar
Back Neck Facing

1. With face-sides together, stitch the ends of the front facings to the ends of the back facing at the shoulder seam (ASTM stitch type 301, seam type SSa-1; Figure 7.8). Press the seams open.
2. Finish the edges of the facing using one of the seam/edge-finishing methods in Chapter 3. Using a contrast fabric in a Hong Kong finish makes an attractive addition here.
3. Face-sides together, pin the facings to the front and back neck edges, covering the collar and keeping all the edges even (Figure 7.9). Stitch.

jacket. Take care not to attach the interlined edge between the clips to the neck (Figure 7.7).

FRONT FACING

A front facing on a jacket or blouse is another way to finish the front edges of the garment while adding body to the area.

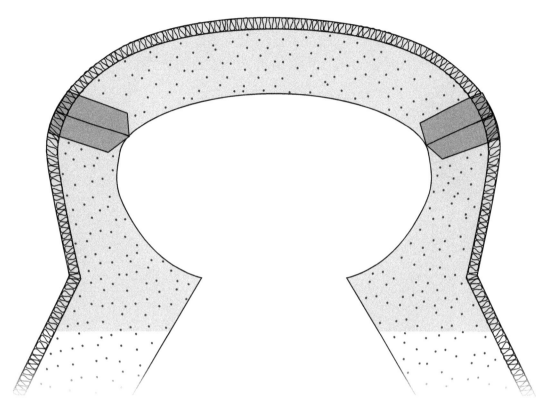

FIGURE 7.8 Stitching the facings together.

4. Press the seam to one side using a seam-roll or point-pressing board to support the fabric; then press from the facing on the outside, making sure that the facing stays inside the garment.

5. Understitch the facing to the seam allowances or topstitch the entire facing.

6. Topstitch the collar edges, starting and ending at the facing seam.

No Back Neck Facing

1. Finish the shoulder ends and outer edges of the facing (ASTM stitch type 504 or 504). Note: If you are applying a zipper to the front of the jacket, do so before applying the facing. Information about this is included later in this chapter.

2. Pin the facing to the front edge of the jacket over the collar ends to the snip at the shoulder line. Stitch the facing to the neck edge (seam type 301).

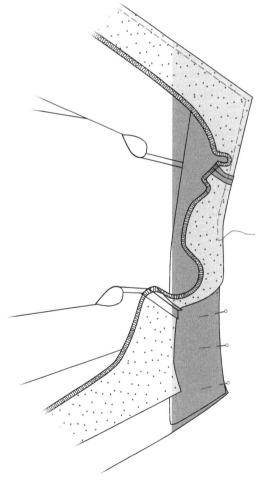

FIGURE 7.9 Attaching a front and back facing to the neck.

FIGURE 7.10 (left)
Stitching the facing to
the jacket front with
no back facing.

FIGURE 7.11 (right)
Sewing the collar to
the back neck edge.

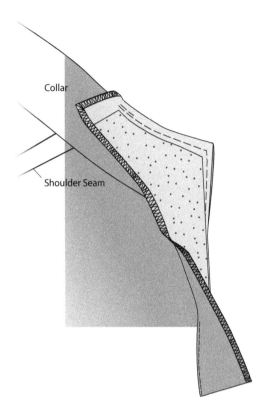

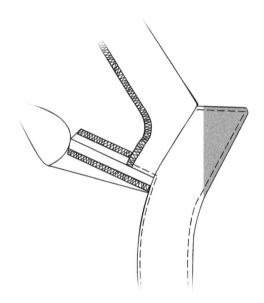

3. Press the seam to one side and then on the outside of the garment; press the facing so that it remains inside the front. Understitch or topstitch the facing (Figure 7.10).
4. At the back neck edge, fold the seam allowance of the collar under to the inside of the collar so that the fold covers the seam line. Pin if necessary, and then stitch in the ditch between the collar and the neck edge to secure the fold (Figure 7.11).
5. Topstitch the collar edges.

CENTERED ZIPPER APPLICATION

This application works for a separating zipper in any style of jacket with or without a lining attached to the facing. Prepare the garment pieces up to the point of adding the facing before applying the zipper.

1. Place the zipper face-side down on each half of the front, making sure that the edges of the zipper tape are even with the seam allowance of the jacket front edge. Fold over the top of the zipper tape diagonally so that the end will be concealed in the seam. Also, make sure that the bottom end of the zipper is at least ½ inch above the bottom edge of the jacket front so that you do not have to sew through the hard plastic or metal (Figure 7.12). Pin in place.
2. Place the jacket facings face-side down over the zipper and pin in place. Also pin the back neck facing if there is one (Figure 7.13.)
3. Stitch the facing and zipper to the jacket front (ASTM stitch type 301), taking care to sew consistently in the middle of the zipper tape. If you sew too far away, too much of the zipper tape will show. If you sew too closely,

TIP | Look in the Appendix for sources of basic zipper styles and lengths, custom-made zippers in your color at your length, and specialty zippers such as those with rhinestone teeth.

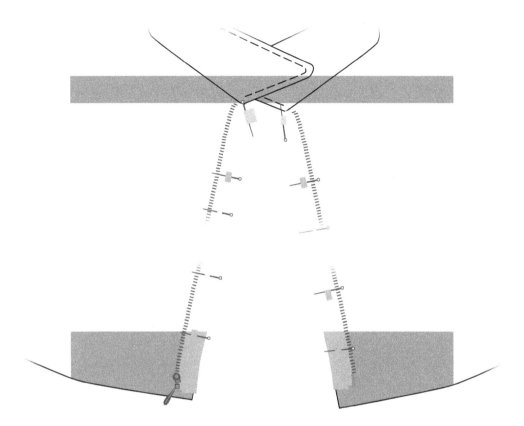

FIGURE 7.12 Placing the seperating zipper on the jacket front.

the pull will get stuck on the fabric. Turn the facing to the inside of the jacket, and press the seam from the inside (Figure 7.13). You may tug

gently on the zipper teeth to avoid pressing in an unnecessary fold. Note: The bottom of the zipper seam will be finished when the jacket is hemmed.

FIGURE 7.13 Placing and sewing the front facing over the zipper and pressing the seam.

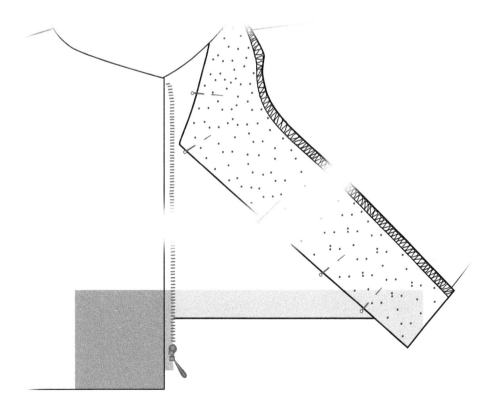

TAILORED SLEEVE PLACKET

As mentioned in Chapter 6, "Ladies' Blouse," the jacket sleeve is completed before applying it to the jacket. Part of that process is to construct a placket to allow easy entry and to pull in the sleeve at the wrist. A tailored placket, which is frequently seen on men's long-sleeve dress shirts, makes an attractive treatment for many tailored styles and gives the garment a higher-quality look. It requires more fabric; more interlining; and more cutting, fusing, and sewing time than most other sleeve plackets, so it is seen mostly in moderate to designer signature brands. It still binds a slash starting at the sleeve end, but the slash is usually longer, necessitating the addition of a button along the placket, which adds still more expense and time to production. Of course, there are specialized machines that accomplish this task in just a few minutes. The placket can be constructed with one finishing piece for both sides of the slit or with two pieces, one for each side, and should be completed before the underarm seam is sewn, no matter the sleeve style. The underlap placket piece should be at least 1¾ inches wide (this will produce a 3/8-inch-wide placket). The length should be the length of the slit plus ½-inch seam allowance to finish the upper end of the placket.

After drafting and cutting out your placket pieces, follow the instructions below to attach them to the sleeves. The pieces of a two-piece tailored placket are shown in Figure 7.14.

1. Apply interlining to the back side of the overlap placket piece.

FIGURE 7.14 The garment pieces needed to sew a tailored sleeve placket.

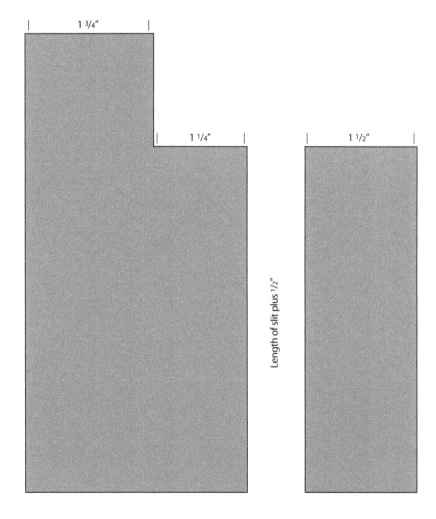

1 3/4"

1 1/4"

1 1/2"

Length of slit plus 1/2"

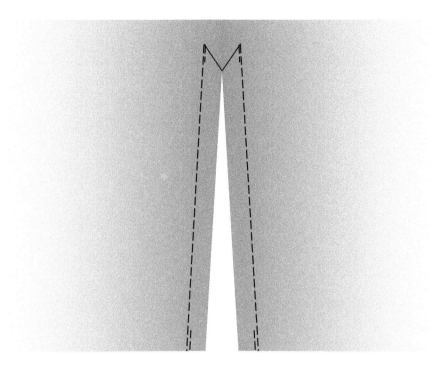

FIGURE 7.15 Beginning the lap attachment process.

2. Cut the slash in the back of the sleeve.

3. Place the overlap and the underlap pieces face-side down on the *back* of the sleeve, aligning the sides of the placket with the slit. Make sure that the overlap placket piece is on the front of the sleeve and that the narrower underlap placket is on the side of the slit closest to the underarm seam (Figure 7.15). Stitch both using a ¼-inch seam allowance, ending ¼ inch above the end of the slit with back tacking (ASTM stitch type 301).

4. Make two tiny clips from the end of the slit to the ends of the stitching, as seen in Figure 7.15.

5. Attach the underlap placket, as explained in Chapter 6 in the section on lap seam sleeve plackets, using a 3/8-inch seam allowance. Stitch only to the end of the clip. When completed, the underlap will extend beyond the slit, as seen in Figure 7.16.

6. Fold the overlap around to the face of the sleeve, folding under ¼ inch for a seam allowance; make this fold even with the fold on the inside of the sleeve. Pin if necessary. Edge stitch the fold to the sleeve, sewing through all layers and ending the stitching even with the top of the

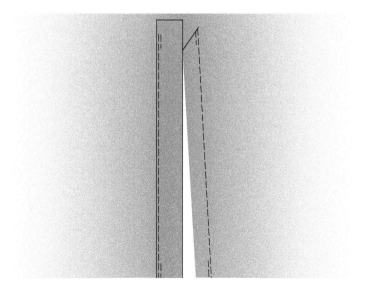

FIGURE 7.16 Finishing the underlap on the sleeve placket.

FIGURE 7.17 Sewing the overlap.

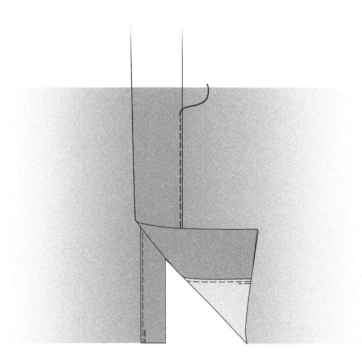

stitching on the underlap. Do not back tack (Figure 7.17).

7. Arrange the underlap so that the edge is vertical and that the loose end slips above the clips between the overlap and the sleeve.

8. Traditionally, the top of the overlap is pointed. If you want a straight end, fold the end of the overlap under between the sleeve and the overlap. If your design calls for a pointed end, you must fold the fabric in, as seen in Figure 7.18.

FIGURE 7.18 Finishing the overlap.

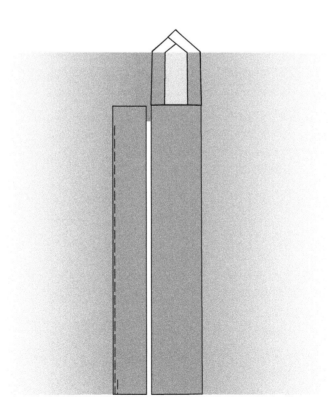

9. Starting a few stitches into the end of the previous stitching, topstitch around the point of the overlap and then down the other side and across the area where the slit ended (Figure 7.19). The stitching should capture the end of the underlap.
10. An extra row of topstitching is optional on the outer fold of the overlap. Note: For a drop-sleeve application, do not sew the underarm seam.

◇◇

DROP-SLEEVE APPLICATION

The drop-shoulder style originated with the looser, more relaxed fit of the early 1980s. It requires that the garment's shoulder seam is extended beyond the ball of the shoulder joint down over the arm, which flattens out the armhole. Also, the length of the armhole is extended down the side of the garment. Therefore, no peaked sleeve cap is needed to allow movement of the arm. The sleeve head will be flattened so that it is almost or exactly straight across. A dropped shoulder is most frequently used in knit casual wear but can also appear in woven blouses, overcoats, and jackets.

1. Prepare the jacket front and back, leaving the side seams and bottom treatment (hem, waistband, etc.) undone.
2. Turn the jacket face-side up, center the sleeve over the shoulder seam, and pin if necessary (Figure 7.20).
3. Stitch the sleeve to the armhole. Possible seams include those listed below:
   - Seam type SSa-1 with seam type BSc, also known as a Hong Kong finish (see Chapter 3 for instructions); high to moderate price point; more labor-intensive
   - Seam type SSA-2 with stitch type 301 or 401 and an overlock finish, stitch type 504; requires two passes through

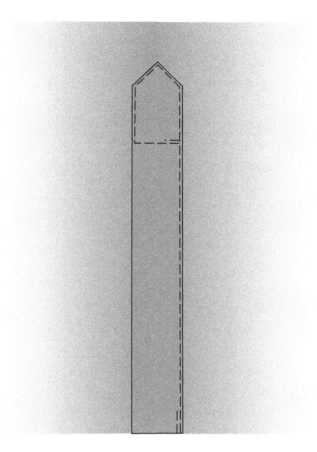

FIGURE 7.19 Stitching the overlap.

the machines but may be perceived as cheap; bridge to budget price point
   - Seam type SSA-1 with stitch type 516; very inexpensive to manufacture, as it only requires one pass but may be perceived as being cheap; better to category-killer price point
   - Seam type LSq-2, stitch types 516 and 301 or 401 to make a mock lap seam; a little better quality but the overlocking still shows
4. Place the bodice and sleeve of the blouse face-sides together, matching the shoulder seams.

FIGURE 7.20 Sewing the sleeve on the jacket.

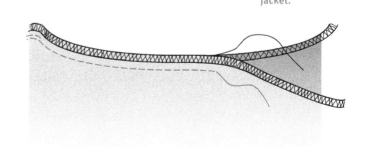

FIGURE 7.21 Stitching the underarm and side seams.

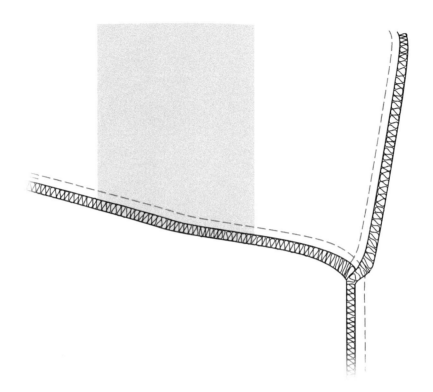

5. Stitch the underarm and side seams, starting at the underarm each time. Any of the seam and stitch combinations mentioned above will create a side/underarm seam as well. On lighterweight fabrics, a French seam, seam type SSae, or seam type SSp also works well and is associated with high-quality construction (Figure 7.21).

Cuff

Prepare and stitch the cuffs to each sleeve using the method described in Chapter 6.

FINISHING THE LOWER EDGE

There are a variety of finishing choices for the lower edge of the jacket. These choices can be combined with a full lining or used on an unlined style. A facing gives a dressier look. It also helps stabilize and add fullness to the edge. A waistband gives more of a casual, jean jacket styling. A basic hem is also used, especially with a lining. That treatment is covered in Chapter 8, "Tailored Jacket."

Facing

The facing at the bottom edge of a jacket should be shaped the same as the edge of the jacket, just like any other facing. The facing for the lower edge on the front of the jacket is usually drafted as part of the front facing. Then there is a seam in the facing at the jacket's side seam where the front facing might connect to the back facing or where the end of the front facing will be covered by the back hem. If the back has its own facing, then the side seams should be sewn before attaching the facing to the jacket. The remainder of the facing application is the same as the facing application in Chapter 4, "Basic Straight Skirt," or in this chapter's section on attaching the front facing.

Waistband

A woven fabric waistband can be just as simple as that: a straight band seated at the waist. It needs no shaping and can consist of one straight band cut on the lengthwise grain that is twice the width of the finished band plus seam allowances. Depending on the jacket style above the band, the jacket

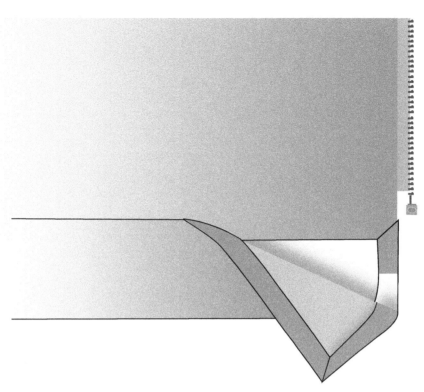

FIGURE 7.22 Positioning the waistband to the jacket.

can have minimal shaping or can be gathered or pleated before the band is applied. The band can have a set of tabs with holed buttons or tack buttons at the side seams to allow a bit of shaping. The application is simple and is described below, along with instructions for a tab. These tabs may also be altered to act as an epaulet or a buttoned tab on the front of a jacket or on a bag.

1. If the band fabric is not stiff enough, add interlining to keep the band from crushing when worn.
2. Press the seam allowances to the inside of the band and press the band in half lengthwise.
3. Enclose the bottom of the jacket in between the layers of the band, pinning if necessary. If you are using a zipper, take care not to enclose the bottom of the zipper in the band (Figure 7.22).
4. Topstitch near the outer edge of the band. Topstitch again just below the first line of stitching. A row of topstitching can also be added at the lower folded edge.

5. To add a tab, follow the steps below:
   - Cut four tab pieces.
   - Face-sides together, stitch two of the tab pieces together as shown, then turn face side out. Repeat for the other 2 tab pieces (Figure 7.23).

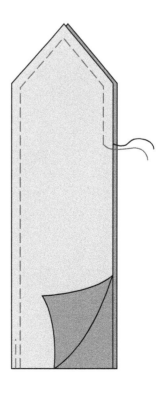

FIGURE 7.23 Stitching the tabs.

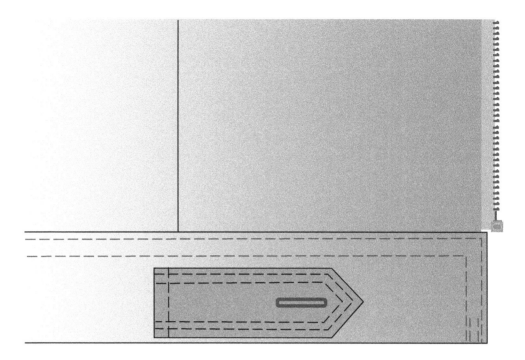

- Topstitch the tabs and add buttonholes.
- Center the tabs vertically on the waistband at the side seam (Figure 7.24).
- The tab end should point toward the front of the jacket. We will use ASTM stitch type 301 and seam type LSbl-2. Stitch the tab down using a ¼-inch seam allowance.

Trim the seam allowance so that it is slightly less than ¼ inch wide (see Figure 7.24).
- Fold the tab back tightly on the stitching so that it is now pointing toward the back of the jacket, and press.
- Stitch through the band again just beyond the seam allowance to enclose it (Figure 7.25).

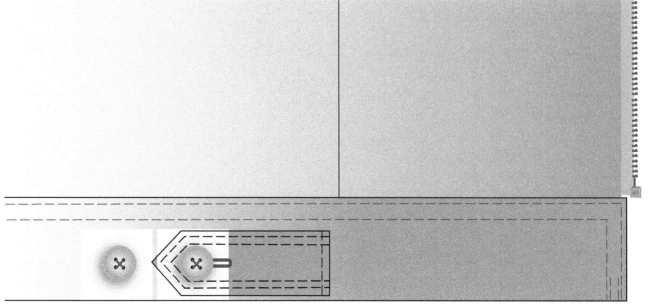

• Add two buttons for each tab, one just under the tab buttonhole and one 2 inches or so away toward the back of the jacket. Buttoning with the second button will allow the wearer to make the waistband smaller (see Figure 7.25).

Hem

The application of a hem should follow the same directions as the straight skirt in Chapter 4.

TAILORED JACKET CONSTRUCTION ORDER

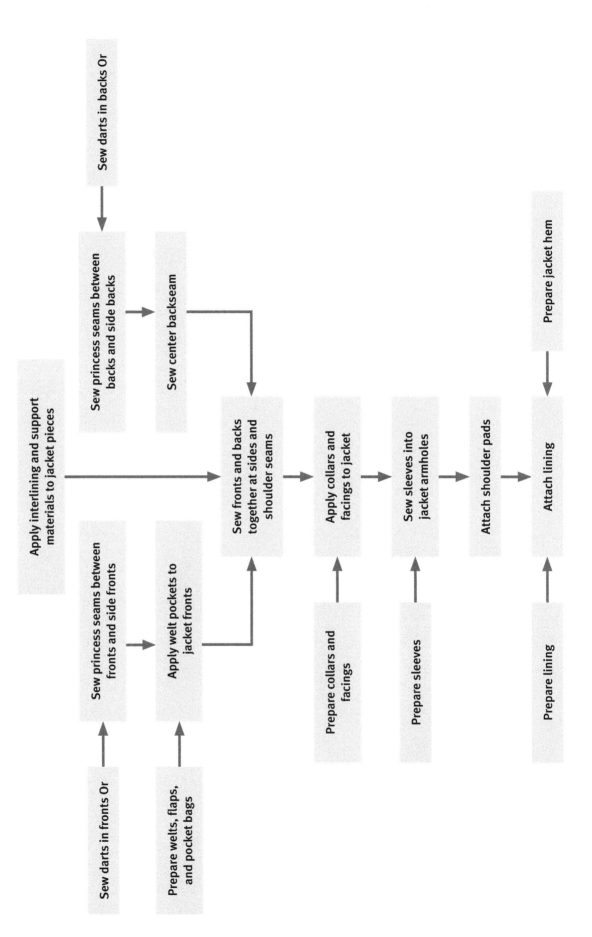

8

Tailored Jacket

◇◇

I n the workplace, a woman uses her suit to present a professional image to those around her whom she wishes to impress and feel comfortable with. A properly fitted, well-constructed, tailored jacket should be seen as an investment when advancing one's career. Many designers prefer to adhere to the basic collar, lapel, one- or two-button

front jacket. But women whose careers are in such fields as the performing and visual arts, nonprofits, publishing, and marketing long to find alternatives to the basic styles waiting for them on the racks of their favorite designers. These styles contain unique silhouettes, fabrics, and construction details to attract and maintain a loyal customer base that finds a kinship with an alternative fashion voice. This chapter contains instructions on constructing a basic, tailored jacket with

- a collar and lapel,
- a single-welt pocket,
- a double-welt pocket,
- a welt pocket with a flap,
- a two-piece sleeve with a vent,
- a corded buttonhole, and
- a machine-set lining using predominant ready-to-wear machine techniques.

This chapter will also show you how to apply sleeve heads and shoulder pads and how to sew on a shank button.

◇◇

INDUSTRIAL METHODS FOR JACKET INTERFACING APPLICATION

As discussed in Chapter 2, "Garment Manufacturing Materials," interlinings can be separated into two groups: those that need to be sewn in and those that can be fused to the back of the fabric with heat, pressure, and moisture. Tailored fashions depend on interlinings to give the fabric the stiffness to stand away from the body. Interlinings for tailored jackets range from sew-in hair canvas to lightweight knit fusible. They may be layered or overlapped to provide just the right amount of body for a certain area of the jacket, such as the upper back or the area around a welt pocket at the hipline. Choosing the right product is crucial to the salability and longevity of the garment and is obviously crucial to consumer satisfaction and brand-image maintenance. An "Interlining Types and Uses" table is located in the Appendix, will help you make the correct choices.

There are many good resources on the hand application of interlinings, stay tape, shoulder pads, and so on, for tailored garments. However, this type of handwork is relegated to couture or very high-end custom apparel because of the extreme amount of time that it takes to complete a jacket using these methods. Custom apparel and designer signature ready-to-wear feature machine techniques for applying these foundation materials and many fusible interlinings to save time and money during production. Although there is no equal to the feel of a hand-made suit jacket, few consumers could or would want to make the kind of investment necessary to have a hand-tailored jacket fitted and then made. Some may opt for a fairly recent solution known as *demicouture*. This level of make involves some individual measurements, resulting in a customized garment but employing machine techniques like those used in standard ready-to-wear.

The construction order and methods described in this chapter, as in all of the chapters, follows as closely as possible the speediest order and methods that could be used at the factory to construct a lady's tailored jacket. However, in this chapter, we must adjust the order a bit to conform to the list of machines presented in Chapter 1. For instance, lining sleeves can be attached to the jacket sleeve at the armhole by using a specialized sleeve-setting machine before the lining is attached to the end of the jacket sleeve. Our sewing order calls for the jacket and lining sleeves to be joined before the lining is tacked to the jacket armhole.

Application of Nonfusibles

Nonfusible interlinings are applied using a felling machine (also known as a *blind-stitch machine*; see Figure 1.3). When the fashion fabric, back-side up, and the interlining are passed through the machine, the stitch just catches the back side of the fabric while sewing through the interlining, securing the two together. Multiple layers of interlining and stay tapes at a roll line can be applied in the same way.

Application of Fusibles

Fusible interlining, as explained in Chapter 2, is fused to the back of the fabric. Interlining may be fused to a block of fabric before garment pieces are cut or before the interlining is cut to the appropriate shapes for the areas where it is applied. Those areas include the jacket front and shield area; upper back; collar and collar stand; lapels; front facings and back facing if used; pocket welts, flaps, and placement areas; sleeve vents; hem; and back vent.

The application of all these pieces will be described in the sections on constructing that part of the jacket. Keep in mind that sewing order is governed by the pieces + pieces = parts concept and that parts are completed simultaneously before being assembled into a garment.

WELT POCKETS

Welt pockets are the standard for most tailored jackets and coats, plus they routinely appear on the hips of many pairs of dress pants. A welt is a narrow strip of material that can be cut out of the garment fabric or a contrast material. It adds definition to the pocket and reinforces the edge. Pockets may be constructed with one welt on the bottom edge of the opening, extending upward to cover the pocket, or with two welts, one on each side. A flap may be added to the top of the pocket between the welt and the opening. Pocket openings and their welts may be straight on the vertical or horizontal grain, may be on the bias, or may be curved. Welts may be two separate pieces of fabric or, for a quicker method, may be constructed of one folded piece of fabric. Highly specialized machines in the garment industry will construct a welt pocket in just a few seconds. All the operator need do is place fabric in the proper locations on the machine. The pocket bags can be made of two pieces of fabric, which will need to be sewn together at the bottom, or they can be made of one strip, which will have a fold at the bottom. The single-welt pocket instructions use two pocket pieces; the double welt pocket uses one piece. Lightweight fusible interlining is fused to the jacket front after any darts or princess seams are sewn to help stabilize the area.

This is an especially important step for loosely woven fabrics.

The following directions are for use with a lockstitch sewing machine.

Basic Construction for a Single-Welt Pocket

The pieces of a single-welt pocket are shown in Figure 8.1. They are the welt, the pocket pieces, an underlap, and the jacket front. The drafted pattern should show the length of the pocket opening and the placement of the welt. When finished, this welt should cover the opening.

1. Interface the back side of the welt and the underlap of the fashion fabric with a lightweight fusible interlining.

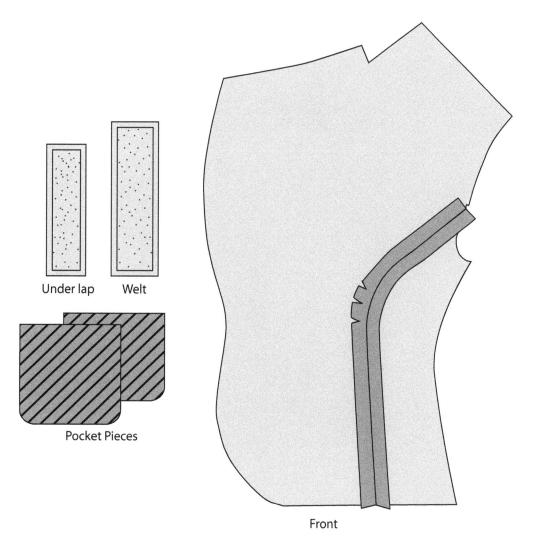

FIGURE 8.1 Pieces of a single welt pocket.

Under lap   Welt

Pocket Pieces

Front

FIGURE 8.2 Sewing the underlap to the pocket lining.

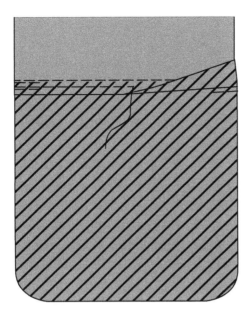

FIGURE 8.2 Sewing the underlap to the pocket lining.

3. If it suits the look of your jacket, edge stitch and/or topstitch the welt.
4. Face-sides together, sew the underlap to one of the lining pieces; then press the seam allowance down toward the lining, and edge stitch through the lining into the seam allowances (Figure 8.2). This underlap of the fashion fabric will create a finished look inside when the pocket is opened.
5. Place the welt on the jacket front, with the basted edge toward the top of the jacket and lined up with the centerline of the pocket.
6. Position the underlap opposite the welt face-side down, lined up with the centerline of the pocket, as shown in Figure 8.3.
7. Stitch across the welt and underlap through the jacket front, following the

2. Fold the welt in half lengthwise and stitch across the ends. Trim the seam carefully (ASTM Stitch type 301). Turn the welt face-side out and press. Baste the open ends together.

FIGURE 8.3 Positioning and sewing the underlap and welt.

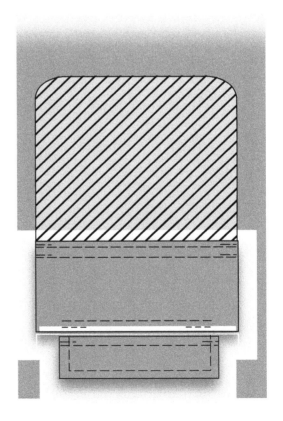

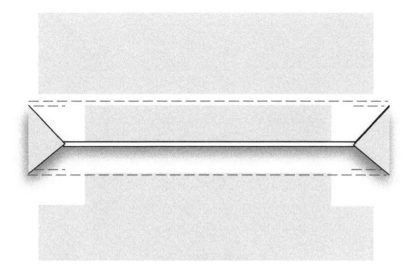

FIGURE 8.4 Clipping the pocket opening.

guidelines from your pattern using a ¼-inch seam allowance (ASTM Stitch type 301). (see Figure 8.3).

8. Carefully cut the centerline of the pocket, and then cut diagonally to the ends of the stitching lines (Figure 8.4).

9. Flip the underlap in through the hole and flip the tiny triangles at the pocket corners out toward the sides of the jacket. Press the welt toward the top of the jacket. Be careful not to stretch the area out of shape while pressing.

10. Position the remaining lining piece back-side down to the inside of the jacket at the bottom welt. Using a ¼-inch seam allowance, stitch the lining piece to the bottom seam allowance of the pocket, keeping the jacket away from the stitching (ASTM Stitch type 301) (see Figure 8.5).

11. Flip back the jacket to expose the outer edges of the underlap/pocket and the triangles on top of the opening ends. Keeping the jacket out

of the way, stitch across the triangles, making sure to catch all the layers as close to the jacket fabric as possible (ASTM Stitch type 301). Bowing in slightly by just a few yarns on this seam can actually make the seam look

FIGURE 8.5 Attaching the other half of the pocket.

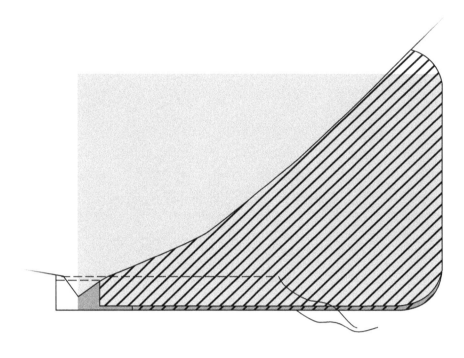

FIGURE 8.6 Stitching the pocket corners and pocket bag.

straighter on the outside of the jacket (Figure 8.6).

12. Stitch around the remainder of the pocket edges (ASTM Stitch type 301). If the jacket is unlined, the pocket edges will need to be overlocked (see Figure 8.6).

13. Finish your single-welt pocket by neatly slip stitching the welt ends to the jacket front. Give the pocket a final press.

Double-Welt Pocket

A double-welt pocket has two welts on either edge of the center slit. The welts are very thin and meet at the center of the pocket opening. The drafted patterns should show the length of the pocket opening and the placement of the welts. The pieces of a double-welt pocket are shown in Figure 8.7. Follow the instructions below for constructing this pocket.

FIGURE 8.7 Pieces of a double welt pocket.

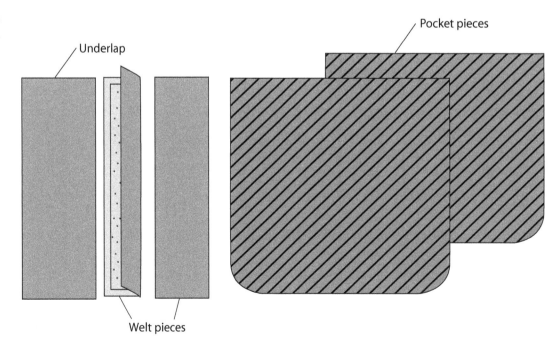

Underlap

Pocket pieces

Welt pieces

1. Fuse interlining to the back side of each welt and to the underlap of the fashion fabric.

2. Press each welt in the lengthwise direction with the interlined sides together. The pressed fold should be ¼ inch from one long edge and ½ inch from the other edge. Baste the cut edges together.

3. Place the welts with the ¼-inch seam allowances edge-down on the face of the fabric, even with the centerline of the pocket (Figure 8.8).

4. Stitch the welts to the jacket front ¼ inch from the center placement line, making sure to stop at the ends of each welt and back tack (ASTM Stitch type 301). (see Figure 8.9).

5. Snip the jacket front only on the centerline. From the insides of the jacket, make two clips at each end toward the ends of the stitching line (Figure 8.9).

6. Turn the pressed edges of the welt to the center of the opening, folding the seam allowances inside. Gently press. Whip stitch the pressed edges of the welts together, making sure they just touch and do not overlap each other.

7. Stitch one end of the lining piece to the ½-inch welt seam allowance on the lower welt, face-sides together, using a ¼-inch seam allowance (ASTM Stitch type 301). Press the seam toward the lining piece.

8. Stitch the fashion fabric underlap to the other end of the lining piece, face-sides together (ASTM Stitch type 301). Press the seam allowance toward the lining.

9. Stitch the other edge of the underlap to the ½-inch seam allowance on the upper welt, face-sides together, using a ¼-inch seam allowance (ASTM Stitch type 301). Press the seam up

toward the top of the jacket so that the underlap is hanging down over the pocket opening. Pin the sides of the pocket together.

10. Flip back the jacket to expose the outer edges of the underlap/pocket and the triangles on top of the opening ends. Keeping the jacket out of the way, stitch across the triangles, making sure to catch all the layers as close to the jacket fabric as possible (ASTM Stitch type 301). Bowing in slightly by just a few yarns on this seam can actually make the seam look

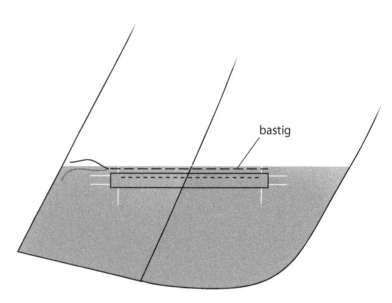

bastig

FIGURE 8.8 Marking the jacket front for welt placement and placing the welts for stitching.

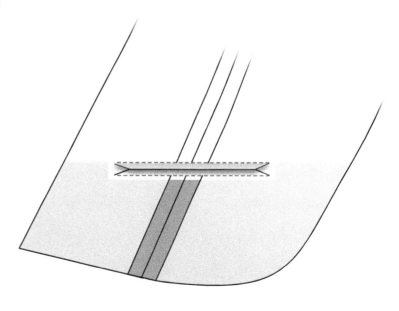

FIGURE 8.9 Stitching the welts to the jacket front and clipping the jacket fabric.

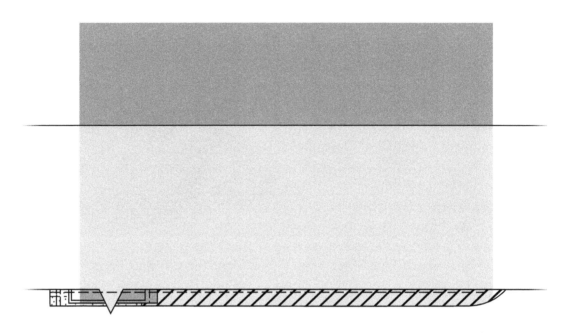

FIGURE 8.10 Sewing the welt corners and the pocket.

straighter on the outside of the jacket (Figure 8.10). Continue the stitching down the sides of the pocket. Finish the sides of the pocket if the jacket will not be lined.

11. Flip the jacket face-side up and give the pocket a final press. Leave the welts sewn together.

Double-Welt Pocket with Flap

A double-welt pocket with a flap is basically constructed the same way as a double-welt

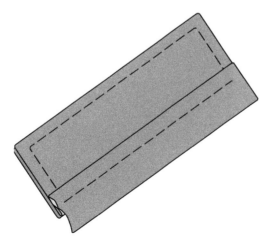

FIGURE 8.11 Welt and flap.

pocket without a flap. The flap is constructed and then placed on top of the welt before the welt and pocket are sewn to the jacket front (Figure 8.11).

Flap construction is covered in Chapter 7, "Fashion Jacket." You may choose to use two layers of fashion fabric for the pocket or to cut the inside of the same lining, as used for the pockets. Topstitching the flap is optional and lends a more sporty look.

CONSTRUCTION AND SHAPING OF COLLARS AND LAPELS

A lot of materials, time, and energy should be spent on constructing and forming the collar and lapel of a tailored jacket. In the manufacturing of moderate to designer signature apparel, these areas are formed around pressing bucks to give them the proper shape and silhouette so that they lie comfortably and present a flattering profile around the wearer's neck. The following instructions detail how to construct and shape a standard collar, lapel,

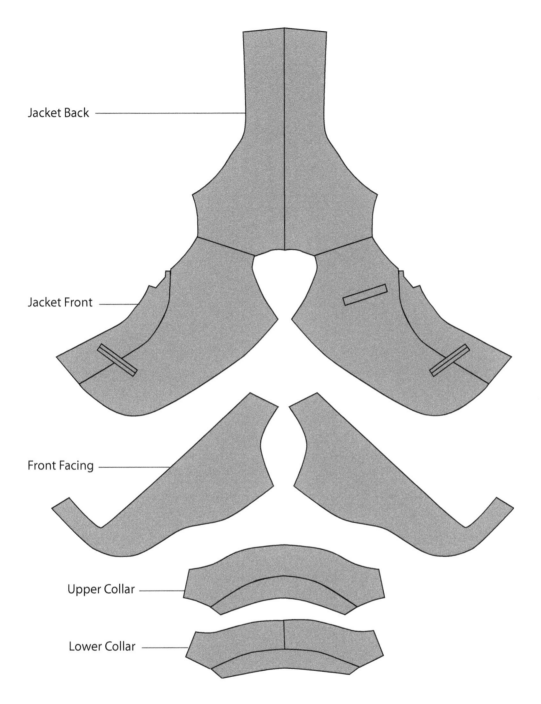

Jacket Back

Jacket Front

Front Facing

Upper Collar

Lower Collar

FIGURE 8.12 Pieces for a jacket collar and facing.

and front and back facings. Figure 8.12 shows the pieces needed to complete the collar and front facing.

1. Apply fusible interlining. Make sure that all of the pattern markings are transferred from your drafted pattern to the interlining side of the cut fabric pieces. The interlining and the lower pockets are not shown in the next illustration for clarity.

2. Stay stitch the neck edge of the jacket to prevent it from stretching while applying the undercollar.

3. Center the curved edge of the undercollar on the jacket neck face-sides, and pin. You will need to clip the neck edge to the stay stitching to allow it to stretch so that the edges of the neckline and undercollar stay even

FIGURE 8.13 Sewing the undercollar to the jacket neck edge.

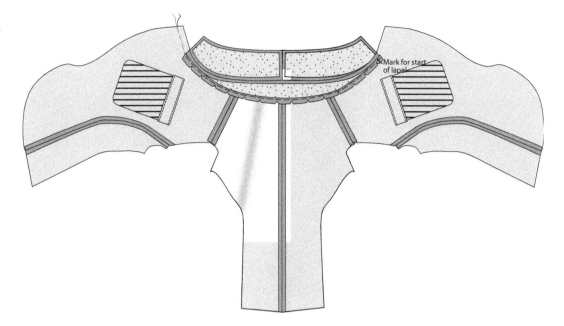

Mark for start of lapel

(Figure 8.13). Make sure that the seam allowance of the undercollar end is pinned at the mark on the neckline for the start of the lapel.

4. Stitch using ASTM Stitch type 301. Your stitching should end at the marks, not at the end of the collar.

5. Press the seam open on a tailor's ham to set the curve, and then clip the jacket neckline to the end of the stitching (see Figure 8.13).

6. Sew the front and back neck facings together at the shoulder seams, and then press the seams open (ASTM Stitch type 301, Seam type SSa-1). Stay stitch the inner neck edge of the facings.

7. Pin the upper collar convex edge to the neck of the facing, snipping if necessary to allow the concave edge of the facing to expand to the convex edge of the collar (Figure 8.14). Make sure that seam allowances at the end of the upper collar pieces are positioned at the marks on the facing edge.

8. Stitch the seam, making sure to back tack at each end and to stop your stitching at the marks (ASTM Stitch type 301). Do not stitch to the end of the collar.

9. Press the seam open on the tailor's ham to preserve its form. Snip through the facing's seam allowance to the end of the stitching (Figure 8.14).

FIGURE 8.14 Attaching the uppercollar.

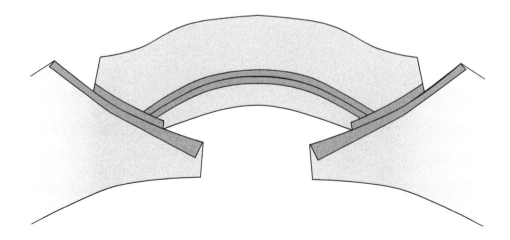

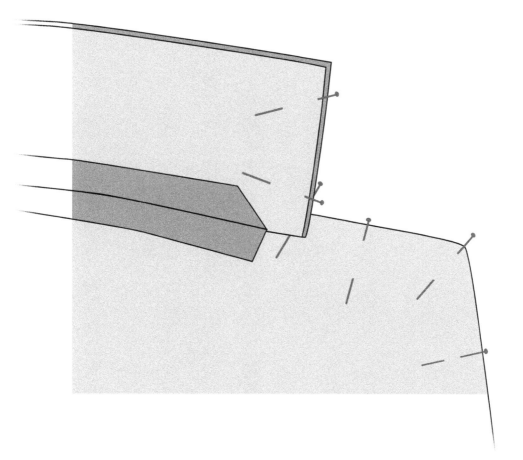

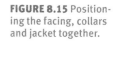
FIGURE 8.15 Positioning the facing, collars and jacket together.

10. If you used ½-inch-wide seam allowances on the jacket, collar, and facing pieces, you must trim the seam allowances down to ¼ inch on the undercollar seam and to 3/8 inch on the upper collar seam.

11. Carefully pin the undercollar, jacket, upper collar, and facing together along the outer edges, starting at the center back and pinning toward the lower fronts. Make sure that the ends of the stitching attaching the upper and undercollar meet at the corner between the collar pieces and the lapel. Insert a pin through this area and then place a thread tack to hold the corner in place so that the seam lines stay on top of each other (Figure 8.15).

12. Keeping the seam allowances out of the way, put your needle down as close to the joint between the collar and the lapel as possible. Do not start stitching past the seam line. Start stitching the seam down toward the point of the lapel turn, and stitch down the outside of the jacket to the bottom of the

TIP | Tips on sewing, trimming, turning, and pressing points

- Seam allowances in areas that will be covered—such as collars, waist facings, cuffs, and vent corners at hems—should be between ¼ and 1/8 inch wide.
- When a corner is particularly narrow, such as at a jacket lapel, extra trimming will be needed in the corner area to allow it to turn neatly and smoothly.
- Sewing two or three very short (stitch length 1) stitches across the end of a narrow point also helps it appear more pointed when completed.
- When turning the point manually, use a professional point turner to speed the process and help keep the point from looking stretched out.

FIGURE 8.16 Stitching the jacket from the collar/lapel corner down along the front of the jacket.

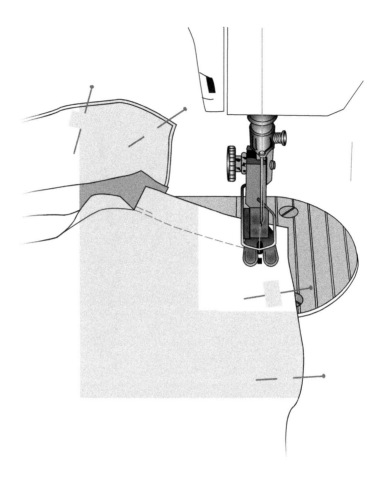

facing (ASTM Stitch type 301). (see Figure 8.16).

13. Stitch the collar and undercollar together, starting from the center of the collar to the joint between the collar and the lapel, keeping the seam

allowances out of the way (ASTM Stitch type 301) (see Figure 8.17).

14. Repeat for the other side of the jacket. Note: Measure the other lapel seam from the joint to the point so that when sewing the other lapel,

FIGURE 8.17 Stitching the lapel and collar.

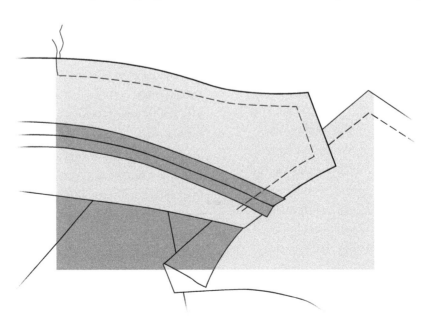

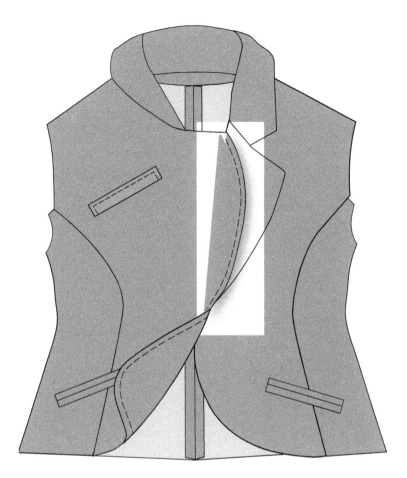

FIGURE 8.18 Under-stitching the lapel and collar.

you make them the same length. Trim the seam allowances to ¼ inch from the lapel; collar joint and grade the seam allowances along the facing and collar seams. Pay special attention to the inner and outer points.

15. Press the seam open on a pressing board to maintain the curved edges and to press into the point.

16. Turn the collar and lapel to the outside of the jacket, and press again along the outer edge from the outside of the jacket. Understitch or topstitch the facings and collar, depending on your fashion statement. If understitching, you must only stitch up to where the lapel breaks at the roll line. If the understitching goes above that point, it will be seen. If topstitching, make sure that the needle and bobbin thread tensions are set so that the joint of the stitches meets inside the

fabric layers. This will prevent the topstitching from looking different than the bottom stitching when the lapel rolls. See Figure 8.18 to find out how the topstitching should look at the joint between the lapel and collar.

17. Reach under the facing and loosely whip stitch the seam allowances of the undercollar and upper collar to each other.

TWO-PIECE SLEEVE WITH VENT

1. Apply interlining to sleeve areas.
2. Face-sides together, stitch the front sleeve to the back sleeve (ASTM Stitch type 301, Seam type SSa-1). Press seam open over a tailor's ham to maintain the curve in the seam.
3. Press up the hem, press in the vent, and finish according to the steps for mitering a skirt vent in Chapter 4. Hand

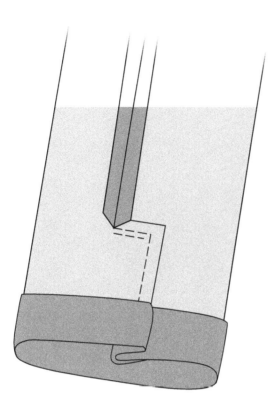

FIGURE 8.19 Sewing the sleeve vent seam.

freedom of movement to the wearer's arm without binding.

Easing means pulling in one layer of a seam to fit another, shorter area. Easing uses the same techniques as gathering to shorten the edge, except that there is less fullness with easing. The lower edge of the sleeve is reinforced with twill or seam tape at the seam line. Before beginning the easing process, all the vertical seams of the sleeve should be sewn, and the hem or end treatment of the sleeve and the lower edge of the sleeve should be reinforced on the seam line up to the point where the shaping will start for the sleeve's top (Figure 8.20). Buttons should also be applied to the vent if your jacket calls for that.

baste the lining to the jacket ½ inch up from the hem. This is in preparation for attaching the sleeve lining.

4. Sew the vent seam and press the seam open on a seam roll (ASTM Stitch type 301, Seam type SSa-1). Clip the seam allowance at the top of the vent extension so that the seam allowance can be pressed flat (Figure 8.19).

◇◇

SLEEVE INSERTION
Applying the Sleeve Head and Shaping the Sleeve Cap

Shaping the sleeve head for a suit is similar to shaping a sleeve head or a blouse, which is featured in Chapter 6. Frequently, however, the shaping that creates an attractive shoulder on a jacket should be invisible. Also, a shoulder pad is always involved, and often a strip of lightweight bias or nonwoven material called a *sleeve head* is used. The top of the sleeve is eased in to fit the size of the armhole and to give more

1. Complete the rows of gathering stitches as described in Chapter 4.
2. Pin the sleeve into the jacket, adjusting the gathering threads as necessary. Avoid having too much fullness in one area so that no gathers or small tucks of fabric will be sewn into the seam. The sleeve shaping should be invisible from the outside once the outer gathering thread is removed (see Figure 8.20).
3. Center the sleeve head over the sleeve fabric at the shoulder seam, with the edge of the sleeve head next to the edges of the sleeve and armhole, and pin. Baste the sleeve head to the sleeve while removing the pins.
4. Stitch the sleeve to the jacket armhole, taking care not to stitch in unwanted parts of the sleeve or jacket (ASTM Stitch type 301).
5. Remove the basting stitches and gently steam the shoulder area from the outside of the jacket with the seam allowances toward the sleeve. Steam over a tailoring board or tailor's ham

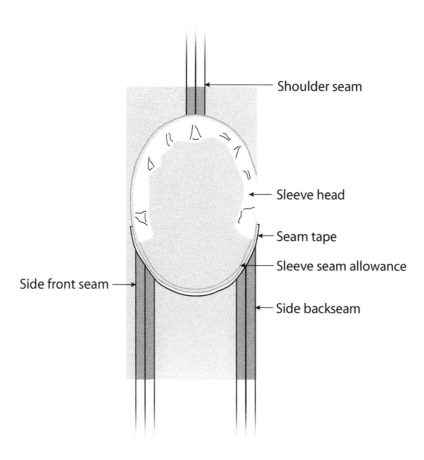

FIGURE 8.20 Setting in the jacket sleeve.

Shoulder seam

Sleeve head

Seam tape

Sleeve seam allowance

Side front seam

Side backseam

to maintain the shape of the shoulder (Figure 8.21).

6. Turn the jacket inside out and lightly press the lower portion of the seam.

Applying Shoulder Pads

1. Pin the shoulder pad to the shoulder seam of the jacket so that the straight edge extends ½ inch into the sleeve.

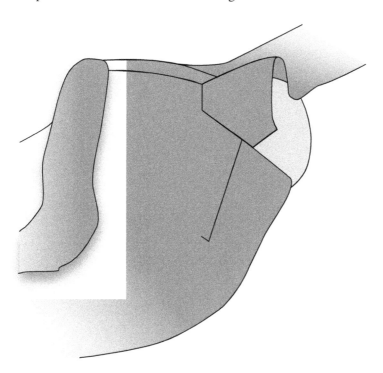

FIGURE 8.21 Steaming the shoulder.

FIGURE 8.22 Positioning and securing the shoulder pad.

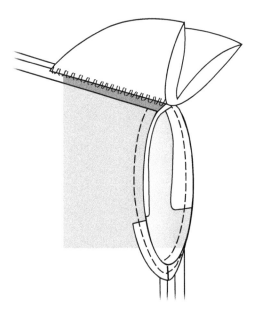

2. Blind stitch or slip stitch by hand the top of the shoulder pad only to the shoulder seam allowance.
3. Tack the corners of the shoulder pad to the sleeve seam allowance (Figure 8.22).

HEMMING

1. Apply interlining to the jacket hem in the areas noted in Figure 8.1.
2. Finish the edge of the hem with an overlock stitch type 504.

FIGURE 8.23 Sewing the area around the end of the front facing and the bottom hem.

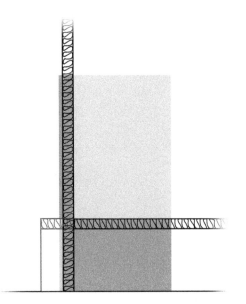

3. Hem the jacket using the methods described in Chapter 4 for skirt hemming if you are not lining the jacket, are lining it with a half lining, or are applying the lining by hand. Remember to extend the hem allowance under the facing and to seam the bottom of the facing if you did not do so when applying the facing before (Figure 8.23).
4. If you are applying a hem using the following machine method, do not hem the lining. Iron up and then pin the hem after applying the interlining. Steam out any fullness at the upper edge. Overlock the edge and hand baste the hem to the jacket about ½ inch above the bottom hemline.

LINING

A lining helps preserve the jacket. The lining takes some of the stress of movement and body contact off the jacket fabric and its construction. Linings also make it easier to put on the jacket over other clothing. Some well-made jackets in timeless styles will outlive more than one lining before wearing out. The lining will also enclose parts of the jacket construction that aren't

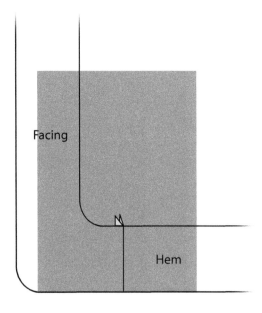

Facing

Hem

attractive and that would be uncomfortable next to the wearer's skin. Unfortunately, linings in budget and category-killer apparel will often be hiding cheaper fabrics and construction inside the jacket. It costs less to add the lining than it does to increase the quality of the jacket construction. Generally, consumers equate linings with higher quality. The lining for a jacket will be created in the factory on the line or in the lean manufacturing pod while the jacket is being sewn so that both will be ready to seam together without having to wait for the other. The method of lining insertion we will use is a version of one used on the factory floor but without the specialized sleeve-setting machines that might be available. We will first construct the lining and then attach it to the jacket.

Constructing the Lining

1. Sew and press any style lines, such as darts, princess seams, and pleats at the center back, in the front or back of the lining. Create or attach any pockets that are being added (ASTM Stitch type 301).
2. Sew the fronts and backs together at the shoulder and side seams, pressing these seams open (ASTM Stitch type 301). It is not necessary to finish these seam allowances, but they may be overlocked with stitch 504 for a quick addition of quality.
3. Press up the hem allowance at the bottom of the jacket.
4. Sew the vertical seams in the sleeves (ASTM Stitch type 301). Make sure to leave an 8- to 10-inch section of one underarm seam open to turn the jacket face-side out through. Press the seams on a sleeve roll.
5. Press up the hems on the bottoms of the sleeves. Note: You may apply the facing and upper collar to the edges of

the lining before applying the lining to the jacket.

Attaching the Lining

1. Lay the jacket down face-side up.
2. Lay the lining face-side down on top of the jacket, sandwiching the collar between the jacket and the lining.
3. Pin the center back of the lining to the center back of the jacket facing. Begin pinning the lining to the jacket, taking care to keep the fabric layers flat so that the jacket or the lining are not shrunken or stretched into the other layer (Figure 8.24).
4. Stitch all of the pinned edges, starting at the lower edge of the facing and sewing across the back neck and down to the front end of the other facing (ASTM Stitch type 301) (see Figure 8.24).
5. Pull out the hem edge of the lining and place it and the jacket hem edge face-sides together. Stitch across the hem and then press the hem open (ASTM Stitch type 301). There will seem to be extra fabric in the lining at the facing seam. This will disappear when the jacket is turned face-side out and the lining hem has a chance to hang down.

FIGURE 8.24 Pinning and stitching the lining to the jacket.

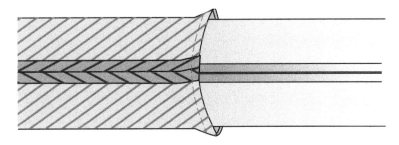

FIGURE 8.25 Attaching the lining sleeve to the jacket sleeve.

6. Pull the jacket and lining sleeves inside out. Line up and pin the ends of the corresponding vertical seams, making sure that neither sleeve is twisted. The face-side of the lining sleeve should be touching the face-side of the jacket sleeve (Figure 8.25).

7. Pin around the rest of the sleeve hems and then sew (ASTM Stitch type 301).

8. Reach in through the hole in the sleeve seam and gently pull the jacket face-side out.

9. Reach back inside the sleeve opening, position the lining underarm and the jacket underarm together, and stitch the seam allowances together to prevent the lining from shifting while the jacket is being worn. Repeat with the other sleeve. Take care not to stitch unwanted bits of the lining or the jacket in this stitching.

FIGURE 8.26 Keyhole button hole with gimp.

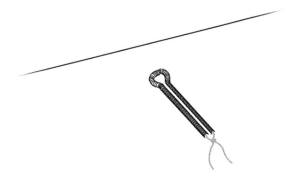

10. Check the jacket to make sure no twisting, puckering, or gaping is occurring between the lining and the jacket. Also check the hems of the lining to make sure that the prepressed hems are hanging above the jacket and sleeve hem.

11. Position the sides of the sleeve-lining opening together and edge stitch the opening closed.

BUTTONHOLES
Corded Keyhole

Keyhole buttonholes are used on some suit coats, overcoats, and jeans. The hole at the rounded end of the keyhole is there to fit a shank button for a coat or a tack button on a pair of jeans so that the buttonhole will not be stretched out (Figure 8.26). Buttonhole machines can be programmed to create this buttonhole and those with double square ends. Also, keyhole buttonholes with tails can be made in overcoats for extra strength. A corded buttonhole has the added strength of a heavy thread-like material such as gimp. The gimp is positioned so that it is stitched over when the buttonhole is being formed.

SEWING ON SHANK BUTTONS

Buttons with holes can be found on women's tailored jackets, and shank buttons can be found on blouses. We have already covered attaching holed buttons in Chapter 6. Now we will cover sewing on a shank button, because these are frequently found on suit jackets and overcoats.

1. Mark the positions of the buttons on the jacket's left side, using the buttonholes as a guide.

2. If you don't have a button-sewing machine for shank buttons, thread

a needle with heavy thread such as
buttonhole twist, double it, and knot
the ends.

3. Begin sewing through the facing
of the garment from the bottom,
using a backing button if desired.
Start your stitching a 1/2 inch or so
from the button position. Take two
small stitches on the outside of the
jacket in the fabric directly under
where the button shank will be.
Then cut your knot off on the inside.
(This is called a *waste knot* and can be
used in any hand-sewing application
for a neat beginning.)

4. Stitch through the hole in the shank,
passing down through the fabric and
keeping the stitching neat in the back
and the stitches slightly loose.

5. After passing through the hole in
the shank four or five times, come
up to the surface of the fabric and
use the thread to wrap the stitching

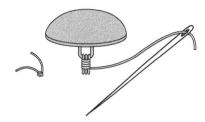

between the shank and the fabric
(Figure 8.27).

6. Pass the thread back down to the
bottom of the fabric and take a few
neat stitches, running your needle
through the loops of the stitches to
make a knot. Pass the thread
through the fabric between the facing
and the garment to bury it. Clip off
the thread.

7. Sew the number of buttons your jacket
style requires onto the vent overlap.

FIGURE 8.27 Sewing on a shank button by hand.

SEWING ON A BUTTON WITH HOLES AND A THREAD SHANK

If you are using a button with holes instead of a shank on a jacket or other garment
with thick fabric, it is necessary to raise the button off the surface of the garment with
a thread shank. This makes it easier for the consumer to fasten the button and keeps
the jacket fabric from looking distorted when the jacket is worn. In the industry, this
operation is done by machine.

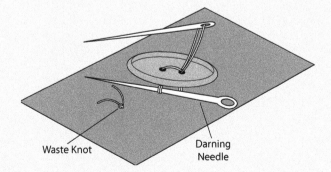

Waste Knot

Darning
Needle

- Mark the position of the button on the front of the garment.
- Using a doubled length of button-sewing thread, make a waste knot before
  coming up to the surface of the fabric where the button is to be sewn on.

SEWING ON A BUTTON WITH HOLES AND A THREAD SHANK (continued)

- Place the button on the garment front with a large darning needle centered under the button to raise it off the surface of the fabric.
- Stitch through the holes on the button, past the darning needle, and through the garment front, keeping the thread tension consistent.
- After taking three or four repeats through all the holes, remove the darning needle and bring the thread back down between the button and the surface of the garment, tightly wrapping the remaining thread around the stitches to create a neat "stem" for the button.
- Bring the thread to the back of the fabric and knot off neatly.

MAKING AND APPLYING PIPING.

Many moderate- to designer-price-point jackets with linings have piping attached to the facing before the application of the lining. The piping adds stability and body to the edge of the facing but is primarily there as a design detail to accent the seam between the jacket fabric and the lining.

Piping accents the seams in your garment, giving a linier effect that can often make the difference between a boring garment and an interesting fashion statement; sometimes it can even give the garment added value in the mind of the consumer. It can be purchased in generic solid colors or can be custom made, and it is easy to construct and apply. Of course, there are specialized machines to create and work with piping, but custom piping in small amounts can be made on a conventional lockstitch machine with either a zipper foot or a piping foot. The piping foot will have a slot through which the center cording of the piping travels to keep the product consistent. Piping feet are manufactured for specific diameters of cording. Bias fabric covers the special cording to give a smooth finish, especially when the cording is curved during application.

To construct piping, follow these steps:
- Measure the length of the seams you wish to add the piping to.
- Cut bias strips that are the correct width to cover the cording you are using to make your piping. The width should go around the cording snugly while providing a ½-inch seam allowance.
- Cut bias strips that will cover the length of seams you are adding piping to; seam them if necessary.
- Wrap the bias strips, face-side out, around the cording so that both long edges of the strips are even. Both long edges should be ½ inch wide from the cording to the edge of the strip.
- Using a thread that matches or is slightly darker than the fabric covering the piping, sew close to the cording through all layers (the piping foot will help with this) without sewing into the cording itself. Take care not to stretch the bias.

MAKING AND APPLYING PIPING (continued)

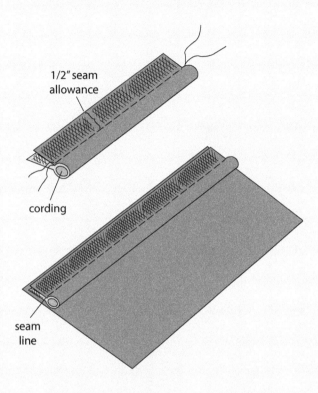

1/2" seam allowance

cording

seam line

- Place the piping on the face-side of the garment at the seam line, keeping the cut edges of the bias even with the edge of the garment piece. The cording should be just inside the seam line so that it will show when the seam is completed.
- If you have a piping foot, a reasonably straight seam, and a good eye, you can layer the coordinating garment piece on top, face-side down, and sew the piping in while sewing the seam at the same time.
- In a complex seam with curves or a lot of layers, you will need to temporarily baste the piping to the garment edge before sewing on the other fabric layers.

VEST CONSTRUCTION

Sew darts or princess seams in vest and lining → Apply pockets, flaps, embellishments → Sew vest fronts and backs and lining fronts and backs together at shoulder seams → Sew vest to lining at armholes, back bottom edge, front neck down to front bottom edge → Sew vest front and back and sew lining front and back together at side seams → Make buttonholes → Apply buttons

Sew pocket pieces and flaps → Apply pockets, flaps, embellishments

Sew back waist belt → Apply pockets, flaps, embellishments

Temporarily attach back belt at waist to side seams → Apply pockets, flaps, embellishments

Vest Construction

ooooooooooooooooooooooooooooooooooooooooooooooooooooooooooooooooooooooooooooooooooooooooooooooooooooooo

Formerly the exclusive style of men, the vest continues on as a fun, versatile layering piece and slimming accessory for the modern woman of any age or figure. Traditional vest designs use a lightweight lining fabric for the vest back and the entire inside. A suiting or fashion fabric is used for the vest fronts. But in fashion, traditions

were made to be ignored, and the vest is a great place to experiment with unconventional and unfamiliar materials and embellishments, because they are quickly and easily sewn. This chapter contains the instructions for applying piping in a seam, and bias binding embellishments to the surface of the vest, which are easy ways to accent all the curves of a vest.

In a man's styled vest, a narrow, adjustable belt of the lining fabric with a special vest buckle usually extends across the back from one side seam to the other to allow a more fitted silhouette at the waist. In this chapter, the inside of the vest is referred to as the *lining*; the outside is referred to as the *vest*. This chapter also contains the steps for constructing a simple, lined, darted vest with button fastenings and an optional back belt. We also discuss the basic techniques for sewing lightweight leather, which may be applied to constructing any leather garment.

Completing Interior Styling

1. Sew darts in the vest front and back using the steps mentioned in Chapters 4 and 6.

2. Add any welts or pockets to the vest or lining as described in Chapters 6 or 8.
3. Add any embellishments to the vest front or back.

Completing the Shoulder Seams

1. Sew the vest front and back together at the shoulder seams (ASTM Stitch type 301).
2. Sew the lining front and back together at the shoulder seams (ASTM Stitch type 301) (Figure 9.1).
3. Press seams open.

Sewing the Neckline and Armhole Seams

1. Lay the vest lining down over the vest with the face of vest to the face of the lining, matching the shoulder seams.
2. Sew the vest to the vest lining along the lower front edge, starting about 3 inches from the side seam, along the front neck edge, around to the back neck edge, and at the arm openings (ASTM Stitch type 301; Figure 9.2).
3. Pull the vest fronts out through the lower back opening until the vest is completely face-side out.

FIGURE 9.1 (left)
Sewing the vest
shoulder seams.

FIGURE 9.2 (right)
Sewing vest lining to
vest at the neck and
arm hole.

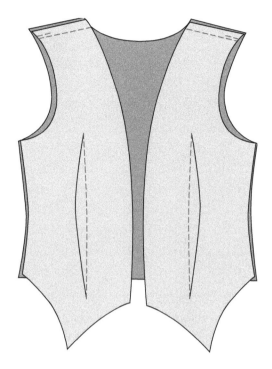

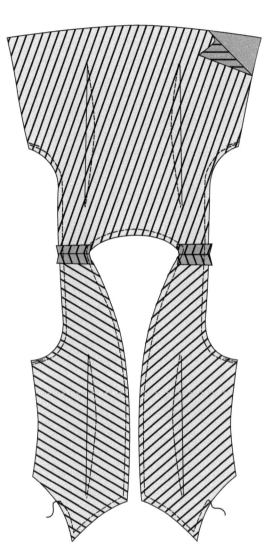

4. Press edges. When pressing the seams, make sure the lining of the vest cannot be seen from outside the garment (Figure 9.3).

Adding a Back Belt

1. Cut two strips of lining fabric for the belt that are twice the finished width plus ½ inch for seam allowances. Each will be about 14 to 20 inches long, depending on the size of your vest. The length of each piece should be half the width of the back plus another 4 to 6 inches for slipping through the buckle.
2. Fold belt strips in half along the long edge.
3. Sew along the open long edge and along one short end. Repeat with the other half of the belt (ASTM Stitch type 301).
4. Turn both belt pieces face-side out. Press, making sure the seam remains along the edge.
5. Add the vest buckle to left-hand closed end of belt piece by slipping the fabric through the buckle and using a zipper foot to stitch the end neatly to the belt.

6. Before sewing the side seams between the vest's back and front, pin the unfinished end of each belt piece onto the seam line at waist level, adjusting them so that they meet in the center and the right belt piece has enough length to thread through the buckle (Figure 9.4).

Sewing the Side Seams

1. At the side seam, place the front and back of the vest lining and the vest face-sides together, making sure that the armhole seams are on top of each other and that the pressed seam allowances remain open (Figure 9.5).

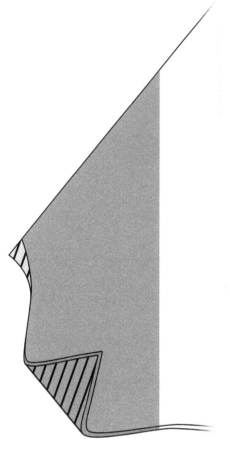

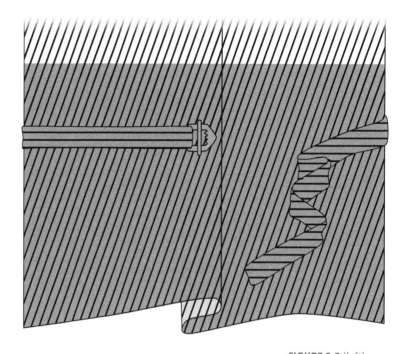

back and the lining together. Sew the back together, leaving a 4- to 6-inch opening in the center through which to turn the vest face-side (ASTM Stitch type 301; Figure 9.6).

FIGURE 9.3 (left)
Pressing the vest seams.

FIGURE 9.4 (right)
Placing the belt on the vest back.

2. Begin sewing from the lower edge of the front, across the armhole seam, and down to the lower edge of the back (ASTM Stitch type 301; see Figure 9.5).

Starting the Lower Edges

1. Turn the vest back-side out again, and align the lower edge of the vest

Turning the Vest

1. Pull the vest face-side out through the hole in the lower back. Press the sewn edges, making sure to keep the lining slightly to the inside of the vest.

FIGURE 9.5 (left)
Sewing the side seams.

FIGURE 9.6 (right)
Sewing the lower back together.

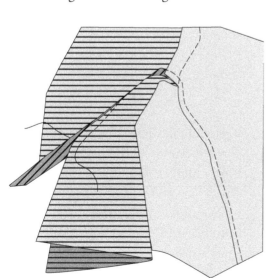

FIGURE 9.7 Finishing the center back seam.

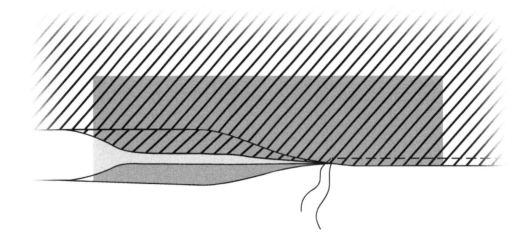

Finishing the Lower Back Edge

1. Press the seam allowances inside the vest, and then slip stitch or edge stitch the opening closed. Top-stitching around the pressed edges of the vest lends a finished quality to the garment and helps to keep the lining from showing on the outside (Figure 9.7).

Adding Buttonholes and Buttons

1. Apply buttonholes to the right-hand side of the vest and attach buttons to the left-hand side using the methods described in Chapter 6, "Ladies' Blouse." Vest buttons are horizontal to allow expansion when worn. Depending on the fabric and styling of the vest, either a square-ended buttonhole such as on a blouse or a keyhole buttonhole such as on an overcoat will be appropriate.

SEWING LEATHER

- Leather has two sides: the skin side and the suede side.
- Use the narrowest seam or hem allowance possible to reduce unnecessary trimming and bulk in seams. One-quarter to a 1/2-inch seam allowance is the standard.
- If you are sewing with the skin side of the leather up and the presser foot is getting stuck, substitute a Teflon foot for your regular foot, or add a Teflon sticker to the bottom of a standard foot. If neither is available, layer a piece of tissue paper under the foot to help it slide more smoothly. Tear away the paper once the seam is sewn.
- Use a leather needle of the proper size for the thread that you are using.
- Sewing-machine needles leave permanent holes in leather. Therefore, accuracy in seam sewing is essential.
- Layers of leather may be temporarily held together with paper clips or bulldog clips while sewing to avoid marking the leather with pinholes.
- Leather cannot be pressed with a steam iron. Use these steps instead to flatten seams:
  - After sewing the seam, use a clapper to pound the seam allow-ances at the seam line on the back of the fabric. This must be done on a hard surface that is clean and smooth to avoid marking the face-side of the leather. Avoid overworking the leather. Cover it with a clean cloth before pounding to avoid marking it.

- After pounding, use rubber cement or leather glue to glue the seam or hem allowances to the back of the fabric. Apply glue neatly to both the underside of the seam allowance and to the back of the fabric. Let dry until tacky, and then press the two areas together carefully to get a smooth, firm bond

- Feed teeth can also mark the surface of the leather. If you absolutely need to topstitch with the skin side of the leather down, you may use the tissue-paper trick mentioned above between the feed teeth and the leather to protect it.

TO APPLY A BIAS-BINDING EMBELLISHMENT ON THE FABRIC SURFACE BY MACHINE.

1. Purchase premade, single-fold bias binding or make your own using a bias-tape maker. Bias-tape makers are sold in a variety of widths so that custom, single-fold bias can be made. If attaching bias to an edge, it is not necessary to use a bias-tape maker. The bias binder attached to the machine creates double-fold bias tape while the tape is being sewn around the edge.

2. Glue or pin the bias to the surface of the fabric where desired. Bias may be curved by pressing the tape into the shape desired before applying it to the fabric surface. Tight curves can be made by sewing a gathering thread in the pressed ditch. The thread is then pulled to cause the bias to curve tightly. Press the curve in before applying the bias to the fabric surface.

3. Using ASTM stitch type 304 at a width of 2 or 3, stitch each edge of the bias to the fabric, making sure to catch the folded edge of the bias.

JUMPER WITH ALL-IN-ONE FACING

Apply interlining → Sew inner shaping → Prepare the facing ← Finish lower edges, if necessary

Prepare the facing → Prepare the bodice ← Sew stay stitching at neck and armhole edge

Sew inner shaping → Prepare the bodice

Prepare the bodice → Join bodice and facing ← Apply pocket or other embellishments

Join bodice and facing → Prepare the skirt ← Sew inner shaping

Prepare the skirt → Attach bodice to skirt → Insert zipper → Hem skirt

Ladies' Jumper with All-in-One Facing

T his chapter describes how to construct a jumper with an all-in-one facing that finishes the front and back neckline and the armholes. You can also use these techniques to create a shift-style sundress, an evening gown, or a top in a symmetrical or asymmetrical style. Although these garments may be constructed with separate facings

for the neck and armholes, the all-in-one facing has a smoother finish and can serve as a lining if extended to the length of just the top part of the garment or the entire length. When the facing has extended to the waistline or beyond, it has essentially turned into a lining, but for clarification, we will continue to call it a facing.

For this chapter, we will be constructing a top with an added skirt. There are instructions for adding an invisible zipper to this garment in Chapter 4.

PREPARING THE FACING

1. Prepare the facing pieces for the front and back of the bodice by applying interlining to the back of each fabric section. If the facing has been extended to become a lining, then the interlining should only be applied around the neck line and armholes out to a distance between 1 1/2" to 3".

2. Sew the shoulder seams together (ASTM Stitch type 301,

Seam type SSa-1). Press the seams open.

3. Finish the lower edge of the facing front and back only if it extends part of the way down the bodice. An entirely lined bodice or a full-length lining will have the lower edge finished later. On a loose-fitting garment, you can use a narrow hem such as the shirttail hem in Chapter 6, but this creates a slight ridge at the pressed edge. The lower edge may be overlocked with stitch type 504, but this may lower the customer's perception of the garment's quality. A combination of an overlock finish with a narrow hem is a quick, higher-quality, lightweight solution. A Hong Kong finish also works well and implies a higher level of quality.

PREPARING THE JUMPER
Bodice

1. Stay stitch the garment neck edge and armholes inside the seam line to

prevent stretching them out when applying the facing. This also helps prevent the neck edge from drooping after the facing is attached.

2. Sew any interior shaping such as darts or princess seams as detailed in Chapter 6 on the sections for bust darts, waist darts, and princess seams. If you are facing a dress, do the same for the entire length of the garment.

3. Sew the shoulder seams of the bodice together and press the seams open (ASTM Stitch type 301, Seam type SSa-1). If the bodice is not fully lined, you will need to finish the seam allowances using one of the methods in Chapter 3. Do not sew the center back seam. The zipper

will go in here after the skirt is attached.

4. Pin the neck edge of the facing face-side down on the face-side of the bodice, matching the shoulder and side seams.

5. Stitch the neck edge (ASTM Stitch type 301, Seam type SSa-1). Your seam allowance should only be ¼ inch, so trimming should not be necessary to have the facing lie flat, but you may need to clip as shown in Figure 10.1.

6. Flip the facing out away from the neckline, and press the seam with the tip of the iron; take care to not press any unnecessary creases into the garment.

7. Understitch the neck facing to the seam allowance (Figure 10.2).

FIGURE 10.1 Clipping the neck edge.

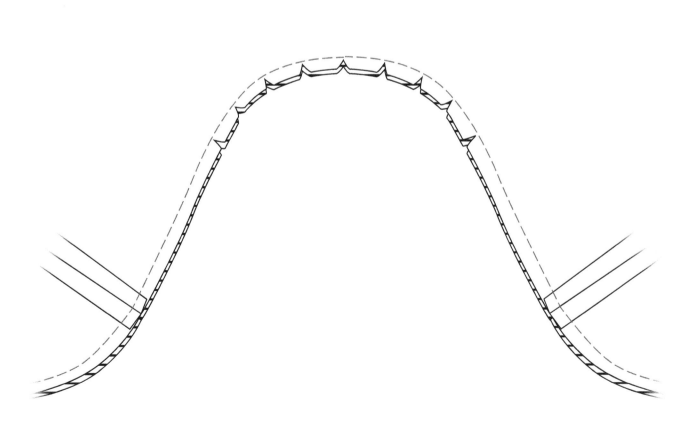

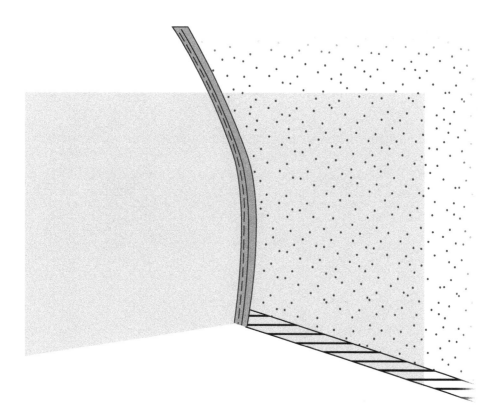

FIGURE 10.2 Under-stitching the neck edge.

8. Lay the garment down with the back sides up so that you can see the shoulder seams of the facing and bodice (Figure 10.3).
9. At the armhole, match the shoulder seams then pin the seam allowances of the bodice and the facing together, continuing across the seam (see Figure 10.3).
10. Stitch the seam, (ASTM Stitch type 301, Seam type SSa-1). Repeat this process with the other armhole, and

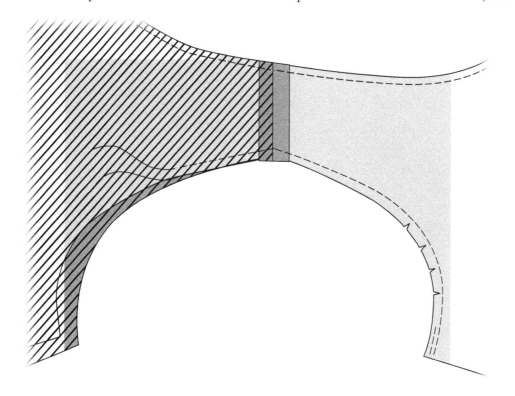

FIGURE 10.3 Preparing the armhole seam and sewing.

FIGURE 10.4 Preparing for and sewing the bodice side seam.

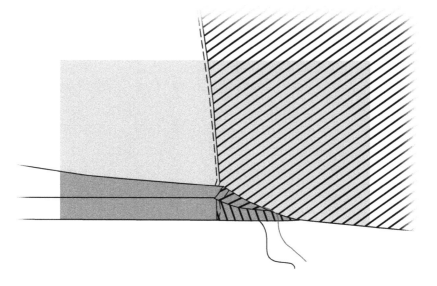

FIGURE 10.4 Preparing for and sewing the bodice side seam.

then press the armhole seams from the face-side of the garment; taking care to make sure that the facing remains on the inside of the garment.

11. Unfold the bodice and its lining and place the side seams of the fronts and backs together. Match the armhole seams. The bodice front and back should be together and the lining front and back should be together.

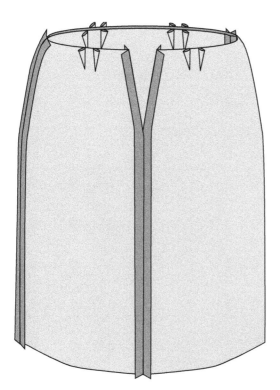

FIGURE 10.5 Joining the bodice and skirt.

(See Figure 10.4) Stitch then press the seam.

Skirt

1. Sew any shaping or other interior seams in each part of the skirt, such as gathering.
2. Sew the side seams of the skirt (ASTM Stitch type 301, Seam type SSa-1). Press the seams open. If the skirt is not lined, you must finish the seam allowances using one of the methods in Chapter 3.

Attaching the Skirt to the Bodice

1. With face-sides together, place the skirt and the bodice together at the unfinished waist area, pinning in place the side seams and any shaping that should match (Figure 10.5).
2. Sew the waistline seam, making sure the darts stay pressed toward the center and the seam allowances stay open (ASTM Stitch type 301, Seam type SSa-1).
3. Press the seam allowance up toward the bodice if the facing will extend to cover this seam. Press the seam allowances down toward the skirt, and finish the seam allowances if the facing does not extend to the waistline.

4. If the facing extends to cover the waist seam, turn up the seam allowance on the facing lower edge, and pin it to the skirt just below the seam line (see Figure 10.6).

5. Stitch in the ditch between the bodice and the skirt to secure the edge of the facing (ASTM Stitch type 301).

FIGURE 10.6 Finishing the waist seam.

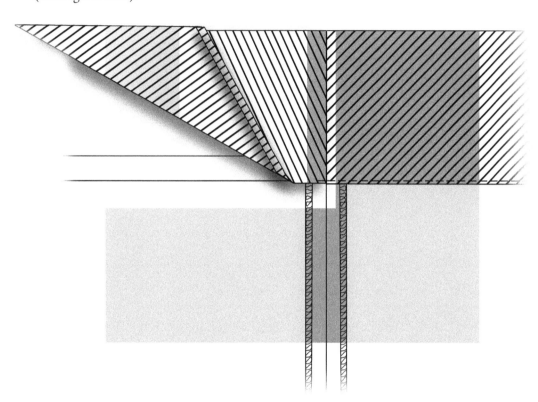

BUSTIER CONSTRUCTION

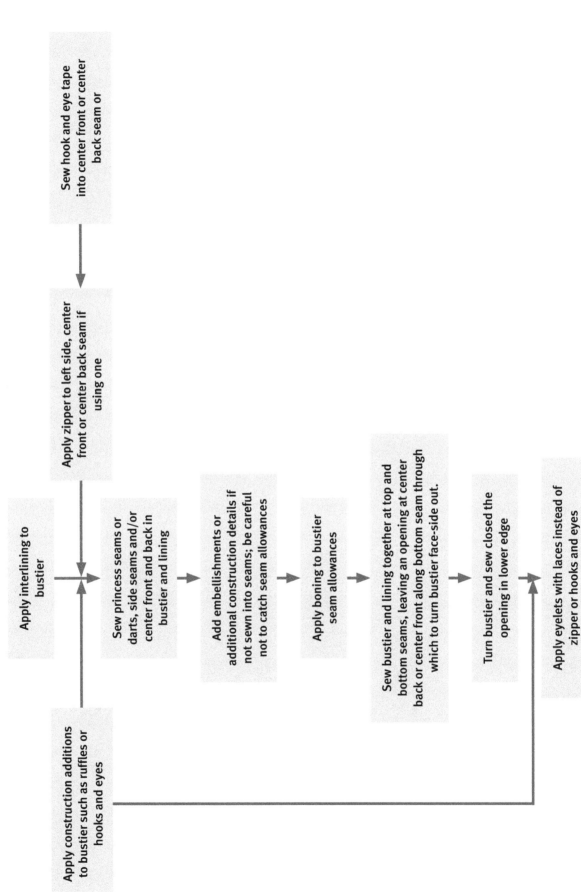

Apply interlining to bustier

Apply construction additions to bustier such as ruffles or hooks and eyes

Sew princess seams or darts, side seams and/or center front and back in bustier and lining

Apply zipper to left side, center front or center back seam if using one

Sew hook and eye tape into center front or center back seam or

Add embellishments or additional construction details if not sewn into seams; be careful not to catch seam allowances

Apply boning to bustier seam allowances

Sew bustier and lining together at top and bottom seams, leaving an opening at center back or center front along bottom seam through which to turn bustier face-side out.

Turn bustier and sew closed the opening in lower edge

Apply eyelets with laces instead of zipper or hooks and eyes

Lined Bustier

B ustiers bare the skin while lifting and enhancing the bust by using a combination of tightness around the rib cage and support materials such as boning. A bustier says a lot about the women who wear them. Perhaps they are going to a first prom, getting married, or wanting to surprise a certain someone. No matter the

occasion, a woman in a bustier will get attention.

This chapter will feature the techniques used to

- add backing and a lining to a bustier,
- apply boning,
- insert a separating zipper, and
- add eyelets to a bodice.

These steps may be used to create a separate bustier or to create a dress by attaching a skirt.

Foundation Material Choices
Bustiers should be lined to protect the wearer from the inner structure of the garment. This inner structure can include

backing, buckram, interlining, boning, and the seam allowances of the fashion fabric. If the fabric is lightweight, a backing will keep the inner structure of the garment from showing through to the outside and will help stiffen and smooth the fabric without changing its texture. Interlining and buckram may be added to increase stiffness and help the garment retain its shape, especially at the upper edges. Boning inserted at the seams will help keep the fabric flat and lift the bust. For opening the garment, a zipper may be added at the center back or front or at one side seam. Also, eyelets may be added, or you can use hooks and eyes. Eyelets will allow the wearer to adjust the fit of the garment.

ALTERNATIVE BUSTIER CLOSURES

A decorative hook and eye tape may be sewn on the outside of the bustier at the center front or center back seam to add a design detail. Zippers with rhinestone-studded teeth and jeweled pulls will also add some bling. In the Appendix, you can find a list of specialty zippers and suppliers.

In Figure 11.1, you will see the pieces of a bustier with a center back seam and a separating zipper. Usually a bustier will have princess seams in the front and back, a center back seam and side seams. The princess seams serve as positioning for the boning and can make the shape more formfitting. However, the opening can be switched from the back to the front, creating a solid center back and a seam in the center front. Or the seam may be placed in the side, in which case the center front and back would not have an opening. The instructions shown are for a bustier with a center back seam and a separating zipper.

1. Apply any shaping materials such as interlining to the lining.
2. Sew the bustier pieces together in the fashion fabric, lining, and backing at the side front, side back, and side seams, following the steps for princess seams in Chapter 6, "Ladies' Blouse"

(ASTM Stitch type 301, seam type SSa-1). Press the seams open. The boning may now be sewn to the backing fabric. If no backing fabric is used, you may sew the boning to the back side of the lining. If your boning has a casing, you may use this casing to attach the boning. If not, you may make a casing from a bias strip of the lining fabric at approximately 1¼ inches wide by the length of all the seams where the boning is to be applied. For the best fit, the boning should be sewn to all the seams mentioned, or it may be sewn only onto the side front and side back seams. To sew on the boning, use the following steps:

3. Measure the length of each seam and cut the boning so that it is ½ inch shorter than the seam. If you are using plastic boning, round the ends by snipping off the corners.

FIGURE 11.1 The pieces of a bustier.

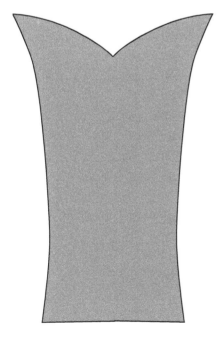   

Center Front	Side Front	Side Back	Center Back
cut 1 each of fashion fabric, lining and backing	cut 2 each of fashion fabric, lining and backing	cut 2 each of fashion fabric, lining and backing	cut 2 each of fashion fabric, lining and backing

4. For boning with a casing, center the casing on top of the seam line and pin down. Sew the edge of the casing to the seam through all layers of the fabric (ASTM Stitch type 301).

5. If you are making a casing, cut a strip of the lining or other lightweight fabric that is the width of the boning plus ¾ inch and the length of the seam plus ½ inch. Press under ¼ inch on each long edge of the strip and ¼ inch across the ends of the strip. Pin the strip over the seam line and edge stitch the strip through all layers (Figure 11.2).

6. Insert the boning into the casing. Edge stitch by machine or hand whip the ends of the casings closed.

7. Baste the backing to the fashion fabric along all edges within the seam allowance, making sure the seams are aligned. The backing fabric should be between the boning and the fashion fabric. This will disguise the boning from the outside of the garment. If using a lining, skip to the next step.

8. Separate the zipper and pin each side facedown on top of the fashion fabric at the center back; make sure that the bottom of the zipper is at the bottom

of the bustier and that the bottoms are ½ inch up from the bottom of the fabric. This is so you do not try to sew through the metal at the bottom of the zipper when stitching the bottom seam of the bustier (Figure 11.3). Note: You may substitute a tape of hooks and eyes for the zipper; just make sure that the hooks and eyes are face-side down and lined up so they will meet when the bustier is finished. Basting the zipper is a wise choice here.

FIGURE 11.2 Sewing the casings to the lining or backing of the bustier.

FIGURE 11.3 Positioning the zipper at the center back of the bustier.

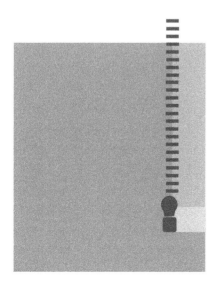
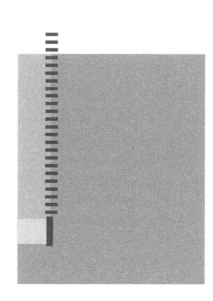

FIGURE 11.4 Sewing the bustier across the top.

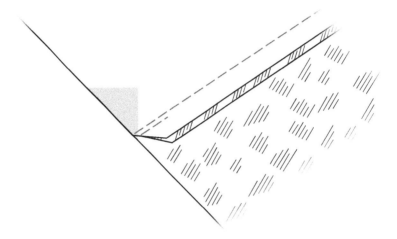

9. Place the lining face-side down on the face of the fashion fabric; align the seams and pin across the top.

10. At the top only, sew the lining to the bustier and then press the seam open (ASTM Stitch type 301, seam type SSa-1). If your bustier has a curved seam at the top, then press the seam on a tailor's ham to prevent pressing in unwanted creases. Trim the backing fabric from the seam allowance to reduce bulk in the seam (Figure 11.4).

11. Understitch the lining to the seam allowances.

12. Place the lining back down on the fashion fabric, face-sides together, and pin the remaining edges. Stitch the sides, center back, and bottom seams, leaving a 3- to 4-inch opening in the bottom seam at one side (ASTM Stitch type 301, seam type SSa-1).

13. Trim the corners and trim away the backing fabric from the seam allowances to reduce bulk.

ADDITIONAL INFORMATION ABOUT FOUNDATIONS FOR BUSTIERS

- Backing choices for bustiers range from the thickest, medium-weight flannel—including lightweight cotton or poly batting—to the lightest weight of plain-woven cotton fabric. All backings should be preshrunk before using them in the garment to prevent the garment fabric from puckering during cleaning.
- A stiff interlining may be added across the top of the bustier to help a sculpted edge lie flat against the body or to stand out away from it. Adding interlining at the closure area is especially important when applying eyelets; this prevents the eyelets from pulling out of the fabric and keeps the fabric edges from distorting when closed.

14. Turn the bustier out through the opening in the bottom seam and press; encourage the lining to move to the inside to keep it from showing on the outside of the garment.

15. Hand stitch or, for a cheaper alternative, edge stitch the opening closed.

Adding Eyelets and a Cord

If you are using eyelets, you will attach them—after you complete the bustier—on both sides of the opening, in this case the center back. Follow the steps below. You will need a marking pen for fabric, the eyelets, an awl, and the appropriate eyelet setter. Mark the location of each eyelet and attach them carefully, because they are not removable after you have attached them.

1. Mark the locations of each eyelet. To fully close the opening, start your eyelets about ½ inch below the top of the bustier and end them about ½ inch above the bottom. How far apart you place them is a design decision, but the farther apart they are, the higher the chance of gaping between them when the garment is laced. If they are too close together, you will be wasting time and materials on setting too many. Usually about 1½ to 2 inches apart is a good amount. Each eyelet should have a mate on the other side directly across from it (Figure 11.5).

2. Use the awl to pierce a hole at each mark.

3. Insert an eyelet into the hole from the outside of the bustier toward the inside. Use the eyelet tool to crush the back of the eyelet to secure it.

4. Lace a length of ribbon or cord through the eyelets, starting at the bottom; make sure to leave enough length on the cord to be able to expand the bustier enough to get in and out of it.

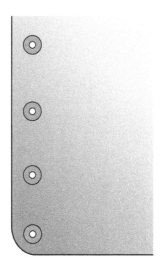

FIGURE 11.5 Eyelet placement on the finished bustier.

Appendix

SEAMS

The following diagrams and descriptions provide guidelines on different types of stitches and seams. Reprinted, with permission, from ASTM D6193-09 Standard Practice for Stitches and Seams, copyright ASTM International, 100 Barr Harbor Drive, West Conshohocken, PA 19428.

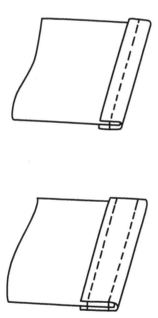

BSa—Bias edge binding using a single layer of trim that does not need to have the edges turned under, such as knit or leather.

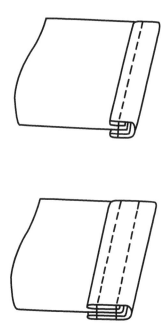

BSc—Sleeve placket with bias folder attachment.

BSc—Bias binding edge finish done with a folder attachment.

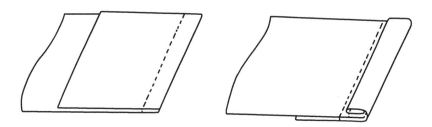

BSf—Bias binding quicker method done with bias or nonwoven trim and no binding attachment.

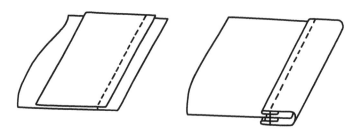

BSo—Bias binding edge finish done without a binder attachment.

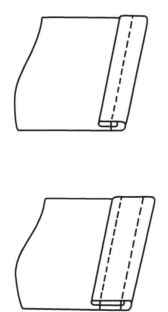

EFb—Hem for a shirttail or jeans with topstitching.

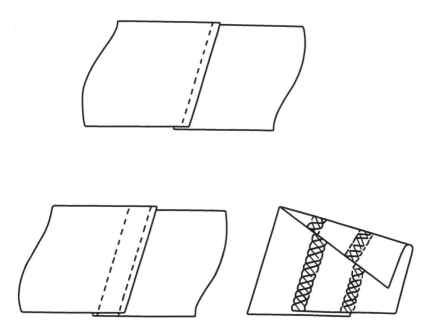

Lsa—Leather or suede real or synthetic seam.

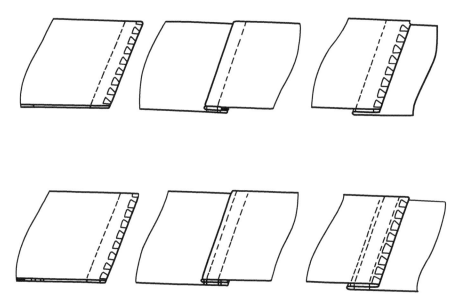

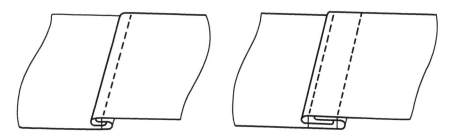

LSbm—Mock flat fell seam can be done with stitches 301 or 401 combined with 504, 512, 514, or 516.

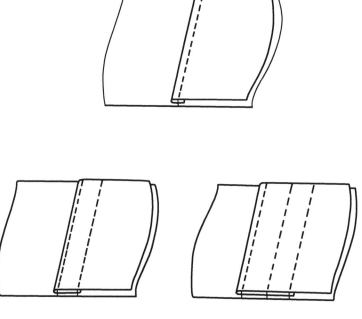

LSc—Men's dress shirt "single needle" tailoring.   **LSc**—Flat fell seam classic version.

LSd—Setting a patch pocket and sewing on labels.

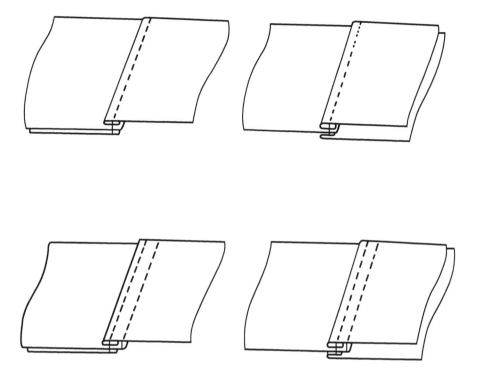

LSf—Yoke seam of a dress shirt or a skirt.

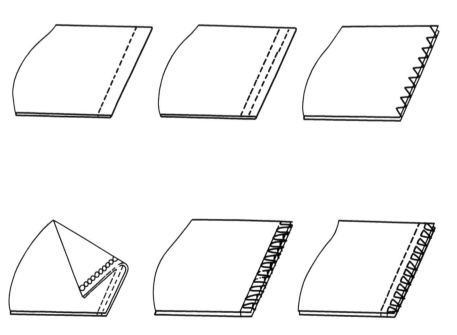

Ssa—Plain seam can be done with stitch 301, 401, 512, 516.

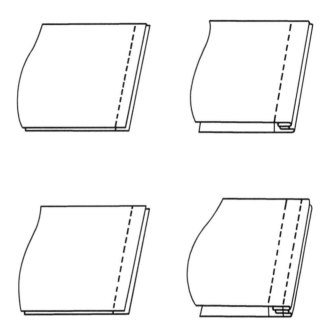

SSae—French seam.

SSe—Enclosed seam at edges of collars, waistbands, and cuffs.

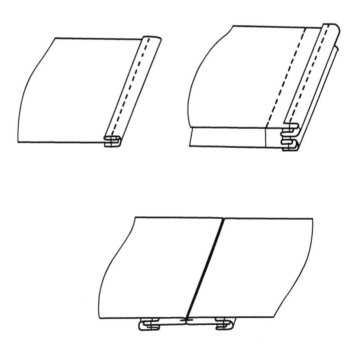

SSbh—Hong Kong seam traditional method done with a bias folder attachment.

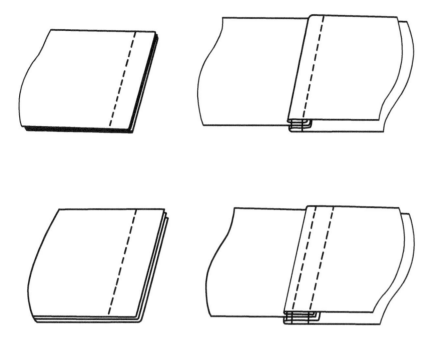

SSq—Waistband setting.

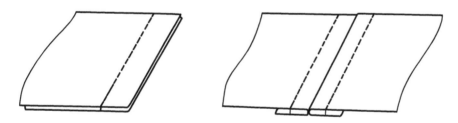

SSz—Plain seam with topstitching on both sides for decoration.

STITCHES

STITCH DRAWING (TOP VIEW AS SEWN / BOTTOM VIEW AS SEWN)	ISO 4915 NUMBER	COMMON APPLICATION	REQUIREMENTS	STITCH DESCRIPTION
Single Thread Chainstitch	101	Basting Stitch for Tailored Clothing; Bag Closing	Specify SPI	Stitch formed by a needle thread passing through the material and interlooping with itself on the underside of the seam with the assistance of a spreader.
Single Thread Chainstitch or Lockstitch Buttonsew, Buttonhole, or Bartack / *304 Lockstitch is preferred when stitch security is a must.	101 or 304	Buttonsew, Buttonhole, or Bartack	1) Buttonsew—specify stitches per cycle (Ex. 8, 16, 32) 2) BH—specify length and width (1/2", etc.) 3) Bartack—specify length and width of tack.	*Knit Shirts*—Buttonhole length generally is 1/2 inch, is placed horizontally, with approximately 85–90 stitches.
Single Thread Blindstitch / No stitch visible on the Bottom or Outside of Sewn Product	103	Blindstitch Hemming, Felling, Making Belt Loops	Specify 1) SPI 3–5 SPI 2) Non-skip or 2 to 1 skipped stitch	Stitch is formed with one needle thread that is interlooped with itself on the top surface of the material. The thread passes through the top ply and horizontally through portions of the bottom ply without completely penetrating it the full depth.
Lockstitch—Most Common of All Stitches / Bobbin Thread on Bottom	301	Topstitching, Single Needle Stitching, Straight Stitching	Specify SPI	Stitch formed by a needle thread passing through the material and interlocking with a bobbin thread with the threads meeting in the center of the seam. Stitch looks the same top and bottom.
Zig Zag Lockstitch	304	Intimate Apparel, Athletic wear, Infantwear, Exercisewear	Specify 1) SPI 2) Throw or width Zig-Zag (1/8", 3/16", 1/4")	Stitch is formed with a needle and a bobbin that are set in the center of the seam and form a symmetrical zig-zag pattern. Also, used to identify bartacking and lockstitch buttonsewing and buttonholing.
Chainstitch / Looper Thread on Bottom	401	Single Needle Chainstitch—Mainseams on Wovens	Specify SPI	Stitch formed by 1-needle thread passing through the material and interlooped with 1-looper thread and pulled up to the underside of the seam.
Zig Zag Chainstitch / Looper Thread on Bottom	404	Zig-Zag Chainstitch for Infantwear and Childrenswear: Binding,	Specify 1) SPI 2) Throw or width Zig-Zag (1/8")	Stitch is formed with a needle and a looper that are set on the underside of the seam and form a symmetrical zig-zag pattern.

STITCH DRAWING		ISO 4915 NUMBER	COMMON APPLICATION	REQUIREMENTS	STITCH DESCRIPTION
TOP VIEW AS SEWN	BOTTOM VIEW AS SEWN				
2 Needle Bottom Coverstitch	Looper Thread on Bottom	406	Hemming, Attaching, Elastic, Binding, Coverseaming, Making Belt Loops	Specify 1) Needle spacing (1/8", 3/16", 1/4") 2) SPI	Stitch formed by 2-needle threads passing through the material and interlooping with 1-looper thread with the stitch set on the underside of the seam. Looper thread interlooped between needle threads providing seam coverage on the bottom side only.
3 Needle Bottom Coverstitch	Looper Thread on Bottom	407	Attaching Elastic to Men's and Boy's Knit Underwear	Specify 1) Needle spacing (1/4") 2) SPI	Stitch formed by 3-needle threads passing through the material and interlooping with 1-looper thread with the stitch set on the underside of the seam. Looper thread is interlooped between needle threads providing seam coverage on the bottom side only.
2 Needle Chainstitch with Cover Thread	Looper Thread on Bottom	408	Attaching Pocket Facings to Jeans and Chino Casual Pants		Stitch formed by 2-needle threads passing through the material and interlooping with 2-looper threads with the stitches set on the underside of the seam. A top spreader thread is interlaced on the top side of the seam between the two needle threads.
2 Thread Overedge	Single "purl" on Edge	503	Serging and Blindhemming	Specify 1) Width Bite (Ex. 1/8", 3/16", 1/4") 2) SPI	Stitch formed by 1-needle thread and 1-looper thread with purl on edge of seam for serging or blindhemming ONLY.
3 Thread Overedge	Common Overedge Stitch	504	Single Needle Overedge Seaming	Specify 1) Width Bite (Ex. 1/8", 3/16", 1/4") 2) SPI	Stitch formed with 1-needle thread and 2-looper threads with the looper threads forming a purl on the edge of the seam. For overedge seaming and serging.
3 Thread Overedge	Double "purl" on Edge	505	Serging with Double purl on Edge	Specify 1) Width Bite (Ex. 1/8", 3/16", 1/4") 2) SPI	Stitch formed with 1-needle thread and 2-looper threads with the looper threads forming a double purl on the edge of the seam for serging ONLY.
Mock Safety Stitch	2 Needle Overedge	512	Seaming Stretch Knits, Wovens	Specify SPI	Stitch formed with 2-needle threads and 2-looper threads with the looper threads forming a purl on the edge of the seam. 512—right needle only enters the upper looper loop. Stitch does NOT chain-off as well as 514 Stitch.

STITCH DRAWING		ISO 4915 NUMBER	COMMON APPLICATION	REQUIREMENTS	STITCH DESCRIPTION
TOP VIEW AS SEWN	BOTTOM VIEW AS SEWN				
2 Needle 4 Thread Overedge	2 Needle Overedge	514	Seaming Stretch Knits, Wovens	Specify SPI	Stitch formed with 2-needle threads and 2-looper threads with the looper threads forming a purl on the edge of the seam. 514—both needles enter the upper looper loop. Preferred over 512 Stitch because it chains-off better.
4 Thread Safetystitch		515 (401+503)	Safetystitch Seaming Wovens and Knits	Specify 1) Needle spacing and bite—Ex: 1/8"–1/8", 3/16"–3/16", 3/16"–1/4" 2) SPI	Combination stitch consisting of a single-needle chainstitch (401) and a 2-thread Overedge stitch (503) that are formed simultaneously. Uses less thread than a 516 stitch; however, many manufacturers prefer a 516 stitch.
5 Thread Safetystitch		516 (401+504)	Safety Stitch Seaming Wovens and Knits	Specify 3) Needle spacing and bite—Ex: 1/8"–1/8", 3/16"–3/16", 3/16"–1/4" 4) SPI	Combination stitch consisting of a single-needle chainstitch (401) and a 3-thread Overedge stitch (504) that are formed simultaneously.
2 Needle 4 Thread Coverstitch		602	Binding A Shirts, Infants Clothing, etc.	Specify 1) Needle spacing (Ex: 1/8", 3/16", 1/4") 2) SPI	Stitch formed with 2-needle threads, a top cover thread and a bottom looper thread.
3 Needle 5 Thread Coverstitch		605	Lap Seaming, Coverseaming, Binding on Knits	Specify 1) Needle spacing (Ex: 1/4") 2) SPI	Stitch formed with 3-needle threads, a top cover thread and a bottom looper thread.
4 Needle 6 Thread Coverstitch	Flatseamer/Flatlock	607	Flat or Lap Seaming Knit Underwear, Fleece, etc.	Specify SPI	Stitch formed with 4-needle threads, a top cover thread and a bottom looper thread. Preferred over 606 stitch because machines are easier to maintain.

WORKING WITH TRICKY MATERIALS

MATERIAL	PRESSING TIPS	NEEDLE	MACHINE FOOT	UPPER THREAD TENSION	TYPE OF STITCH	STITCH LENGTH	ADDITIONAL TIPS
VELVET AND OTHER NAPPED FABRICS	Always press from the fabric back side. Over pressing will flatten the nap, steam with the iron above the fabric or use just the tip; use a damp press cloth over the fabric; use a needle board or a piece of heavy fleece on top of the pressing surface to prevent ruining the nap; can also use strips of heavy paper bag wider than the seam allowance between the seam allowance and the garment when pressing to prevent marking on the face side; the nap may be steamed then brushed and left to air dry to raise it if necessary.	12–14 standard	Roller foot or dual feed is best to prevent the layers from shifting	Balanced	301 or 401	2.5 to 3.5	Napped fabrics are one way. Pining also helps reduce layers crawling; if the napped surface will touch the feed teeth during stitching, put tissue or toilet paper strips between the fabric and feed teeth to avoid marking the nap.
FAKE FUR	Avoid melting the fabric by testing the iron temperature before pressing; always press from the back of the fabric with the tip of the iron.	14–16 standard	Standard	Balanced	301 or 401	2.5 to 3.5	Fake furs are one-way fabrics; clip fur from the seam allowance area before sewing; pull out any hairs that get caught in the stitching with a blunt needle.
TAFFETA	Avoid over pressing by testing the temperature of the iron on a swatch; also, check for water spotting from steam before using a wet iron to press; use strips of paper between seam allowance and garment to prevent marking.	Standard or ball point size 9–11 if yarns pull on the crosswise grain.	Standard	Balanced or loosened slightly if the fabric puckers along the seam	301	1.5–2.5	Taffeta is a one-way fabric due to the surface treatment, especially if it has a moiré pattern.
PLASTIC AND VINYL	Pressing has no effect on plastic and vinyl other than melting it.	14–16 leather helps avoid skipped stitches; may also need a needle lubricant.	Teflon standard foot, roller foot, or dual feed	Balanced	301 or 401	2.5–3.5	Plastic and vinyl will stick to a standard foot causing uneven and skipped; stitches, using the feet listed helps combat this; can be marked by the feed teeth so use strips of paper to protect the surface when top stitching.

MATERIAL	PRESSING TIPS	NEEDLE	MACHINE FOOT	UPPER THREAD TENSION	TYPE OF STITCH	STITCH LENGTH	ADDITIONAL TIPS
FINE KNITS	Pressing temperature depends on the content of the fiber; do a test and avoid over pressing; press lightly from the back, taking care not to press the seam allowance into the fabric so that it marks the face side.	8–10 ball point or stretch needle for lock stitch or overlock.	Standard for both machines	Balanced but loosened if the fabric puckers in the direction of the stitching.	401, 504, or 512	2.0–2.5	A polyester knit may be pressed with a damp press cloth to help set the press in the synthetic fiber.
LEATHER	Do not press, it will damage the leather; use the gluing method described in Chapter 9.	10–16 leather point	Standard or Teflon foot	Balanced	301 or 401	2.5–3.5	See Chapter 9 for more tips on working with leather
CHIFFON AND OTHER EXTREMELY THIN FABRICS	Set the iron temperature according to the fiber of the fabric; avoid over pressing.	8–10 standard or ball point if the fabric yarns pull in the crosswise grain.	Standard straight stitch foot and plate will prevent the material getting pushed down into the feed plate.	Balanced or slightly loosened if the fabric puckers along the seam.	301, 504, or 512	1.5–2.5	A shorter stitch length will help eliminate puckering along the seam.

INTERLINING TYPES AND USES

The products in this chart are representative of the hundreds of types of interlinings available to the apparel industry. These interlinings are manufactured as "Vilene," a division of the Fruedenberg Group, a worldwide manufacturer of interlinings.

PRODUCT DESCRIPTION: PRODUCT NUMBER, COLOR, WIDTH, BASE, WEIGHT (g/m²)	ATTACHMENT METHOD	FIBER CONTENT	USE
955—white, 60", random/binder, 130 g/m²	Sew in	100% polyester	This is a heavier interlining used for the chest pieces of men's suit jackets.
AO247—white, 60", criss-cross binder, 85 g/m²	Sew in	100% polyester	A medium interlining used for causal shirts and pant waistbands.
AO403—white, 60", random/binder, 38 g/m²	Sew in	100% polyester	A lightweight interlining for ladies blouses and dresses.
DO208—white, 48", cross laid thermal bonded, 59 g/m²	Sew in	100% polyester	A medium-weight interlining for the collars and cuffs in woven shirts.
2500—white, 60", random thermal bonded, 34 g/m²	Fusible	100% polyester	A lightweight interlining for application in blouses or dresses.
CE3023—white, 60", random thermal bonded, 32 g/m²	Fusible	50% polyester, 50% polyamide	A lightweight, multipurpose interlining for women's apparel.
CE 6035—white, 60", random thermal bonded, 46 g/m²	Fusible	70% polyester, 30% polyamide	Interlining for multiple uses in men's tailored clothing.
CE 9023—white, 60", random thermal bonded, 34 g/m²	Fusible	85% polyamide, 15% polyester	This interlining works well for the small parts in tailored clothing and women's wear. It has an extra concentration of fusing material per square centimeter to ensure a secure bond.

MACHINE NEEDLE TYPES AND THEIR USES

A common method for testing if the thread and the needle size are compatible is to thread the needle and then hold the thread taught while tilting it at a 45-degree angle. If the needle slips down the thread under its own weight, then the needle eye is large enough. The correct size needle will be the smallest one that works with the thread diameter. If the needle is so small that it breaks because the fabric is dense or many layers are being sewn, then the needle size used must be bigger.

NEEDLE TYPE	POINT SHAPE	USE ACCORDING TO TASK, FABRIC TYPE, OR THREAD DIAMETER	SIZES AVAILABLE AMERICAN (EUROPEAN)
Standard/universal	Sharply pointed to slightly rounded.	Basic sewing of knits or wovens of fine to heavy weights. As with all machine needles, the thickness of the fabric or the increase in thread diameter means a larger needle size (larger number). The thinnest possible needle should be used. If the needle breaks, then move up to a larger size.	8–30 (60–330)
Ballpoint	Differing degrees of rounded end from slightly pointed to very rounded.	Ballpoint needles have many uses, including sewing on fabrics woven or knitted from very fine yarns, such as microfibers and elastic materials, to avoid skipped stitches or snagging yarns. They also can aid in producing smooth embroidered patterns.	9–22 (65–140)
Leather	Sharpened wedge shape for cutting through the leather.	Leather needles are designed to cut a slash into the leather to allow the thread to pass through. Using a leather needle will help avoid skipped stitches and shredded thread while sewing.	9–23 (65–160)
Machine embroidery	Rounded with a larger and/or elongated eye.	Machine embroidery needles create smooth stitching, especially satin stitching. They also eliminate skipped stitches. The larger eye helps avoid shredding your thread.	7–18 (55–110)
Topstitching	Round with a larger eye.	Topstitching needles are especially designed to function with the thicker threads used to create topstitched design details, such as on jeans.	14–21 (90–130)
Blind stitching	Curved needle available either in a sharp point for wovens or sturdy knits, or a ball point for hemming fine knits.	Needles for blind stitch machines are curved to allow the machine to catch a few threads of the fabric being hemmed. This reduces or eliminates the amount of each stitch that will appear on the outside of the garment.	9–18 (65–110)

ADDITIONAL SEWING TIPS

Sewing a curved hem (also see *roping*): Curved seams are on the bias so they are prone to distortion when sewing.

- Keep curved hems narrow, no more than ½" wide.
- Stay stitch the hem inside the hem allowance before sewing the hem to the garment to prevent the bias edge from stretching. You can use this line of stay stitching as a guide for pressing the hem up.
- Press the hem up with the tip of the iron before hemming. This helps prevent pressing unnecessary creases.
- If time permits, pin the hem to the garment before stitching by hand or machine.
- Avoid pulling on the hem while stitching to prevent it from becoming stretched out.

Sewing inside corners.

- As you approach the corner, stop at the seam allowance line for the next edge and put the needle down into the fabric.
- Turn the fabric to your right so that the next edge of the fabric lines up with the stitching line on the feed plate of the machine.
- Continue sewing down the next edge of the fabric.

Sewing outside corners.

- As you approach the corner, stop at the seam allowance line for the next edge and put the needle down into the fabric.
- Turn the fabric to your left so that the next edge of the fabric lines up with the stitching line on the feed plate of the machine.
- Continue sewing down the next edge of the fabric.

Sewing a convex curved seam.

- Sewing a convex curved seam is similar to sewing many tiny outside corners.
- If the curve is tight, you must put the needle down into the fabric and make many slight turns to keep the seam curving smoothly.
- It's important to keep the edge of the fabric touching the correct line on the feed plate for the seam allowance width you're using.
- If the curve is shallow, you may be able to simply rotate the fabric to keep the seam smooth.

Sewing a concave curved seam.

- The quickest way to conquer a concave curve is to gently pull the fabric edge straight while sewing. This will cause ripples to form in the body of the fabric, so be careful not to catch these in the seam.

- It also helps to gently push the fabric to the right so that the edge of the seam stays at the correct seam allowance line on the feed plate.

Controlling a creeping upper fabric layer. Fabric layers that are slippery (e.g., silk), thick (e.g., hand woven material), napped (e.g., velvet); or stick to the foot (e.g., leather or vinyl) may not feed evenly with the lower fabric layer, resulting in excess fabric at the end of the seam. This also may occur on very long seams.

- Choose a machine with a dual feed or a walking foot attachment, which feeds the top layer as well as the lower layer of fabric.
- Use the tip of an awl to coax the upper layer of fabric under the toes of the foot.
- Reduce the presser foot pressure to allow more room for the fabric to feed.
- If you have lots of time, pinning the seam also helps, as does using basting tape.

Easing a layer of fabric with the machine feed teeth.

- If you are easing one layer of fabric into another, such as at a sleeve head or a skirt to a waistband, put the layer to be eased on the bottom next to the feed teeth. This will help smoothly shrink the longer layer to the shorter one on the top.

Alternative seam finishes with bias binding or other trim. These can be used in Hong Kong seams or to decoratively finish edges on the inside or outside of garments.

- **BSc**—Bias binding edge finish done with a bias binding attachment in one pass.
- **BSo**—Bias binding edge finish done without a binder attachment.
- **BSf**—A quicker bias binding method done with bias or nonwoven trim, with or without a binding attachment, and can leave a decorative single layer of fabric on the outside of the garment.
- **BSa**—Bias edge binding using a single layer of trim, such as knit or leather, that does not need to have the edges turned under. Applied in one pass with a binding attachment.

WHOLESALE SUPPLIERS
No endorsement of products or services is implied by inclusion in this list.

List of resources for:
Sewing/alteration supplies including linings, interlining, tools, notions, elastic, thread, zippers, etc.

B. Black and Sons
548 South Los Angeles Street
Los Angeles, CA 90013
Phone: 213-624-9451
Toll Free: 800-433-1546
Fax: 213-624-9457
www.bblackandsons.com

Charles Zarit Co.
624 S. 5th St.
Philadelphia, PA 19147
Phone: 1-800-523-0686
Fax: 215-627-5927
www.charleszarit.com

A Feibusch Corp
27 Allen Street
New York, NY 10002
Phone: 1-212/226-3964
Fax: 1-212/226-5844
eMail us at: afeibusch@prodigy.net

If Outside New York State,
Call Toll-Free at:
1-888/ZIPSUSA
1-888/947-7872
www.zipperstop.com

Steinlauf and Stoller Inc.
239 West 39th St.
New York, NY 10018
Phone: 212-869-0321
Fax: 212-302-4465
Toll Free: 877-869-0321
Email: steinlauf@rcn.com

Buttons and trims

Buttonology, Inc.
264 West 40th Street
Suite 404
New York, NY 10018
www.buttonologyinc.com
Phone: 212-768-3342
Fax: 212-768-4395
info@buttonologyinc.com

Roth International
13 West 38th St.
New York, NY 10018
Phone: 212-840-1945
Fax: 212-391-1033
www.rothinternational.net
roth.import@verizon.net

Waterbury Button Company
1855 Peck Lane
Cheshire, CT 06410
Phone: 203-271-9055
Fax: 203-271-9280
www.waterburybutton.com
info@waterburybutton.com

Sewing machinery

New York Sewing Machine, Inc.
2011-15 85th Street
North Bergen, NJ 07047
Call toll free 1-800-225-2852, in
NJ 201-809-2009
email: machines@nysmac.com
nysmac.com
www.mansew.com

Advanced Sewing Technologies Corp.
Piedmont Sewing Supply
704 Main Street
Pittsburgh, PA 15215
Phone: 412-781-3222
Phone: 800-626-0823
Fax: 412-781-3245
Email: advsew@aol.com

200 Heywood Ave. Suite # 1402
Spartanburg, SC 29307
Phone: 864-804-2559
Fax: 864-573-9729
Email: kevin.advsew@live.com
www.advancedsewing.com

Collier Equipment Company
PO Box 175
Anderson, AL 35610
Phone: 256-229-6595
Fax: 256-229-6779
Randy@CollierEquipment.com
www.collierequipment.com

Sewing machine attachments

Civit
2 Maple Street
East Rutherford, NJ 07073
Phone: 201-896-9292
Fax: 201-896-8588
Civit.com; stephanie@civit.com

W.S. Bessett
1923 Main Street
Sanford, ME 04073
Phone: 207-324-9232
Fax: 207-324-1702
bessett@wsbessett.com
www.wsbessett.com

Cutting equipment

Central Penn Sewing Machine Company
351 E. 7th Street, Box 278
Bloomsburg, PA 17815
Toll Free: 800-547-3859
Phone: 570-784-1312
Fax: 570-784-3312
Mike Criqui: Mcriqui@centralpennsewing.com

Cutting/Sewing Room Equipment
1816 Briarwood Industrial Ct.
Atlanta, GA 30329
Phone: 404-321-3607
www.cutsew.com

Dress forms

PGM-PRO INC.
5041-5047 Heintz St.
Baldwin Park, CA 91706
info@pgmdressform.com
Phone: 626-338-1990
Toll Free: 888-818-1991
Fax: 626-338-1995
www.pgmdressform.com

Wolf Form Company, Inc.
P.O. Box 510, 17 Van Nostrand Avenue
Englewood, NJ 07631
info@wolfform.com
Phone: 201-567-6556 or
201-567-6572
Fax: 201-569-9023
www.wolfform.com

Pressing equipment

Hoffman/New Yorker, Inc.
25 Lackawanna Place
Bloomfield, NJ 07003-2401
Phone: 973-748-0500
Fax: 973-748-1341
info@hoffman-newyorker.com
www.hoffman-newyorker.com

Pleating services

Regal Originals
247 West 37th St.
New York, NY 10018
Phone: 212-921-0270
Fax: 212-575-1893
regaloriginals.com

Pattern Making and Grading services

AAA Pattern and Marking Services
347 N. Merrick Ave.
Ozark, AL 36360
Phone: 334-445-4870
Fax: 334-445-3910

Tukatech
5527 E. Slauson Ave.
Los Angeles, CA 90040
Phone: +1 323-726-3836
Fax: +1 323-726-3866
tukateam@tukatech.com
Contact: Kabeer Lal
www.tukatech.com

Computer programs for the fashion business including marker making, design, grading and communication programs

Tukatech
5527 E. Slauson Ave.
Los Angeles, CA 90040
Phone: +1 323-726-3836
Fax: +1 323-726-3866
Email: tukateam@tukatech.com
Contact: Kabeer Lal
www.tukatech.com

Gerber Technology
24 Industrial Park Road West
Tolland, CT 06084
Phone: +1-860-871-8082
Phone: 1-800-826-3243 (USA only)
Fax: +1-860-872-6742
info@gerbertechnology.com
www.gerbertechnology.com

Browzwear
3 Nirim Street
Tel Aviv, Israel 67060
Phone: +972-3-688-5556
Fax: +972-3-688-0635
www.browzwear.com

Lectra
New York
25 West 39th Street, 4th Floor
New York, NY 10018
Phone: +1-212-730-4444
Fax: +1-212-730-4344

OptiTex USA
325 W 38th Street
Suite 1107
New York, NY 10018
Toll free (US & Canada):
1-877-RING-OPT
Phone: 212-629-9053
Fax: 212-629-9055
www.optitex.com

International Advanced Technology
Center—North America
889 Franklin Road, SE
Marietta, GA 30067-7945—USA
Phone: +1-770-422-8050
Fax: +1-770-422-1503

Call Center–North America
Phone: +1-8774-LECTRA/+1-877-453-2872 (Free call)
Fax: +1-800-746-8760
www.lectra.com

REACH Technologies
Head Office
Bangalore
49, First Main, Third Phase, JP Nagar, Bangalore- 560 078, India
Phone: 91-80-65996111, 65996112, 65996113
Fax: 91-80-26585744

U.S.A. Offices
New York
1133 Broadway, Suite 706
New York, NY 10010

Los Angeles
Wilshire Blvd Suite 200
Beverly Hills, CA 90211
sales@reach-tech.com
www.reach-tech.com

Research and Training

$[TC]^2$
5651 Dillard Dr.
Cary, NC 27518 USA
Phone: 919-380-2156
Toll Free: 800-786-9889
Fax: 919-380-2181
www.tc2.com
Karen Davis, 919-380-2177, or email
kdavis@tc2.com

$[TC]^2$ provides a range of solutions for the global soft goods industry specializing in technology development and supply chain improvement. Its initiatives include the broad investigation and demonstration of advanced technologies, education, training, and consulting for brands, retailers, manufacturers, and suppliers. It is well known for its ability to strategically and tactically align business practices, to implement 3D body scanning and related fit/shape analysis methodologies, and to help companies streamline operations to reduce nonvalue-added activities and processes.

BASIC METRIC CONVERSION TABLE

DISTANCES	
English	**Metric**
1 inch	2.54 centimeters
1 foot	0.3048 meter / 30.38 centimeters
1 yard	0.9144 meter
Metric	**English**
1 centimeter	0.3937 inch
1 meter	3.280 feet
WEIGHTS	
English	**Metric**
1 ounce	28.35 grams
1 pound	0.45 kilogram
Metric	**English**
1 gram	0.035 ounce
1 kilogram	2.2 pounds

General formula for converting:

Number of Units × Conversion Number = New Number of Units

To convert inches to centimeters:

[number of inches] × 2.54 = [number of centimeters]

To convert centimeters to inches:

[number of centimeters] × 0.3937 = [number of inches]

To convert feet to meters:

[number of feet] × 0.3048 = [number of meters]

To convert meters to feet:

[number of meters] × 3.280 = [number of feet]

To convert yards to meters:

[number of yards] × 0.9144 = [number of meters]

To convert ounces to grams:

[number of ounces] × 28.35 = [number of grams]

To convert grams to ounces:

[number of grams] × 0.035 = [number of ounces]

To convert pounds to kilograms:

[number of pounds] × 0.45 = [number of kilograms]

To convert kilograms to pounds:

[number of kilograms] × 2.2 = [number of pounds]

Bibliography

Abernathy H., Frederick, John Dunlop, Janice Hammond, and David Weil. *A Stitch in Time: Lean Retailing and the Transformation of Manufacturing—Lessons from the Apparel and Textile Industries.* Oxford: Oxford University Press, 1999.

Abraham-Murali, L. "Consumer's Perception of Apparel Quality Over Time; An Exploratory Study." *Clothing and Textiles Research Journal* 13, no. 3 (1995): 149–158.

Agins, Teri. *The End of Fashion.* New York: Harper Collins, 1999.

Barbee, G. "Getting the Most from Your Sewing Room; Small-sized Sewn Products Manufacturers Often Face Big Challenges in the Sewing Room." *Bobbin* 40, no. 2 (1998): 24–28.

Betzina, Sandra. *Power Sewing.* Newtown, CT: Taunton Press, 2002.

Brown, Patty, and Janett Rice Pearson. *Ready-to-Wear Apparel Analysis.* 3rd ed. Upper Saddle River, NJ: Pearson Prentice Hall, 2000.

Burman, Barbara. *The Culture of Sewing: Gender, Consumption and Home Dressmaking.* New York: Berg Publishers, 1999.

Bye, Elizabeth K, and Kathryn Reiley. "Comparison of Information About the Quality of Apparel in Three Retail Formats." *Perceptual and Motor Skills* 96, no. 31 (2003): 839–846.

Calasibetta, Charlotte Mankey, and Phyllis Tortora. *Fairchild Dictionary of Fashion.* 3rd ed. New York: Fairchild Publications, 2003.

Cavallaro, Daniel, and Alexandra Warwick. *Fashioning the Frame Boundaries, Dress and the Body.* Oxford: Berg, 1998.

Cunningham, Patricia. *Reforming Women's Fashion, 1850–1920.* Kent, OH: Kent State University Press, 2003.

DesMarteau, K. "Liz Launches Global Quality Coup." *Bobbin* 40, no. 11 (1999): 34–38.

Eicher, Joanne B., Sandra Lee Evenson, and Hazel A. Lutz. *The Visible Self.* 2nd ed. New York: Fairchild Publications, 2000.

Forsythe, Sandra, K. Wilson, and Ann Beth Presley. "Dimensions of Apparel Quality Influencing Consumer's Perceptions." *Perceptual and Motor Skills*, no. 83 (1996): 299–305.

Frings, Gini Stephens. *Fashion from Concepts to Consumer.* 9th ed. New York: Pearson Prentice Hall, 2008.

Gimlin, Debra. *Body Work: Beauty and Self-Image in American Culture.* Los Angeles: University of California Press, 2002.

Gioello, Debbie, and Beverly Berke. *Fashion Production Terms.* New York: Fairchild Publications, 1979.

Glock, Ruth E., and Grace I. Kunz. *Apparel Manufacturing Sewn Product Analysis.* 4th ed. Upper Saddle River, NJ: Pearson Prentice Hall, 2005.

"Integrating Quality into the Textile and Apparel High School Curriculum." *Journal of Family and Consumer Sciences* 93, no. 4 (2001): 84–87.

Kaiser, Susan B. *The Social Psychology of Clothing.* 2nd ed. Fairchild: New York, 1998.

Klerk, Helena M, and Stepna Lubbe. "Female Consumers' Evaluation of Apparel Quality; Exploring the Importance of Aesthetics." *Journal of Fashion Marketing and Management* 12, no. 1 (2008): 36–50.

Levine, Gene. "Implementing Cost Effective Quality Assurance Programs." *Bobbin* 38, no. 12 (1997): 116–118.

Mannie, Ken. "Skill Development: An Open and Closed Case." Psychomotor Skills National Guidelines for educating EMS instructors. *Module 17: Teaching Psychomotor Skills* (August 2002): 140.

McBride, David. "The 7 Manufacturing Wastes." EMS Consulting Group, August 29, 2003, accessed 1/3/09. emsstrategies.com

Proctor, Robert, and Addie Dutta. *Skill Acquisition and Human Performance.* New York: Sage Publications, 1995.

Romano, Pietro, and Andrea Vinelli. "Quality Management in a Supple Chain Perspective; Strategic and Operative Choices in a Textile-Apparel Network." *International Journal of Operations and Production Management* 21, no. 4 (2001).

Schiffman, Leon, and Leslie Kanuk. *Consumer Behavior.* 9th ed. Upper Saddle River, NJ: Pearson Prentice Hall, 2006.

Shaeffer, Claire. *Sewing for the Apparel Industry.* Upper Saddle River, NJ: Prentice Hall, 2001.

Singer Sewing Reference Library. *Sewing for Style.* Minnetonka, MI: Cy Decosse Inc., 1985.

Singer Sewing Reference Library. *Tailoring.* Minnetonka, MI: Cy Decosse Inc., 1988.

Standard Practices for Stitches and Seams. ASTM International West Conshohocken, PA, 1997.

"Stitch Type Matrix Flyer." American and Efird thread company, accessed 1/09/09, amefird.com

Stone, Elaine. *The Dynamics of Fashion.* 3rd ed. Fairchild: New York, 2008.

Staff report. "[TC]² Offers Sewability Analysis." *Bobbin* 42, no. 12 (2001): 96–99.

"Technologie + Praxis Blouses." Durkopp-Adler, accessed 3/29/09. duerkopp-adler. com/en/main/applications/ladieswear/

"Technologie + Praxis Jackets." Durkopp-Adler, accessed 3/29/09. duerkopp-adler. com/en/main/applications/ladieswear/

"Technologie + Praxis Pants." Durkopp-Adler, accessed 3/29/09. duerkopp-adler. com/en/main/applications/ladieswear/

"The Unification of Quality and Productivity Parameters with Eco Friendliness." *Apparel News* (January 2009): 54.

Thomas, Dana. *Deluxe: How Luxury Lost its Luster.* New York: The Penguin Press, 2007.

Scheller, Heidi P., and Grace I. Kunz. "Toward a Grounded Theory of Apparel Product Quality." *Clothing and Textiles Research Journal* 16, no. 2 (1998): 57–67.

Vogue and Butterick. *Designer Sewing Techniques.* New York: Simon and Schuster, 1994.

Index

Printed in the USA
CPSIA information can be obtained
at www.ICGtesting.com
LVHW070759100823
754828LV00012B/86